# NGATI DREAD

## Volume One
## Footsteps of Fire

### ANGUS GILLIES

Rogue Monster Books

ISBN 978-0-473-13522-5

## Dedication

For my wife Tui
and my sons Rogie,
Pele and Cassius and
my daughter Aroha

## Acknowledgements

The author would like to thank everyone who was willing to be interviewed, all the family and friends who supported him during this project and the staff and management of The Gisborne Herald newspaper, which provided the photos and the use of its archives.

# Author's Note

Ngati Dread is a complex story so it needed a structure
that would keep it as simple as possible for the reader.
Nevertheless, it still needs some explaining. There were
too many events and too much time between alleged
crimes and their court trials to keep it strictly
chronological. At a certain point I decided to deal with
one strand of the story in its entirety before going back in
time and starting on the next strand. I also decided that
Part 2 would precede Part 1. In other words I took the
chronological start of the story (Part 1) and inserted it
halfway through the book. That way I could plunge the
reader straight into the mayhem of Part 2. The author's
voice is always in present tense and printed in italics.
That's so it isn't confused with the many voices of the
interviewees as I cut between them and me. I apologise if
you're a Rasta and I quoted a cop, fireman or farmer
calling you an effin c, or vice versa. But this is a story
that engenders strong emotions. You shouldn't be
shocked. When relevant, I've noted my connections to
people quoted or written about in this book. It gives
readers an insight into the interconnectedness of people
in Gisborne and the East Coast. It's not us and them.
Firemen fight fires lit by their sons. Cops are mates with
Rastas. Some claims I've quoted are possibly inaccurate.
Often two versions of the same incident are completely
different. But I believe the version of the Ruatoria
Troubles collected in this and the next two volumes of
Ngati Dread is more complete and closer to the truth
than anything previously recorded.

## WELCOME

**May 7, 1988, The Gisborne Herald, Staff Reporter:** Ruatoria is unique in New Zealand's history – this reign of terrorism against the town's homes, farm buildings, businesses, churches, schools and symbols of authority, is unmatched by anything police have had to deal with in this country.

**Interview with Rasta leader John Heeney in early 2000:** Mate, if we're not gonna get justice from them (for the Rastas who've been killed) you watch this in our lifetime, Angus, we're gonna turn this mountain into our own country. We're gonna make another country in this country in our lifetime. And in our lifetime, if it don't happen, we'll certainly die trying to do it. We paid the price. Look, we've got martyrs just on our little shed wall. Just imagine if our house was *that* big, how many photos of martyrs we'd have. In our lifetime period. And not martyrs from, you know, outside it, ay. Because we're the builders of our place now. We are the builders. And we're not gonna be dictated to from them outside people because they are the ones dangling the purse strings in front of us and saying, "Hey, you jump *when* we say and *where*."

*Question: It's died down and been quiet for so long now. Isn't the quiet life kind of attractive?*

No (softly, while breathing out a lungful of thick smoke) not really. You know, they say there's peace but there's no peace, ay. They say it's quiet but these things are still going down and we're not the ones doing it. They're doing it to us, ay. And when we stood up at the start, when we started seeking our God, course, we wanted justice. And we loved it, ay, because we loved our Lord and we wanted equality. But amongst ourselves we never knew these outsiders existed and had all these big ideas for our whenua (land) that didn't include us until we started running into it. But we started running into that after we clashed with our parents. Because you look at that as the right way, ay. We had to go through our parents cos our parents knew what was going on behind the hills with the land. But we didn't know. We were wanting to know. And then as we started climbing up the hills we started getting a bit more wiser and seeing a bit more of what was going on, who we were up against.

**The Bible, The Book of Micah:**
Chapter 7, verse 5:
Put no trust in a friend,
Have no confidence in a companion;
Against her who lies in your bosom,

Guard the portals of your mouth.
For the son dishonours his father,
the daughter rises up against her mother,
The daughter-in-law against her mother-in-law,
And a man's enemies are those of his household.

**Former Detective Sergeant Laurie Naden:** I remember I locked up one joker for one of the arsons and his father was one of the volunteer firemen. Anyway, I went round and told his father. I'd known this guy ever since I was a mechanic up there. And he just looked at me shaking his head and he said, "Mate, he lights 'em, I fight 'em." And I felt so sad for him. But it was so intertwined. Most of the guys in the fire service up there had sons or relations who were in the Rastas.

**Former Ruatoria policeman Steve Tresidder:** Ruatoria was the sort of place where everybody was connected with everybody else. And that was what made it hard there. No one really wanted to tell on anybody else because everyone, virtually everybody there, to a person, was doing *something* they *weren't* supposed to be doing. Whether it was shagging the next door neighbour's wife, ripping off the social welfare, pinching stock, or driving around in a hot car, they were virtually all doing something they weren't supposed to be doing. They all had something to hide, so they all didn't want to dob each other in. No one really wanted to tell you anything in case someone dobbed them in for something else in retaliation.

# PROLOGUE

*Between 1985 and 1990, Ruatoria, a town of about eight hundred residents on the East Coast of the North Island, was terrorised by a religious sect calling itself the Rastafarians. But although it shared many of the beliefs and customs of the Rastafarian religion, the Ruatoria sect was unique. Its members wove together Rastafarian teachings with local Maori beliefs and prophecies.*

*They believed they were descended from Dan, one of the ten "lost tribes of Israel", which was forced into exile when Assyrian warriors captured the kingdom in 722 BC. They referred to Ngati Porou's sacred mountain, Hikurangi, as Mount Zion, the house of God in the Bible's Old Testament. They believed, as all Rastafarians do, that the late Ethiopian emperor Haile Selassie was the Second Coming of Christ. But, in keeping with local traditions, they also believed that a great spiritual leader would be born on the East Coast of New Zealand. This belief was a huge driving force behind the Ruatoria Rastafarians. And it is my belief that three of their members – Chris Campbell, John Heeney and Beau Tuhura – all thought at one time or another: "I am that leader."*

*How special was this prophesied leader to the Rastas? John Heeney describes Haile Selassie as the Second Coming, and the much-anticipated Ngati Porou leader as "the third advent of the Most High".*

*So why did the Rastas – as they came to be known – believe such a divine leader would appear in their midst? Because they were on a divine mission: to drive off the white settler families and return all the land around Ruatoria to the original Maori owners.*

*How did they plan to do this? Their main tactic was to cut down fences and burn buildings on farms.*

*But as the Ruatoria community – both Maori and Pakeha – rose up in shock and anger, the Rastas found themselves even more isolated. Before long they were burning down anything that represented authority and the establishment, as well as the properties of Maori they believed had wronged or slighted them.*

*So what happened while this process was playing itself out? Well, about forty buildings were destroyed in suspicious fires, including houses, farm buildings, the fire station, the primary school, the police station-cum-courthouse, main street businesses and even churches and marae. One Rastafarian , Joe Nepe, killed another, Lance Kupenga, in a ritual beheading. Five Rastas – John Heeney, Cody Haua, Chris Campbell, Hata Thompson and Dick Maxwell – stood trial over the death of a horse (they claimed they were trying to break it in by dragging it along the road behind their car). Three Rastafarians – Chris*

Campbell, Cody Haua and John Heeney - were jailed for "beating the devil" out of a fellow Rasta, Junior Paul. Five Gisborne CIB detectives were charged with kidnapping and assaulting a Rastafarian, Dick Maxwell. They were found not guilty. Numerous other police officers were charged with assaulting Rastafarians. They were all found not guilty. Three Rastafarians - Chris Campbell, Hata Thompson and Cody Haua – were jailed for kidnapping the head of the Gisborne Armed Offenders Squad, Detective Sergeant Laurie Naden. And two other Rastafarians, Chris Campbell (widely regarded as the group's leader) and Dick Maxwell, were killed. The men who killed them, Luke Donnelly and Watene Wanoa respectively, got off on self-defence.

Two other things need to be mentioned to fill out this quick overview of the Ruatoria Rastafarians: they grew out of New Zealand's gang culture (mainly Black Power) and they grew, sold and smoked a lot of cannabis.

Things have quietened down in Ruatoria in recent years. The crime spree tapered off after the death of Chris Campbell in 1990. A Rastafarian community of about thirty members still lives and worships in Ruatoria. But if they're in the newspapers these days, it's usually a feature article about the adobe brick houses they're building.

Some of the original hard-core members like Cody Haua and Hata Thompson have drifted away from the movement and moved on philosophically. But John Heeney, often considered Campbell's right hand man, is still very much involved and just as fanatical as ever. He says that one day all of Ruatoria will be adobe houses inhabited by Rastas, once they get rid of the rest of the town. He says sending the Rastas to jail helped them forge connections in the gang world. Thanks to that, they'll be fully armed next time there's a confrontation with the establishment. He says the moko he's tattooed on the Rastas' faces are their "number plates". That's how God will recognise them as the chosen ones when the end of the world comes. And he says that there is an utu on Luke Donnelly. Joe Nepe, the man who beheaded Lance Kupenga, agrees. Chris Campbell's death will be avenged, he says. It's not a question of **if** it'll happen, but of **who** will do it. I met Joe at his father's house in Hillsborough, Auckland, in November, 2000. "Well," he said, "we're still trying to work out something between us and the Mongrel Mob doing it. They're working out whether it's gonna be the Mongrel Mob to do it first or the Rastas."

Maybe the comments of Heeney and Nepe are the rantings of a couple of dope-fuelled middle-aged criminally inclined religious fanatics. But many in Ruatoria still remember all too vividly the way the Rastas terrorised the town. For many the wounds from that time haven't yet healed. They are suspicious of anything that might encourage the Rastas into another uprising. And, because of that, some at the top of the Ngati Porou heirarchy didn't want this book written, particularly by someone who was not of Ngati Porou descent.

It's hard to imagine the Rastafarians regaining the terrifying momentum they had in the mid-to-late 1980s. But I do think that a few violent or destructive incidents are quite possible. And, like the residents of Ruatoria, I sometimes have nightmares that I am the victim of one of these.

I really wondered whether I should leave in that last sentence about my nightmares. Was it relevant? Was it necessary? Did it fit? Was it appropriate? Was it too personal? How did it affect the tone of everything else I'd written? How did it resonate? Did it work?

I tried it out on my younger brother, Duncan, who's naturally more circumspect, responsible and respectful. He agreed. The line had power, like the first rub of a genie's lamp or the first curious glance at Pandora's box. But he wondered, too.

Having said that, I'm going to take that sentence a step further. And then I'm going to shut up and concentrate on helping the characters tell the story themselves, those that will speak to me. After all, this is their story. (Those that won't speak to me will be quoted anyway if they ever expressed themselves in the newspapers. I have all the clippings.)

I've just been jolted awake. It's 1.29am on Tuesday, September 30, 2003, and I'm going to share something with you. Sometimes I ask: "Is it me or is it the book?" It's true. I do have nightmares. They're the deranged offspring of my fear: "The Rastas won't like what I've written and will seek revenge."

But that's nothing. At other times I get really paranoid. And I wonder if I'm just going mad or deliberately being driven mad. I wonder if some disgruntled Maori elder has put a curse on me. I wonder if someone's sicked a hound of hell or set an evil spirit upon me. And sometimes, when I'm working deep inside some dark shaft of this story, mining, drilling, picking away, I look back and realise how far I've come and how isolated and vulnerable I am. And I imagine that I've uncovered or even unwittingly created an evil spirit that resides **in this book**. I am in awe of this material. I respect it. I revere it. I venerate it. And I am frightened of it. Sometimes I feel like Aladdin in the cave full of treasure, at others like the drunken village idiot mistakenly left alone in the gelignite room.

I have these crazy dreams. And I don't know what they mean. But I keep writing. I'm sure I'm under a spell of some sort. Even the sceptics would agree with that.

# PART 2  SHOCKING & BIZARRE

# CHAPTER 1

### THE RASTAS BEAT THE DEVIL OUT OF JUNIOR PAUL

*On Saturday, June 1, 1985, the Ruatoria Rastafarians are involved in a shocking and bizarre incident at a hut on Whakaahu Station. They badly beat up a Maori youth from Te Teko in the Bay of Plenty who's been hanging out with them. Junior Paul is beaten with fists and sticks, pushed underwater, stood in a fire and defecated on. The beating lasts a day and a night and into the following day. Paul is left badly bruised, concussed and with broken fingers. He leaves the area but doesn't complain to police. Eventually the police hear about what happened in the course of other investigations. But it's ten months before any of the Rastas appear in court over the incident.*

**Detective Sergeant Gary Condon (retired):** They did some pretty bizarre things. One of the Rastas had erred in his ways so they decided they had to beat the devil out of him. To do that, they tried to drown him in a bath. They put him in a fire with gumboots on. They had him dancing around in the fire with his gumboots on. And I know he ended up with a broken finger.

As far as I'm concerned they became Rastas and followed the Rasta beliefs purely to enable them to grow dope and smoke it. But as for them being true Rastas, to me it was just a joke. They just used it as a front and as a way of justifying their dope growing and smoking.

**Detective Sergeant Hemi Hikawai (retired):** With their philosophical attachment to the Ringatu religion (which was started by the 19th century rebel prophet Te Kooti) the Rastas then began searching for their true identities, for want of a better phrase. They immersed themselves in things Maori, as far as the supernatural and tohunga-ism was concerned; so much so, that they nearly killed a person.

They beat him with sticks. They threw him in the bloody fire. They did everything with him. They immersed him in fuckin' hot water.

John Heeney told me that he could smell evil on him and that this guy had Johnny Too Bad, the devil, inside him.

Anyway, they nearly killed this guy - Junior Paul was his name - when they tried to beat the devil out of him. And Heeney explained to me in an interview that he became convinced that Junior Paul had the devil in him when he, Heeney, fell down Junior Paul's throat. He was talking to this guy once and this guy actually opened his mouth and Heeney believed he actually fell... inside... this guy's... throat. And he said the guy tried to close his mouth behind him and he had to struggle to get out of his mouth. He felt the devil inside Junior Paul was trying to suck him in. This is how fucked in the head they were with the dope and everything. And Heeney to this day would say that that is what happened. And when that happened there was only one option left and they had to get this devil out of him.

They then went and sought some advice from some of the elders as to how you dealt with this, how you got the devil out of people the Maori way. And as a result they came across the advice that they were given and they then started trying to beat it out of him.

And that was the dangerous thing. As they began to delve into things Maori they began dealing with something that was too much for them. This coupled with their addled brains as a result of all this dope use that they were going through brought about this warped view of things. And what they did was they selectively chose passages from The Bible, which gave them the authority to do whatever they wanted.

**Gordon Sutton, childhood friend of Rastafarian leader Chris Campbell:** To me Chris was like another Te Kooti, mate, a rebel leader. He was one of those guys that you think, "Shit, this guy's going to turn out to be one of these leaders that's gonna go a long way, and whether it's the right way or the wrong way, Christ knows." He obviously went *both* ways. But at the end of the day I think he was trying to stand up for his rights. He was a very strong character and a lovable guy as well. He was like someone who'd been born in the wrong time. He should have been with Te Kooti, when those boys got taken down to the Chatham Islands. He was an outlaw prophet, like Te Kooti. He was just ordinary Chris. But when things started happening in Ruatoria, I thought, "Aw yeah, things are happening now." It didn't surprise me that things were being stirred up and he was in charge.

**Beau Tuhura, one of the early Rasta leaders:** To me Chris was a fulla that was out of the last century. He should have been alive in the 15$^{th}$ century. He was a warrior with the same sort of instincts our tipuna had. And I talk about warrior tipuna. His whole philosophy was an eye for an eye and a tooth for a tooth. And he didn't believe in loving his enemies.

**Former Detective Sergeant Hemi Hikawai:** Chris Campbell had the ability to control people. And that is what made him dangerous. You know you get these people and everyone says, "Aw, get'm on their own and they're all full-a shit." No, he wasn't like that. He was quite capable of physically looking after himself. Plus he could look after himself verbally. Plus he could look after himself mentally.

**Former Gisborne deputy fire chief Lyn Hillock:** I didn't have much to do with Chris Campbell, only to be on the receiving end of abuse from him. He was a real sick guy: smart, but fucked in the head, lost it, like a lot of the kids up there, too doped up. People who say marijuana doesn't affect you, they really want to go and have a look up at Ruatoria.

**Jeremy Williams, Pakeha farmer:** The Chris that I used to know when I was younger was a different one to the Chris I knew towards the end. Even before he went to jail he'd changed dramatically. He was very militant. He had very strong views. He seemed to be able to persuade people to do things that they wouldn't normally do. Look at this beheading and things like that. I don't know the details behind all that. But somebody was persuading people to do some pretty extraordinary things. So if Chris was still alive, I don't think he would have changed.

I personally saw Willie, Chris's father, whack Chris once. Willie was a big strong man in his day. But Chris had quite an arrogant streak, even as a younger guy. He was confident. He was not afraid of authority. He was not afraid of the police and he wasn't afraid of his elders. He didn't respect anybody really and I guess his father got annoyed with him.

**Beau Tuhura, one of the early Rasta leaders:** There were things about the teachings of Jesus Christ, well, you know, Chris felt Jesus got it wrong. He didn't believe in turning the other cheek. He lived by the old rule. He believed in utu. He was more influenced by the Old Testament than the New Testament, although he acknowledged that Jesus Christ had come to try to save his people and to reveal things, as in Revelations.

He was a very proud man, Chris, very pro Ngati Porou and pro his Te Aowera hapu, or sub-tribe. And I suppose at the time we were all into shearing. And it was also like a sport to us and Chris was the No. 1. He was on the No. 1 stand. So that speaks volumes for the fulla and his ability. It's not an easy thing being there. First you've gotta shear the numbers to get there. Then you gotta stay there. As one of the other shearers, you're chasing the fulla day in, day out through the season. You might get him now and again. But that doesn't constitute that you're gonna get the No. 1 stand. You've gotta be consistent, thereabouts every day. That's how Chris was.

And he was a fighter. I've had confrontations with him though they never came to much. But he wouldn't back down to anybody. He always felt that he was a worthy contender and he placed himself at the top of the list. And if anybody was going to consider himself any better they had to go through him.

By the same token he acknowledged other fighters around. And I suppose rather than contest the fellow he was the sort of joker who would say, "Well it's better to be a friend of that guy than his enemy." He was quite a shrewd diplomat when he needed to be. He wasn't an all-out confrontational guy.

And he was a charismatic fulla too, Chris. When he spoke about things, he spoke with authority. And he read a lot so he was quite a clued-up, clever joker. He gloried in The Bible. He read it constantly, to the point where he could quote freely from The Bible. And that gave him more mana. Anyone that can quote freely from The Bible with the same sort of fervour is a man worthy to be heard and listened to compared to those that just get out of bed and open the scripture in the morning and say, "This is our reading for the day." Sometimes the reading's got nothing to do with what's happening to them right then. But he was able to apply scripture to different situations in day-to-day life. As he confronted a situation he would come out with a bit of scripture that was pertinent.

He was a natural-born leader. And he had some hard lines too, like, "If you're not for me, then you're against me." So rather than having him as an enemy, fullas preferred to have him as a friend. And I suppose, from time to time, he demonstrated his philosophy. And when he did do it, he took it to extremes. He was quite a cruel fellow, a violent fellow. And I suppose to be at the top of your game you had to have some way of showing your followers that you're the man in charge. If anyone fell out of line he would see to it that that fulla learnt a lesson.

I called around to see a cousin of mine who I was told was at this house with the dread, the Rastas. And I went to the house and there was this fulla lying in the bed. He couldn't talk. He was just lying there. And they were gathered around him in prayer. I went to embrace the fulla and I felt all the welts and all the bruising and the swelling of his body. And I realised he'd taken a hell of a beating, this fulla. And he was lucky to be alive. That was Junior Paul.

When I got there I said, "This is not right. You're gonna have to do something about it. This fulla here had better not get any more of a beating than what he's already got."

He'd gone a bit crazy that kid. He was losing it. I had him over at my place one time and he was spitting away there. And I had to tell him to cut it out. He was actually beginning to believe that he was the man, that he was the devil.

Like I said, I hadn't witnessed Chris in action. But I kept coming across the aftermath.

Another instance, when a joker must have crossed him or stepped out of line with him, Chris took a wire to him. He whipped this guy with a piece of No. 8 wire. It just ripped his back up, and ripped his skin open. Chris thought nothing of it really. But I got a shock to see the fulla, cos I ended up taking him home.

I was separate from them, but whenever I came into contact with them these situations would be prevalent. More often than not I had to resolve the issue or clean up the mess.

I never really had words with him about it. I just saw it as how he conducted his leadership. As for myself, I preferred to be a loner anyway. I'm not really a group man, a gang man. I preferred my own privacy and my own thoughts and I didn't really want to have anybody else imposing their thoughts and philosophies on me, although I was prepared to listen.

The guy he whipped with the wire was Tom Moeke. I don't know whether it went to court. Tom and another fulla considered themselves Rasta. They were from that school of Rasta, from an Auckland group, that denounced the taha Maori. And that was like a red rag to a bull for Chris, and myself included. I wouldn't take on a philosophy that meant I had to forsake my Maoritanga anyway. I saw the philosophy of Rastafari as complementing my Maoritanga and enhancing it.

# WHY THE RASTAS REALLY BEAT JUNIOR PAUL

**A tape recording of myself at the end of a day spent talking to Rastas John Heeney and Cody Haua and Rasta Hamana Brown's father, Sonny Brown, in November, 2000:** It's generally accepted that Junior Paul was crazy. John Heeney said he was bad and used to climb in people's windows at night. I'm not quite sure what that means. But if it's true then at best it's an invasion of privacy. Joe Nepe also told me that Junior was climbing in people's windows, or rather, Joe agreed when I told him what John had said. The Rastas believed Junior was suffering from "mate Maori", a Maori sickness of the mind. They believed someone had stuck a curse on him.

Cody Haua reckoned one of Junior's uncles in Te Teko must have done it. Apparently, Junior was at a rugby match and Junior was spitting in front of his uncle. And his uncle told him not to do it, told him not to do it. And eventually his uncle spat back at Junior Paul. And at the end of telling that story at a Rasta meeting (known as "a reasoning") Junior Paul was laid out on the ground on his back, totally incapacitated. That's why the Rastas believed that was *when* the curse was put on him and that it was his *uncle* who put the curse on him.

Sonny Brown, Rastafarian Hamana Brown's father, said that Junior Paul turned up at his house on the corner of the main highway and Whakapaurangi Road one day. Junior wanted to buy his car. It didn't take Sonny long to realise that the guy was stark raving mad. He took Junior up the road to the Rastas and said, "Here, hang out with these guys."

John Heeney recalls Junior Paul as a "fuckin' nutcase". He reckons Tom Te Maro, a well-respected local tohunga, came and had a look at Junior Paul to see if *he* could help him. "But old Tom hardly even bothered to get out of his car. The next thing we saw of Tom was his wheels skidding as he drove off. He obviously didn't think he could do much for Junior." Junior Paul's behaviour was freaking out the Rastas, who were mostly still in their teens and early twenties.

The Rastas reckoned he had a demon inside him. Cody Haua reckons it was Junior Paul and Lance Kupenga, who'd grabbed a bayonet off a headstone in a cemetery, which belonged to one of Joe Nepe's ancestors. And Nepe had warned these guys that something would happen because they were stealing dope and stealing bayonets off headstones.

Also, Cody and Sonny Brown were saying that Junior and Lance had gone climbing down the hole on Whakaahu Hill. And that was something else that had freaked out these guys because, to the locals, there is no bottom to that hole. It wasn't long after this that Joe chopped Lance's head off and put his head down one of the holes on Whakaahu and his body down the other. And they reckon that Lance Kupenga had just been caught on a ledge. Then after that ledge it just goes down. No one's ever reached the bottom. They've tried to reach the bottom, but they've never made it. They believe it's like the hole that leads down to the underworld.

Cody talked about Junior Paul being in behind a horse and putting his head down to look at the hooves and being kicked in the head, and then putting his head straight back there, unconcerned that he might get kicked again.

Cody remembers Junior Paul bending down and looking through a keyhole. "He'd look through the keyhole and start bursting out laughing. And then you'd go and look through the keyhole and there'd be nothing there. Then he'd go back and look through the same keyhole and suddenly he'd start crying. And you'd go and have another look through the keyhole and there'd still be nothing there."

A few people such as Sonny Brown believed Junior Paul should have been stuck on a bus back to his own people in Tuhoe country so that they could take the curse off him. But John Heeney maintains Junior was in no fit state to be put on a bus. He was too far-gone. And the Rastas were scared his sickness would pass on to them.

There was talk that the Rastas had been told by a tohunga that the old way of getting a demon out of someone was by literally beating the devil out of them, and that they acted on that advice. But John Heeney said that wasn't the case. "It wasn't the *old* way. It was *our* way. If someone's losing it and acting crazy, sometimes a good punch in the head snaps them out of it. It's worked plenty of times in the past."

But did it work on that occasion?

"He was different after that. I could hardly believe it was him at the trial. He became a born-again Christian after what we did to him. And last I heard he was a counselor in Australia."

Cody said he was put away for three years for the Junior Paul incident, but reckons he didn't do it. First of all he said, "I got three years for hitting him fifty times with a horse's bridle. But I didn't hit him fifty times." A minute or so later, almost as an afterthought, he said, "I didn't do it."

**Sue Nikora, cited by many as an early influence on the Rastas:** I've never heard of anyone treating mate Maori with violence. I've never seen that sort of treatment where they beat the hell out of them to get the sickness out of them. It's not the normal thing to do.

If someone suffered mate Maori and they brought him here, you'd sit and you'd study him, study it and - it seems ridiculous to you but not to us - we'd get back into a huddle and sort out who's going to attend to the sick person. If there were three of us here we'd decide who's going to take the lead and take over the curing of the poor guy.

There are lots of things you can do. We've just finished doing a mother and nine children who went all berserk. The whole family went berserk. The kids were like dogs and cats. It was just horrible.

We won't say how we cured them. But the first cure is love for all mankind. That's important; not to beat the hell out of them like that. I can't believe for one moment that's what happened. I would say that's experimental. I would say that's sinister because it doesn't really happen like that. But evil spirits do come into it.

What you've got to do though is study the mate Maori, and ask your guides to give you a blessing and the ability to deal with this situation. See, each and every person has what we call a *Maori*, a life-essence. And you're wrapped with that all the time. It's like an aura. You have your guides. I have mine. So you just ask your kaitiaki, or ask your guardian. You look back and ask, "What shall we do in this situation?" And you get told what to do. It changes from situation to situation.

But you've got to make sure that you're covered before you go in, that you're protected. You do your blessings before you go in otherwise you come out affected.

**Interview on November 17, 2000 with Rasta Joe Nepe (who beheaded fellow Rasta Lance Kupenga in 1985):** *So why did you think that giving Junior a whacking over basically was gonna, you know, sort him out?*
We just didn't know what to do, ay.
*You were at your wits end sort-a thing?*
Yeah.
*What sort of stuff was Junior doing that was freaking everyone out?*
Aw, all sorts of shit, all sorts-a shit.
*Do you remember any incident that kind-a...*
Na, I don't know. I just heard one story there how he went to Nanny Peg's and left some stones there or something.
*Nanny Peg? Aw, Peggy Heeney (John Heeney's mum).*
He left some stones at her place from Whakaahu.
*Aw yeah. Why did he do that?*
I don't know. I don't know.

16

*So he went up to Whakaahu and got these stones and left them there?*
I don't know.
*Why would he do that?*
He left them at her house.
*Just to freak her out or something?*
I don't know. That's all I heard.
*So he did all this stuff that no one could understand.*
Aw, he was doing lots of things. He was just playing marbles, ay.
*Just having everyone on? Just playing games with people?*
Playing games with people.
*Mind games and that?*
Mind games.
*Had he done anything to particularly piss off the Rastas, cos he wasn't part of the Rastas as such was he?*
He was joining in. Well after that he got kicked out.
*Yeah. Well he wouldn't-a been that interested after that would he?*
Ha ha ha ha ha ha.
*So whadyu remember out of that incident?*
Nothing much. Can't remember anything out of that. No, we just beat the shit out of him, that's all.
*Yeah. Was the idea to beat the devil out of him?*
Na. I don't know why they said that. We just wanted to beat him up, give him a good fuckin' hiding.
*Did he need one?*
Yeah. After I heard that story of him taking stones off Whakaahu and taking them to Nanny Peg's, fuck, it really drove me crazy.
*Yeah. Why? Because you couldn't understand what he was getting at?*
I didn't know what he was doing at the time, you know, just couldn't quite figure out what he was doing.
*Yeah. John said something, just in passing, and I probably shouldn't even be going down this track anyway but it's just niggling away. He said something about Junior had been climbing in people's windows and that sort of thing.*
Yeah.
*Had he been doing that sort-a shit?*
Yeah.
*And he'd told you guys about it.*
Well that's the kind of shit he was doing, ay.
*And that didn't go down well either?*
No, that didn't go down well.

**More from Joe Nepe:** The hole up there is *the* bottomless pit. That's where souls go down. But there are a lot of traditions to that place. You don't know which ones to believe.

*What did you read when old Junior Paul put those stones down at Peggy Heeney's house, you having been brought up on Whakaahu Hill, knowing what a sacred place it is?*

Aw, I don't know *why* he did that.

*You don't think he made a mistake?*

Well he shouldn't have did that anyway. That's just cursing someone. That's putting a curse on somebody if you're gonna do that.

*Yeah, cos it's such a sacred place?*

Yeah.

*Yeah, yeah.*

We don't know what kind of stones they were. We don't know where they were from. Actually Chris told me about that, what he had done with those stones.

*What was your reaction when Chris told you?*

Fuck I got angry.

*Yeah.*

I wanted to chop his head off too.

*And what did Chris say?*

He said, "Na, leave him alone. We'll deal to him another way."

*Had you been told by your grandfather or something that that's how they used to deal with people who broke the tapu?*

Aw, wouldn't know. Na, not really. Just heard about it from the old people. Actually, they've got a lot of stories to tell, those old people, but which one to believe, you don't know.


## ON TRIAL FOR BEATING JUNIOR PAUL


*The trial into the beating of Junior Paul begins in Gisborne District Court on Monday, April 14, 1986. Christopher Campbell, John Heeney and Cody Haua are jointly charged with assaulting Paul and injuring him with intent. They all plead not guilty.*

*Junior Paul left Ruatoria after he recovered from the beating and moved back to his family in Murapara. (In 2001 he was living in Melbourne and working as a counselor but, unfortunately, the author was unable to track him down for an interview). Paul tells the court that he arrived in Ruatoria in December 1984. He was water boy and first-aid man for the Rastas' Nga Tama Toa (The Young Warriors) rugby team.*

*Campbell, Heeney and Haua played for the team, as did others, including Joe Nepe, Lance Kupenga and a man called Sonny Bartlett.*

*Paul says that some time in May he went to a house in Ruatoria. He was in the sitting room one afternoon when Campbell and Heeney threw him on the floor and held him there. Heeney, Haua and Nepe stamped on his stomach for some time. Then Haua shaved his head, after which he was taken to the bathroom, where Nepe shaved his arms and groin.*

*From there he went back to the sitting room where Bartlett punched him in the head until he was unconscious. Nepe then took him back to the bathroom where he was sat in a bath of hot water up to his waist. Nepe held his head under the water while Haua held his legs. After being allowed to dress he was taken back to the sitting room where Heeney poked him with a stick and taunted him. "What is your name?" he said. "Your name is the devil. You are Johnny Toobad. You are the evil man."*

*Haua then struck him with a bridle so hard and for so long that Paul voided both his bladder and bowels. By now night had fallen. He was exhausted and fell asleep.*

*The next day he was taken to another house. He stayed there for several days. Most of the time he lay on a mattress and could barely get up. And he couldn't eat solid foods. Campbell, Heeney and Haua came to see him. Campbell was all smiles as though nothing had happened. He said they had beaten the devil out of him and that he was now a holy man. After three nights at the second house Junior Paul was driven back to the Bay of Plenty, where a healer treated him for some months. He also went to Whakatane Hospital where the broken index finger on his left hand was operated on.*

*Chris Campbell, John Heeney and Cody Haua elect to defend themselves against the charges of assault and injuring with intent.*

*Campbell is the only defendant to give evidence. He claims Junior Paul was extremely sick and destitute when they found him. Nobody wanted to help him. He was incoherent, had lapses in memory and emptied his bowels and bladder often and anywhere. At one stage he stood in a fire. He believed Junior Paul was suffering from mate Maori, or Maori sickness.*

John Heeney's mother Repeka, known as Peggy, appears for the Crown. She says she went to the house and found Junior Paul lying on the mattresses. She was shocked by his condition. His face was bruised and swollen. He tried to speak but was incoherent. And when she read to him from The Bible, she cried. She says she'd never heard of anyone trying to literally beat the devil out of a person.

Cross-examined by Campbell, Peggy Heeney remembers attending a prayer session at which Junior Paul was present. Afterwards he had cried and kissed her, she says. He looked sick and she could feel his hands shaking. This was before the Rastas beat him.

Junior Paul has the harrowing ordeal of not only facing up to his attackers in court, but also, of being cross-examined by them. To Heeney – who poked him with a stick and taunted him during his humiliation - he explains that he'd been laughing and crying at the same time because he was looking forward to seeing Joe Nepe. He says he doesn't remember standing in the fire while they were on Whakaahu and Heeney pulling him out. But he agrees that he and Heeney had been pretty good friends.

To Campbell – who, along with Heeney, initiated the attack and who later acted as though he'd done him a favour – Junior Paul concedes that he is not a member of the Mongrel Mob. But he admits he gave the Mongrel Mob hand sign to Nepe when he was being held under water and that, when he saw it, Nepe stopped. When asked about a prayer service involving the whole rugby team at the house where the beating took place, he says he can't remember.

Chris Campbell, John Heeney and Cody Haua are convicted of injuring with intent. (An alternative charge of assault is dismissed). They'll be remanded in custody until April 30 for probation reports and sentencing.

Judge J. D. Hole explains that the case revolved around witness credibility. Junior Paul gave his evidence in a hesitant manner and showed little emotion but was still a compelling witness. Peggy Heeney, John's mum, had corroborated evidence of Paul's injuries, saying she was shocked by his condition, while a doctor and a holistic healer offered further corroboration. Having heard all this, Judge Hole says he's satisfied, beyond all reasonable doubt, that the charges of injuring with intent have been proved.

He says he preferred the evidence of Peggy Heeney to that of Campbell, who was reluctant to give clear answers, and was evasive and shifty. Basically, he didn't accept Campbell's evidence.

Campbell, Heeney and Haua are all sentenced to three years in jail, the maximum penalty, for injuring with intent.

# CHAPTER 2

## TALK OF A PLANNED HUMAN SACRIFICE

**Genevieve Westcott, on the Close Up current affairs programme:**
"Twenty one-year-old Junior Paul was beaten so badly he wound up in hospital, unable to walk unassisted for several days. His assailants apparently believed he'd been possessed by the devil. After shaving his head and groin, they forcibly held him under water in a bath, then threw him on the floor, where he was repeatedly kicked and punched. They also defecated on him, forcing him to eat his own excrement. By this time the victim was unconscious. When he came to, the beatings continued with a horse bridle and a wooden stake around his head. His cries for help were ignored. At the time of that beating, a twenty-five-year-old woman who'd been living with the Rastas for several months was warned by one of the sect members to get out of town. The woman, who had her two-year-old son with her, was told the Rastas were discussing a human sacrifice. The woman fled to Gisborne, so frightened she needed police escorts to get her to the airport and on board her flight home in the South Island."

**Excerpt from an interview with Rasta Joe Nepe in 2000:** *There was one thing I heard mentioned in Gisborne. I don't know if there's much in it. I mentioned it to Cody and he said, "Aw, that woman's still in town," and whatnot. But it's one thing that someone had brought up to me. Cody brought it up. He said he was in Rotorua and someone said this. Someone said that the Rastas were planning to do something to a child or something. They said they were gonna sacrifice a child or something like that. And that was preceding what happened with Lance. Do you remember anything about that?*
No. No.
*Cos what I heard was that, well Cody had heard about it –*
Aw yeah.
*And he couldn't believe it – when he was in Rotorua or something. And he reckoned it was a domestic or something like that. Or someone had had a domestic and they'd made a threat or something like that. But I don't know. Do you...*
No.

*Do you remember anything to do with that?*
No.
*Had you heard that story?*
No.
*You haven't even heard that story?*
It's the first time I've heard it.
*Yeah, yeah, cos when I heard it I thought, "What?" you know.*
Ha ha ha.
*You haven't heard anything about that one?*
Na.
*Yeah, yeah.*
But I know the lady that you're talking about is still in Ruatoria.
*Aw yeah. Did she make up that rumour or something?*
I think she just made that up herself to try and get the better of the Rastas, ay. I don't think the Rastas go around sacrificing children.
*Aw, na, na, na. It obviously never happened but I mean...*
You can tell it's a rumour, ay.
*I mean if it had happened it would have been in court and everyone would know about it. But whadyu think she was doing? Where do you think it came from?*
Dunno.
*Is she a local?*
I think she's a local. I don't even know her myself. But I know she's still in Ruatoria.
*And that she'd passed these rumours around?*
Yeah.
*But you'd never heard of them?*
Na. Actually that's the first time I've heard of that. I've heard of it once before but from someone else.
*Aw yeah okay.*
But not a Rasta, ay. He wasn't a Rasta. He was just a normal person.
*Yeah, yeah.*
I said, "Na, Rastas don't go around sacrificing children."
*Ha ha, yeah.*
Ha ha ha ha ha ha.
*Well that's what I sort of thought.*
It had to be a domestic, ay.
*Yeah, something like that. Cos Cody couldn't believe it. I'd heard it in Gisborne. A cop had told me. And he said he'd had to deal with this woman and*

*they'd had to send her out of town or something. I think Laurie Naden or Mal*
*Thomas or someone like that had mentioned it. So I thought, "Well, shit, I better*
*check it out with the Rastas and just see," you know. It's an awkward one to*
*bring up but...*

Na, it's just a rumour.
*Nothing to it.*
Nothing to it, ay. Just wanna get the names in the paper.

**Detective Malcolm Thomas:** By mid-1985 the police are extremely
concerned about the behaviour of the Ruatoria Rastafarians. We keep hearing
stories of increasingly bizarre practices.

One day I'm asked to escort a Ruatoria woman and her child to the Gisborne
airport. A Maori woman from either the Women's Refuge or Rape Crisis is also
there.

The woman from Ruatoria is terrified. She's a Pakeha, who's been living
with one of the Rasta men. Her son is very light-skinned. He's about three or
four years old and has blonde hair.

It's obvious to me the mother's suffered some severe shock or trauma. I take
her to the Air New Zealand shop to get her tickets. But I can't just wait in the car
while she buys them. I have to go inside with her. She's so petrified I can't leave
her side for a minute.

It's the same when we get to the airport. I have to accompany her to the
counter and wait with her until she gets on the plane. She's getting away from
the Coast as quickly as she can, heading back to the deep south, where her
parents live. She has also asked to be met by the police in Wellington while she
changes planes.

I drive the Maori woman who has accompanied us back into town. On the
way she tells me that the Rastas intended to use the young Pakeha woman's boy
as a human sacrifice. She says they were looking for a rock with an eye on it.
And the only way they were going to locate the rock was by first sacrificing this
particular blonde-haired child. And they needed the stone as an indication of the
second coming. They believe the second coming will take place at Mt Hikurangi.
As for me, I don't know what to make of the story.

**Former Detective Sergeant Laurie Naden:** They had this place at the back
of Ruatoria called Whakaahu, which they believed was the site of an ancient
battleground, and hidden up there was a black diamond. Don't ask me the
significance of the black diamond. But they were looking for this black diamond.
And during one of their dope-smoking scenarios they decided they needed a little

bit of *help*. And they read The Bible constantly. They read it all the time and interpreted it the way they *wanted* to interpret it. But there were *sacrifices* in The Bible. I can only assume that they thought, "Well, maybe if we have a human sacrifice we might appease someone and this bloody diamond may appear."

So this woman – I forget her name now, well, I don't know if I ever knew her name – she was approached and told, "We're going to sacrifice your child." And she ran off to the local sergeant at the time who, like most of us, poo-hooed it until she was spoken to at length. And the cop who spoke to her said, "Shit, she's really upset, mate." And she and the child were actually physically removed to Central Otago, where her parents live. Yeah, so that was of major concern to her and she believed they would carry out their plan.


## THE BLACK DIAMOND (1)


*I haven't, by any means, read or heard everything there is to know about the black diamond, but just enough to give an idea what the Rastas were looking for. I was going to add, "without holding up the story too much". But we are going to drift away on the odd tangent in this and, particularly, the other related chapters. People talk about the black diamond and wander off onto other subjects, which I find too interesting to interrupt. Or they tell stories tenuously linked to the black diamond and these are connected to other stories, not related to the black diamond at all, but which offer useful insights to the environment, which spawned the Ruatoria Rastafarians. Or they tell stories that remind me of other stuff I've read or heard and that gets put into the mix as well.*

*Legend has it that the black diamond was worn by the 19th century Maori prophet Te Kooti Arikirangi Te Turuki, who was born among the chiefly ranks of Ngati Maru of Gisborne.*

*Te Kooti was the founder of the Maori faith known today as the Ringatu (or the Upraised Hand). He received his divine message of deliverance while a prisoner of war on the island of Wharekauri in the Chatham Islands.*

*The charges against Te Kooti remain uncertain. At the onset of the Poverty Bay civil war in 1865, he had reluctantly fought for the Government against the Hauhau. And some say he was imprisoned because he was believed to be a spy. Another version has to do with his reputation as a ladies' man: he'd become too*

*friendly with a local chief's wife, so the cuckolded husband laid a false charge
that Te Kooti had been seen supplying gun-caps to the Hauhau.*

*On the schooner that took Te Kooti to the Chatham Islands, he was the
only prisoner who was not a member of the Pai Marire, or Hauhau faith.*

*Pai Marire was the first movement to weave the new Christian God and the
Bible, introduced by Anglican missionaries, into the Maori belief system. The
founder, Te Ua, from the Taranaki tribe, told his followers that New Zealand
was Israel, the Maori were just like the Israelites when they were exiled to
Babylon, and, just like in the Bible, God would return their land to them.*

*Te Kooti himself would carry on this affinity with the Israelites in the Old
Testament, as would all subsequent Maori religious movements, down to the
Ruatoria Rastafarians.*

*Another thing Maori could relate to in the Old Testament was the historical
significance of prophets. Like the Israelites, Maori have always had them. In
1766, three years before Captain James Cook sailed into Poverty Bay, Toiroa,
from Mahia, south of Gisborne, is said to have predicted the arrival of strangers
with white skin. He's also said to have prophesied the birth of Te Kooti.*

**Judith Binney, The Oxford Illustrated Encyclopedia of New Zealand:**
"The role of the prophet in colonial Maori society would be reinforced rather
than undermined by the introduction of Christianity. The Old Testament
prophetic tradition was an integral part of the early Protestant teaching, while the
situational parallels between the Maori and the Israelite tribes became
imaginatively potent as conflicts over land and sovereignty developed in the
mid-nineteenth century... ... Living in a pre-Darwinian world and needing to
explain their different appearance and culture from that of the settlers, they chose
to associate themselves with the early Israelites, probably because they shared a
tribal history of migration."

*Anyway, Te Kooti escaped from the island of Wharekauri with his followers
by hi-jacking a schooner called the Rifleman and forcing the sailors on board to
take him back to the East Coast. He landed at a stony beach called
Whareongaonga, south of Gisborne on July 10, 1868.*

*From that time, Te Kooti and his followers were pursued by the military and,
from February 1870, Ngati Porou warriors led by Ropata Wahawaha, until
given sanctuary in Te Kuiti in May 1872.*

*The story of Te Kooti's black diamond was born during his time on the run in
the bush of Te Wera, near Ngatapa, inland from Gisborne.*

**Judith Binney, Redemption Songs – A Life of Te Kooti Arikirangi Te Turuki:** It was in the darkness of this heavy forest that his followers first noticed that he carried with him the brightest light to guide their way. Ned Brown's narrative of Te Kooti's diamond begins: "Te Kooti... used that diamond to go through a dense bush at Te Wera. And those that followed him saw it. It was in the form of a lamb: the diamond."

... It is told in many areas of the country, where different versions connect the narrative to the particular locality and to the particular people...

... Lena Te Kani Te Ua of Puha also remembered being told by her mother, Arihia, that, when Te Kooti rode on his white horse into Opotiki in the 1880s, he carried the diamond. It was 'as big as a duck's egg' and he wore it in a little flax kit tied at his neck. The kit now kept the light partially hidden, for otherwise people had to turn their faces away from the brightness of the stone... ... Wherever he journeyed in the wars it will be seen that he gave a portion of the diamond to place on the sacred mountains of the people for their protection.

*So where did the diamond come from? Some say from India, on the Rifleman itself. Others say it made its way, from hand to hand, down from Biblical times.*

**Reuben Riki of Ngati Maru, formerly the assistant secretary to the Ringatu church in the Gisborne area (quoted by Judith Binney in Redemption Songs):** People that go out possum hunting, they could see this luminous light coming up from one area, only one area, at night. This one here, it's at Paparatu... This one, here, it is a diamond. He (Te Kooti) came here with a purpose – as the story goes – that he came here to hide all his wealth. If theywere to find the wealth of this country, they will ruin this country. He says, "It's better to be hidden." But there is a day coming. Someone, or somebody, will (be) bound to find this and there will be plenty for all.

*Now Te Kooti prophesied that he would have a successor, who would complete his work. He had a recurring vision that a star appearing in the east would mark the advent of a new leader. And, just before he died in 1893, he predicted the Maori Messiah would show himself within twenty-six years.*

*In the legends surrounding the Knights of the Round Table, the young King Arthur is recognised because he is the only person able to pull the sword from the stone. Likewise, Te Kooti's successor would be recognised by his ability to perform certain tasks (set by Te Kooti himself).*

*Members of Te Haahi o Te Kooti Rikirangi (the church of Te Kooti) accepted that the prophet Wi Raepuku was the successor. The church gathered together seven of Te Kooti's sayings in a manuscript, "The Prediction of One to Follow". The sayings are referred to as the seven seals (a set of tasks and riddles). The Maori Messiah had to prove himself by opening the seals.*

*According to this church, the sixth seal concerns the hidden bones of Te Kooti. Some believe that if the prophet's bones are returned to Gisborne, a diamond of considerable size will be discovered. And then there's this...*

**The Prediction of One to Follow:** 7th Seal. Te Kooti's Word, concerning his Stone. You are laid here in this place by me; it is for my child to unearth you.

**Judith Binney, Redemption Songs:** Juxtaposed with the statement are the scriptural texts of Isaiah 28:16 and Revelation 2:17, which are cited as confirmation. The first describes the precious stone laid as the foundation of Zion, or the corner-stone. The second is an even more famous text: To him that overcometh will I give to eat of the hidden mana, and will give him a white stone, and in the stone a new name written, which no man knoweth saving he that receiveth it.

**Rasta leader John Heeney (interviewed at a time when I knew nothing about the black diamond):** You say (retired Detective Sergeant) Laurie Naden was talking about us searching for the black diamond. Maybe this is what Laurie and them are talking about. "To him that overcometh I will give to eat of the hidden mana and will give him a white stone and in that stone a new name written which no man knoweth saving he that receiveth it." That's Revelations 2, Verse 17.

*So whaddya reckon? Something was given to Laurie?*

Yeah. He got his own gun stuck in his ear (by Chris Campbell). He got his own 357 Smith and Wesson magnum with no safety catch stuck in his ear. "What the fuck's this, Laurie?!"

**Sue Nikora, early influence on Rastas:** The only white stone I can think of is the moamoa stone. Scientists have studied the moamoa stones on Mount Hikurangi. There used to be myths about their curative value. And then in the 1840s the geologists came in and made their discoveries about the flora and fauna of Hikurangi. A man called Stack was one of the scientists.

They did the full research and testing and discovered that these stones came out of the mountain. There are two rivers that come out of the mountain and where the two rivers meet a chemical process occurs. The only minerals that were there were pyrite (iron sulfide or "fool's gold") and iron ore. But a chemical process occurred to formulate these stones they call the moamoa stones. The moa is an extinct bird. The name moa is also the name that is given to a chicken in the islands. And the moamoa name would have been because the shape of the stones is like an egg.

The stones have got healing properties. In some of our books we've got people saying in Maori, "I've got my foot trampling on things that are not visible to the naked eye." They already had a sense of value for those things of yore. So they hid them. They didn't want to expose them until such time as it should come out. I realised afterwards they have a section in the law, in the 1852 constitution, where it says that one foot of your land is yours, what's underneath belongs to the Crown. And that was the reason why our people said, "We'll put our foot on it until such time as that law is taken away, and then we will reveal it."

Well it's already been revealed. But we're waiting for that time when we can ask the Waitangi Tribunal or whatever to uplift it. There are tonnes of these moamoa stones. It's marketable, like quartz crystals. They're useful for stress, arthritis and all sorts of illnesses. You just hang them around your neck. They have remarkable healing powers.

**Rasta John Heeney:** The police came up against a group, which was against their whole movement, and they couldn't handle it. And there was only a handful of us. And yet the New Zealand Police Force couldn't find a solution because they were just looking at it totally wrong.

Like they say, the black stone. "Those Rastas are always talking about the black stone."

*The black diamond?*

Donna Heeney (John's wife): Well, the black stone has been revealed.

John: Like I just showed you in there (The Bible). "To him I'll give him a pure white stone with a new name inside it."

*So it moved on from that?*

Well, *they* can't move on from it. *They* can't move on from the black diamond. They're never gonna pass that stone. That stone is gonna be a stumbling block for them for the rest of their lives. It's not gonna let them go any further in spirituality way of living unless they get on their knees and really give their hearts over to the Lord. Then… maybe… Then maybe...

*Explain this black stone and white stone to me as in, when you say it's moved on from that?*

The kingdom of heaven is like a man walking through a field. And he tripped over a stone. And then when he found and looked at this stone and saw the value of it he went and sold everything he had to buy that field.

*And that's a story in The Bible?*

Yeah.

*Where would I find that? New Testament?*

Yeah, in the Gospels.

*Gospel according to?*

Jesus.

Donna: Jesus is the white stone because he's the New Testament. And the black stone was Te Kooti because he was like the Old Testament.

John, patting his heart: Here it is. Here's the stone here. Here's the stone here.

*So it's all symbolism?*

Yeah. The stone is here. Hence comes the shepherd of Israel. The stone is a person. The stone is not a rock it's a person. It talks about it in The Bible, him being the stone ay, the *rock*. Like Christ is the rock, ay. He's the sure foundation. But he's not a stone, he's a man, he's a flesh and bone. Now the black diamond is a pure stone. The diamond is made out of one carbon and that makes itpure. Purity is also symbolised as white and that's why there's the pure white stone.

*So the black diamond is like the most pure stone you can get is it, or?*

Yeah.

*In science and whatnot?*

Yeah.


*The prophet Rua Kenana Hepetipa claimed he was Te Kooti's "son" after seeing the diamond in a vision on Maungapohatu, the sacred mountain of the Tuhoe, inland from the Bay of Plenty in 1905.*

*Rua said the archangel Gabriel had appeared before him and told him to ascend Maungapohatu. He climbed the mountain with his wife Pinepine. Then the Tuhoe female ancestor Whaitiri appeared and revealed the diamond to Rua. It had been covered by a shawl left by Te Kooti. Rua left the diamond on the mountain. From that day on, he knew he was the chosen one.*

*He gathered followers and took them back to the promised land, Maungapohatu, where he built his own settlement. The two main buildings were called Hiruharama Hou (New Jerusalem) and Hiona (Zion). And for nine years, from 1907 to 1916, Maungapohatu thrived, a bastion of Maoridom against the Pakeha.*

Rua and his followers were committed to Te Kooti's compact with the government for a "long abiding peace". But during the First World War, when the men refused to volunteer, this caused conflict with the law. Rua was eventually arrested during a police raid on the settlement in which two men, including one of his sons, were shot dead. He was imprisoned for "morally resisting arrest".

After Rua's return from prison in 1918, Maungapohatu was reconstructed. In 1927, all the houses were rebuilt in preparation for the end of the world. When God didn't appear, Rua postponed the millennium. He died in 1937 telling his followers, "the Israelites", that he would rise again from the tomb. Apparently, a few believers are still waiting.

# CHAPTER 3

## THE RASTAS TURN ON THEIR RELATIVES

In May, 1985, the Rastafarians move into two houses on Koura Station on Whareponga Road. That particular part of the station is leased from the Crown.

Koura is managed by Kate Walker and her husband. Kate is the sister of Peggy Heeney, who's the mother of Rastafarian John Heeney. Kate and Peggy are also sisters of the late Moana Ngarimu. Moana won a Victoria Cross for bravery with the Maori Battalion in the Second World War, and is venerated as a hero by his nephews in the Rastafarians.

When the Rastas occupy the shearers' quarters, known as the top house, without permission the managers aren't happy.

But the Rastas believe that because Koura Station and all the land around Whareponga once belonged to their tipuna, or ancestors, it's their birthright to come and go on it as they please.

**Rasta Joe Nepe:** After the fence-cutting at Taitai Maunga we did the rustling, cutting fences, ousting. We went to Te Ano then. We were based at Te Ano, down at Whareponga, Koura Station.

There was a family grievance there. John Heeney was supposed to get that house there. That top house was supposed to be John's. That was his family's house. That's one of the reasons why we went there, to grab it actually cos no one was staying in it, ay. That's why Chris and John took over the house, because Chris was going with Tina, John's sister. Michael Heeney was with us then, too. But he's with the Black Power now.

**Sergeant Alex Hope's background report on Ruatoria for Police:** It would appear that the information upon which they based the land claim came from Sue Nikora and the East Coast Genealogical Society.

**Policing the Tairawhiti, a book by former policeman John Robinson:** When Sergeant Nimo Panifasio transferred to the police college in 1983, it was difficult to get a sergeant to take over the station as the "Ruatoria troubles" were just starting. Constable Norm Gray applied for the position and was promoted to sergeant, and took over the position. He transferred in 1985 to Otahuhu and was followed by Sergeant Alex Hope who knew the area well, having previously been stationed as a constable at Te Araroa.

**Tom Heeney, Rasta John Heeney's father and the deputy chief of the Ruatoria Voluntary Fire Brigade:** My wife Peggy hears that the Rastas have kidnapped one of our daughters, Tina, the elder one, who's been going with Chris Campbell. My in-laws, the Ngarimus, have a manager's house in Whareponga. But there's no one living in it and the Rasties have moved in.

So I think, "I'll go down and sort 'em out."

But first I figure I better go down and see the sergeant. So I go down to see this sergeant Gray and say, "Aw, I'm gonna go down and have it out with them."

He says, "Aw no, don't do that." He says he's heard about it and he'll ring Gisborne. "Don't go out. We'll all meet at the station at 8 o'clock and travel out then."

Okay. I get there about quarter to 8 - no one there. Then it's 8. Then at about quarter past 8 I go round and knock at his house to find out what he's doing. His wife says, "Aw, he's gone."

"Where?"

"Aw, he's out doing something."

"Is anyone coming up from Gisborne?"

"I don't know."

So Peg and I get in the truck and I drive out there. There's a big gang of them and they're quite aggressive. They're the types who'll stand up and get cheeky.

31

But I'm the same. I'm aggressive in my own way. And I'm thinking, "If they knock my girl around they're gonna get it."

So I go out there and I get to the door and the door's locked. I give the door a bang. They're having breakfast inside and they've locked all the doors. So I go to one of the windows and lift that up. Of course, I hear all the other windows all flying open. As I'm going in one way they're jumping out the other side of the house. And by the time I get in, there's no one in the house, only my daughter.

They've all taken off and jumped over the fence. They hang around there but they won't come back over because they know if I get hold of them I'll dong them.


## FOURTEEN ARRESTS, TWO HUNDRED CHARGES


**Tom Heeney:** We had our words with John. But he was gonna go his way. He was full of dope and stuff at the time. So I just told him, "We don't want you back in the house. If you wanna go and live with them, you go and live with them chaps. Don't come back here." He just went his own way.

***Sunday, June 2, 1985 (the day after members of the Ruatoria Rastafarians beat up Junior Paul):*** *The Rastas have installed themselves in the "top house" on Koura Station. The managers tell the Rastafarians that they have no permission to occupy the vacant cottage. They're asked to leave the property. The police give the Rastas two days to leave or their gear will be shifted out.*

***Tuesday, June 4:*** *Two Ruatoria police officers visit the top house while the Rastas are away. They turn loose two horses that don't belong to Koura Station. And they load all items not belonging to Koura Station into a car belonging to one of the Rastas. They drive the car to a house where Chris Campbell normally lives and leave it there.*

***Monday, June 10:*** *The number of Rastafarians staying at Koura Station has grown.*

*At mid-day forty police, including eighteen members of the Armed Offenders Squad, start planning Operation Whareponga. Chief inspector Mick Huggard is in charge.*

*Tuesday, June 11:* *The police and Armed Offenders Squad carry out a dawn raid on the cottage at Koura Station. By 7am, fourteen Rastafarians have been arrested. Sergeant Norm Gray is in a helicopter. He's responsible for aerial observation of any escaping group members. He uses the helicopter to contain three trying to get away on horseback but notices others leaving by another route. Cody Haua is arrested in Ruatoria. The police also round up several stolen horses at Koura Station.*

*Wednesday, June 12:* *Fourteen Rastafarians appear in the Gisborne District Court. They all reject the services of a duty solicitor. Instead Chris Campbell speaks for them.*

*"They came with guns, rifles, dogs and brutality," he says. "They busted into our home, assaulted our children and brethren, and threatened us with acts of violence."*

*He says they were crammed into vans and that some were handcuffed too tightly. His own wrists still hurt. It was so hot in the vans that most had stripped to their underwear by the time they arrived in Ruatoria.*

*Anthony Wayne Chambers and Darryl Robert Te Hau are both fined for possession of cannabis.*

*The other twelve face a variety of charges such as being unlawfully in a building, willful damage and stealing.*

*Campbell says the cottage where they were arrested belongs to his brother-in-law (John Heeney) and they had his permission to be there as long as they wanted. In response to references to the men riding horses over other people's land, he tells the court that Whareponga was the land of their tipuna (ancestors) and it was their birthright to move freely on it.*

*He says he knows nothing about nineteen stolen horses or the cutting of fences. Judge R. J. Gilbert is presented with a written submission from the police on why they want the Rastafarians to be remanded in custody. The police say they're processing more charges against the group and are concerned that they won't answer bail bonds. Sergeant Chris Douglas tells the court that numerous threats have been made against police, buildings, vehicles and other people while the Rastas have been in custody.*

*Campbell quotes Psalms 68, verse 4: But the just rejoice and exult before God; they are glad and rejoice.*

*He says The Bible tells them not to be violent and that they do not comprehend violence.*

*Campbell promises that bail will be answered. He tells Judge Gilbert that the Rasta man is a peaceful man who worships God every day and gives his allegiance to Jah. He says all the Rastas have promised on The Bible that they will respect bail.*

*Sergeant Douglas says that when the threats of violence were made in custody, Campbell was the most vocal.*

*Judge Gilbert decides all of the remaining twelve Rastas will be remanded in police custody until June 19.*

**Wednesday, June 19, 1985:** *One of the Rastas, Raymond Gray, is transferred to the Children and Young Persons Court. The other eleven appear in Gisborne District Court. They face between sixteen and nineteen charges each, collectively more than two hundred charges, mostly relating to the theft of twenty-eight horses from Ruatoria.*

*All the men who were refused bail by judge R. J. Gilbert last week, are now released on bail and remanded without plea.*

*Judge J. D. Hole tells the Rastafarians he's been assured there will be no offending before their next court appearance and that they're being released on this condition.*

## "IT WAS ALL ABOUT LAND"

**Wednesday, July 24, 1985:** *A story about East Coast land rights issues appears in The Gisborne Herald. Land is the hot topic in Ruatoria right now. The Rastafarians are fueled by feelings that they've been robbed of their ancestral land by Pakeha landowners, such as the Williams family. And many say that Sue Nikora is quietly feeding the Rastas' fire.*

*The headline reads: Positive reaction to land claims.*

*This is the story:* Research into claims by the Ngati Porou Hikurangi Mountain land claim committee has been completed and two of them have some definite substance, says Maori Affairs minister Koro Wetere.

"We are absolutely thrilled for our sub-tribe, Te Aitanga a Mate and the Ngati Porou people and the committee as a whole," said committee member Sue Nikora.

"Many of the troubles which have arisen could have been prevented if we could have had confirmation earlier."

She pointed out that the committee had 233 affiliated members and chairman Hamana Keelan had been working on the claims for the past 20 years.

Another dedicated member Mrs Waiomaho Kaa had been on the committee for over two years and Mrs Nikora had been on it for ten.

In a letter to the committee Mr Wetere said a detailed report was now being drawn up from all the research and this would be made available to the committee as soon as possible.

"I would ask you to be patient just a little longer while the full details of any possible action on the two claims is fully researched," the letter stated.

All the claims were being thoroughly researched and he would do all he could to settle the successful ones.

In a letter to Mr Keelan, Prime Minister David Lange assured him the return of Hikurangi Mountain and other disputed lands to Ngati Porou is being carefully considered. The matter would be fully dealt with in the final report to Mr Keelan.

*One time while I was up in Ruatoria, Hughie Hughes, the local electrician (with whom my uncle Archie used to work) mentioned that Chris Campbell's brother, Ike, still lived with his partner and kids up at the Campbell family home in Makarika. I decided I'd stop in on the way back to Gisborne. I asked Hughie if Ike had been in the Rastas. No, he said, Ike was friend and family to the Rastas, but had never really been part of the group. Unlike the Rastas, who had the full moko, Ike had only ever had one side of his face tattooed. Hughie seemed to think this symbolised Ike's relationship with the group: sympathetic but not fully immersed.*

*I found the Makarika turn-off just south of Ruatoria. Some people who lived on the corner gave me instructions on how to get to the Campbells. Before long the road turned to loose metal. I drove my little black Honda City as far as it could go, to the edge of a thin, windy river, which flowed over black and brown stones. It was a stinking hot day. I rolled up my jeans to my knees and took off my shoes and socks, carrying them in my hand as I picked my way across. Then it was up through the bush on the steep bank, holding on to manuka trunks and branches and finding my footing on tree roots. The river was so windy I had to cross it three times on foot, putting my shoes on when I left the water and taking them off every time I encountered it again. There was no other soul in sight. The sun was a yellow ball. The air was still and hot, and electric with the rattle of cicadas. The water was cold and the stones hard under my sensitive city feet. I tried to appreciate the uniqueness of my situation. I was discovering a beautiful little pocket of the world that otherwise I'd never have seen. I followed the road around a corner into some waterlogged green paddocks dotted with cattle munching lazily. The house was up on the hill. No one was moving around outside. It looked empty. I jumped from dry spot to dry spot across the paddock with only limited success. Some dogs near the house started barking and leaping against their chains. I noticed a white cross, painted on a door. As I came closer I realised all the doors and windows had white crosses painted on them. "Hello!" I yelled. "Anyone home! Hello! Hello!" I came up to the fence and yelled again. The dogs seemed to be going berserk by now. So I wasn't going to go into the yard. "Hello! Hello!" Oh well. I turned around and made my way back to the car. Fruitless trips like this were a common experience as I made contacts and collected interviews. Even arranged interviews (particularly with the Rastas) were never certain until you were sitting across the table from the person to whom you wanted to speak. It seemed to me that there were no devious or paranoid motives behind this unreliability. People lived on what is commonly known in Gisborne as "East Coast Time". Arrangements seemed to be genuinely forgotten immediately after they were made. But, even when interviewees failed to show, I seldom went home empty-handed. People on the coast are enthusiastic talkers and storytellers. And I always seemed to find someone willing to chat about what had happened in their town.*

*Back at Mum and Dad's in Gisborne a few days later, I was talking to Gordon Sutton, a Maori guy, who at that time was living with my cousin Linda. They'd had three beautiful children together. Gordon had been one of Chris Campbell's best mates as a kid. He offered to take me up in his four-wheel-drive to see Ike and to also introduce me to Chris's other brother, Joe "Boots", who'd been in the Rastas. And that's what he did.*

**Ike Campbell:** There were people we would today consider to be our elders, who were wrong. And it seems that some of them got those fullas all hyped up. And look what happened. Things got out of hand. And when the time came for these guys to pay for their crimes, these so-called elders didn't wanna know them.

I believe that their advisers at the time grossly misguided them. Land was their motivation. I still believe it was all about land.

I disagree with what was happening. Some farmers were getting their fences cut. Horses were being stolen. At the start, that's what was happening. And then it got worse. Houses started getting burnt down.

But it all goes back to the land confiscations around here. That's what it was about. All the land, as far as the eye can see, was confiscated. They'd get it through what they called a breach of the Native Land Court or its agents at that time, *done* by the Native Land Court.

I think Chris did his own research and realised that all this land was confiscated. And the thing is he had a direct descent to it - he was living on his ancestral land, no matter what - if you look at the four sides of h_s two parents, even on the Campbell side. It's common knowledge a lot of what Chris was upset about. Everyone around here knows it.

For Chris, it wasn't a matter of getting guys to follow him. They were all whanau anyway. They're all the same family. They were just hanging out together. Everyone was a brother or a cousin to everyone else. Chris had a bit of a gift of the gab, but he was also a pretty hard-headed bloke.

His whakapapa says that he's the senior line all the way down, male lines. We are a sub-tribe of Ngati Porou. We have our own ancestral and territorial boundaries, which are all you can see. The sub tribe is Te Aowera. That is the head of the maraes in this area here. That's what it's all about. The chief during the late 1800s brought the people up from the beach from Whareponga to Jeru (Hiruharama) to Te Aowera, he was the one who was losing the land, our ancestor, the paramount chief Tuta Nihoniho. He was losing it through the Native Land Court. It was being legislated away from him. They were doing it by passing various acts and just downright dishonesty really. Months on end they'd have to wait outside the courthouse in Waiomatatini, on the other side of Ruatoria.

The Rastas weren't the first people to protest about the land around here. The people have been here down through the centuries. What's happened has come to us. We just happen to be here now. Those problems have come to us.

Taranaki and the Waikato had their land confiscated by the gun, we moreso by the pen, but confiscation's confiscation.


Ike: We've been all over New Zealand and we can't find records of that particular court case. This is a memorandum of transfer of land. It says, "We Hone Hehe and Renata Hape, of the County of Waiapu…"

*Angus: There should have been a record of this. He was pronounced bankrupt and so they took the land off him. How much land?*

That whole hill over there that you're looking at. And that goes right into the next valley, which is Ihungia.

*Who owns that now, the Williams?*

Well it's just been sold under our noses again to another guy a millionaire, who doesn't give a fuck he's got that much money.

*So with Hone Hehe being made bankrupt and this land deal taking place…*

The thing is we can't find any records. We've been all over New Zealand. There should be minutes to that court case. And as far as the Auckland archives are concerned no such court case took place.

*So it could have been someone just sitting at a desk and sending a piece of paper to you.*

We got that from the lands and deeds, from the top drawer, that and Valuation New Zealand.

*Who got the land originally when Hone was found bankrupt?*

The Maori Land Court, who in turn sold it on. That's what they used to do.

*Ike was walking Gordon and me out to the gate. It was a beautiful sunny East Coast day with a slight breeze. Ike's dogs were barking at us, but were tied to their kennels. Ike leaned up against a tanalised pine gatepost. "You see that hill over there?" he asked.*

*"Yeah," I said.*

*"Well at the back of that hill is a block called Orua. That's Makarika Station. Our people have an ancient pa site there. It's called Te Rere E Waho. And in approximately 1890, two hundred men, women and children were forcibly removed from there by the armed constabulary. They owned the land. But it was given to another Maori people.*

*"The Maori people it was given to sold it to the Williams family. And the Williams gave it to the Cotterills as a wedding present. A lot of that went on up here, the Williams gifting farms to their family and friends."*

## ON TRIAL FOR TRESPASSING

**Friday, August 2, 1985:** *Chris Campbell is the first of the Rastafarians to go on trial for trespassing on Koura Station at Whareponga.*

*Central to his defence is the letter sent by Maori Affairs Minister Koro Wetere to the Hikurangi Mountain claims committee (even though the Rastas were arrested for trespass in June and the letter was dated July 18). Wetere sent the letter in response to a petition seeking the return of all lands from Mt Hikurangi to the sea. Committee researchers Sue Nikora and Jill Kaa reveal the contents of the letter to the court.*

*The letter states that research into the claims has been completed and that those in relation to blocks of land at Mohaka and Awapuni appear to have some substance. The witnesses have clearly interpreted this to mean that all other claims have been upheld and the lands returned with the two specified blocks still to be resolved. Campbell and members of the claims committee believe the* letter effectively returned 2.8 million acres of East Coast land to the Maori people. But Judge J. D. Hole does not agree with that interpretation of the letter. He tells Campbell and his defence witnesses that they've completely misrepresented it. Judge Hole says it's clear the letter meant only two claims had any substance, and that it then follows that the other claims had no substance. He's satisfied the evidence before him shows that a trespass notice was entitled to be served on Campbell and that he willfully trespassed after receiving it.

The court hears how Campbell was warned by Koura Station proprietors to stop trespassing. He was served a notice and was later found in a dwelling on the station known as the top house.

Evidence is produced to prove the land belongs to the Crown.

The title of the land is presented to the court. This includes certified copies of consolidation orders of the Maori Land Court. The land in question was vested in the Crown Land and the lease transferred to an incorporation.

In essence, the defence is based on the right of access to ancestral land. It's a right Campbell believes he should be able to enjoy regardless of titles. Tracing his own genealogy Campbell tells the judge that he believes he has a birthright to come and go on ancestral land as he pleases. He says land vested in the Crown by ancestors was leased for ninety-nine years, a lease expiring in 1984. The land involved in the trespass charge was a small part of the Hikurangi Reserve.

Giving evidence for Campbell, Nikora says he was evicted wrongfully from the land. She says it's a matter that should've been thrashed out on a marae rather than in a court. She believes he had every right to occupy ancestral land.

Nikora refutes Crown prosecutor Terry Stapleton's assertion that Wetere's letter clearly stated only two areas had any prospect of successful return to the Ngati Porou people. She and Jill Kaa both claim that the bulk of the land claimed has been returned by the Crown and now belongs to the claims committee's trustees.

In his decision Judge Hole says it's clear there existed a Crown lease on the land and that there's nothing in the certificate of title to say the lease was surrendered or no longer existed. On that alone, he says, the Crown's case succeeds.

But, Judge Hole says, it's also important to look at Wetere's letter of July 18, and that it has been "completely misrepresented". Campbell is found guilty and remanded in custody until Monday on this and other matters for which he faces crown depositions.

***Monday, August 5, 1985:*** *It's the first day of depositions for the other Rastas on charges over Operation Whareponga, which the Rastas' refer to among themselves as Operation Overkill.*

*The Crown is attempting to establish a prima facie case against the Rastas. It alleges they occupied land on Koura Station at Whareponga as an unlawful base from which to steal horses, saddles and other property from neighbouring farms.*

*Lance Kupenga doesn't show up for the trial (he's been killed by Joe Nepe and his body hasn't been found yet). The judge issues a warrant for Kupenga's arrest.*

***Tuesday, August 6:*** *The Rastas' hearing gets underway. Twelve Rastafarians, not counting Lance Kupenga, face one hundred and sixty one charges.*

*By the time depositions is over and the lawyers have pruned out all the charges police can't back up with hard evidence, it's down to ten Rastas facing more than one hundred and twenty charges.*

***Friday, August 9:*** *Chris Campbell's in court again, to be sentenced for trespassing on Koura Station. Campbell is ordered to do ninety-six hours of community work on a marae.*

*The Rastas consider themselves reasonably lucky. They're getting off lightly, considering they took over a farm house when the manager didn't want them there and were caught with thousands of dollars worth of stolen goods. Everyone in Ruatoria knows the Rastas are heavily into theft, but because they work as a group, it's hard to pin any one crime on an individual.*

***Monday, September 30, 1985:*** *The trial of ten Rastafarians facing more than a hundred and twenty charges, following Operation Whareponga on June 11, is due to start today. But there are hold-ups. A one hundred-strong jury panel turns up. But Judge B. O. Nicholson is locked away discussing the case in chambers. Eventually the jurors are sent home.*

***Wednesday, October 2:*** *Joe Nepe is no longer among the Rastas facing trial on theft charges. He's awaiting trial for beheading Lance Kupenga.*

*Two of the Rastas enter pleas of guilty to five of fifteen theft charges laid against them jointly with all but one of the accused Rastas. The remaining theft and fifteen receiving charges are discharged (under section 347 of the Criminal Justice Act). The two Rastas taking the rap are twenty-one-year-old Tiger Hongara and eighteen-year-old Sammy Keelan. Interestingly (perhaps* *conveniently), they're the same two who "found" Lance Kupenga's remains in the two holes on the hillside at Whakaahu, while "walking in the hill country". They are remanded until next Thursday for probation reports and sentence. Convictions are entered against them on the charges to which they plead guilty. These involve theft of horses, saddles, bridles and other riding gear worth about $6000.*

*Alan Kirikino pleads guilty to one of the charges involving a number of horses, while Barney Wharepapa pleads guilty to the theft of one horse.*

*But there are still plenty of charges to come from Operation Whareponga.*

**Auckland, Tuesday, November 17, 2000 (part of an interview with Rasta Joe Nepe):** *It must have been hard for you in the days that followed with old Lance supposed to turn up at court and all that sort of thing.*

Yeah.

*And you had to carry on with your day-to-day life.*

Yeah.

*Did it play on your mind?*

Na. Once it was over that was it.

*Did you tell the other guys about it?*

Yeah. They didn't do anything.

*They were just sort of thinking, "Aw shit, how do we keep this quiet," or...*

It all came out in the end anyway. We found out who it was anyway. It was Sammy and Tiger that took the cops up there, ay.

*I don't know.*

Yeah it was them that took the cops up there.

*Sammy Keelan and Tiger Hongara?*

Yeah.

*That came out in court didn't it?*

Yeah. Ha ha ha ha ha ha ha ha ha. Fuck I don't know what they were up to.

*They just freaked out did they?*

Yeah, I think they just freaked out. I think they freaked out when the twelve told them. When the twelve told them what had happened they freaked out.

*Mmm. So when you say the twelve? Who would-a been the twelve at that stage?*

Chris Campbell, Mahuta, me, John Heeney...

*Who's Mahuta?*

Beau-beau. Beau Tuhura.

*Aw yeah.*

... Diesel Dick, Cody, Hamana, Hata. Who else was with us then? Aw, a few others. Jano Kirikino, young Sammy Keelan, Tiger and Gallace Hongara, Tony Chambers. *(Joe's actually listed 13 names.)*

**Rasta Hata Thompson:** The original twelve would have been Lance, me, Sammy Keelan, Cody Haua, John Heeney, Joe Nepe, Chris, Sonny Bartlett, Beau Tuhura, Hamana Brown, Gallace and Tiger Hongara. We were all related by blood. We were all cousins. We all go back to the ancestor Porourangi. That's who the Ngati Porou come from. But because of our blood ties and land ties, we've all been there for generations.

*Wednesday, December 4: Eleven Rastas are in court. They face a total of ninety-one charges of receiving and ninety of theft relating to horses, saddles, riding and farming equipment.*

*Friday, December 13: Seven Rastafarians facing over a hundred and eighty charges of theft and receiving are found not guilty in Gisborne District Court. The jury of seven women and five men take almost six hours to reach their verdict.*

*Saturday, December 21: Three of the Rastas – Sammy Keelan, Tiger Hongara and Alan Kirikino - are jailed for three months for charges arising from Operation Whareponga. The three had pleaded guilty. All in all, Operation Whareponga and the few paltry convictions that followed amounted to a failure for police and a victory for the Rastas.*

**Farmer Colin Williams:** The police were absolutely incredible considering what they went through. But the judges down here in Gisborne were pathetic when the police brought the boys down. The police had tonnes of evidence. They knew who'd done what. And then the judges would let them straight out on bail. In the end most of them got off.


**THE BLACK DIAMOND (2)**


**Rasta Hata Thompson, interviewed in Gisborne in July, 2001:** *Well what about the black diamond?*

Te Kooti had a black diamond. They reckon the black diamond of Te Kooti is supposed to be a diamond. But I reckon it isn't. I reckon it's a greenstone, and it's probably dark black. Because greenstone in our culture is more highly prized than money, more highly prized than anything. Our people believe that pounamu (greenstone) is the tears of the gods. And these tears come from the face and head and that's a sacred part of the body. That's why greenstone is held so dearly in our tradition. A good pounamu talks to you. It's like a computer chip picking things up. And it talks to you, like a guide. So I reckon the black diamond is a pounamu.

**Api Mahuika, Leadership: Inherited and Achieved (from Te Ao Hurihuri, Aspects of Maoritanga, edited by Michael King):** In Ngati Porou, first-cousin marriages were not uncommon in pre-European times, such was the degree of 'in-marriage'. There is a saying, 'E moe I to tuahine (tungane) kia heke te toto ko korua tonu.' (Marry your sister (brother)so that if blood is to be shared, it is only your own.) This suggests that the situation was not peculiar to Ngati Porou. The inference is that if the 'blood' was 'shared' among close kin, the unity of the hapu would not be jeopardised.

**Notes taken following a conversation with Laura Thompson and her son Chris (Rastafarian Hata Thompson's mum and brother):** Chris and Laura were saying that the diamond occurs over and over in a whakapapa (or family tree), if first cousins are marrying and, in the old days, even brothers and sisters.

Consider this: a woman has a child. That child is the top point of the diamond. That child has two children, who in turn have children of their own. This is the diamond expanding out. Two of the first cousins marry and produce a child of their own, which is the bottom point of the diamond.

**Api Mahuika, Leadership: Inherited and Achieved:** The generally accepted rules in regard to marriage apply within Ngati Porou. Marriage was generally between two people of equal status. Not only were there marriages between first cousins, but also between uncle and niece and aunt and nephew. Such cases are not isolated ones, as a detailed study of tribal genealogies has shown. On this basis, it would seem that marriage was, in the main, endogamous, for the sake of perpetuating the line. It is interesting to note that, as far as I can establish, there was no Maori word meaning 'incest' in pre-European days.

**Conversation with Laura Thompson (Aunty Ga-ga), Hata's mother:** It goes back to that diamond you were talking about: up and down.

*So that's another thing about the diamond: Rangi and Papa (the first man, the sky, and the first woman, the earth)?*

Amen.

*So what's that: the spirit coming into life from the sky is the top of the diamond and the body, which is connected to the earth and returns to the earth, is the bottom of the diamond.*

Yes, and those are the principles I've been brought up with and that I've been teaching my children. And I'm glad I managed to let them see this pathway that I had been down with a man named Hori Gage. He was from Omaio, past Te Kaha. He was half Whanau A Apanui and half the stone people, Ue Pohatu. And he carried that prophecy around the land for people to hear.

*And was there one main prophecy?*

Yes, to expect the coming of the new Messiah. That was it. That was **it**.

*That was it in a nutshell.*

In a nutshell.


**Hata's brother Chris Thompson:** With the prophecy, one of the signs is the person's speech. There shall be something distinctive about the man's speech. That's part of the local prophecy. But there are parallels to Revelations in The Bible. They talk about a man coming out of the clouds in the east on a white horse and upon his thigh is a name that only he can read, and out of his mouth is a sword, a double-headed sword. We believe in a double-headed sword of truth and integrity. It is one of the true signs of the person that wherever they may go they are capable of standing regardless of whatever threats they come across. We also believe that children carry that double-edged sword because they are innocent, they haven't been tainted.


**Hata's mother Laura Thompson:** Hori Gage said that when the morning star is strong over the Mangahanea Marae and the evening star is strong over Mount Hikurangi it will be time. It won't be far from then.

*And the star known as the morning star is the one above the doorway at Mangahanea?*

The star in the east. The prophecy says to look for when the strength of the morning star is like the sun and it's, like, hitting the twin peaks of Hikurangi. And, for me: why is Hikurangi the twin peaks?

*Why's that?*

Cos when you look at it, it's the diamond again. The line of the twin peaks is like the bottom of the diamond. And when the sun shines on it in the early hours of the morning, they call it the children of the first light. And who are the children of the first light? Well that mountain was there when Maui pulled up the land, the fish. And who were the first children to live there?

*Ue Pohatu.*

Yes. Well when they integrated in they were fortunate they got part of that line.

*Mangahanea Marae has the six-pronged star above the door. This is of special significance to the people of that marae, such as Laura Thompson and her sons Chris and Hata.*

**Chris Thompson (Hata's brother):** In the belly of the house that bears the six-pronged star there are two separate lines of descent. The house I'm talking about is called Hine Tapora at Mangahanea Marae.

One line of descent is an integrated whakapapa. The other is from the genuine line of descent regarding Te Ue Pohatu, which is the ancient people, the people of stone.

Te Ue Pohatu goes back to when Maui fished up Mount Hikurangi. But Ngati Porou either choose Mataatua waka or Horouta waka. They, as you will note, also mention their mountain being Hikurangi. And both lines of descent also claim Waiapu as their river. But both lines are also significantly different.

Then the next phase was colonisation and the introduction of The Bible.

Now I'll go back to the prophecy regarding the star, which was: "As sure as the sun shall rise in the east and shall set in the west so shall the coming of the next son of man." The star and the diamond are virtually one thing because the whakapapas stem from the house because she bears both lines of descent. And yet the prophecy also states, "Out of her belly shall come the healing," or the next so-called Messiah or advent. You come back to your bottom point of the diamond again because out of her belly comes that.

And that person will be the bottom point of those three whakapapa of Ue Pohatu, Ngati Porou and the Pakeha.

## NGATI UE POHATU

**Chris Thompson:** There was a series called Landmarks back in the early 80s, produced and narrated by David Attenborough. And on there he talks about his findings regarding Kupe's arrival here. He noted that Kupe arrived, landed and went back again to Hawaiki. But when Kupe arrived back in his native land he told them that there were already people of the land living in New Zealand.

It goes like this. We believe we stem from the tipuna Maui. He was the youngest of seven brothers.

Now when Kupe returned to the motherland he said there were people already in the land that he'd visited. When Kupe went back the likes of Paikea and all of that came about because they also are noted to have come from Hawaiki. And the likes of Paikea, even though he is likened to a god because he arrived on a whale, it was already brought to his notice that there was a land in existence that he was to come and be a part of.

*The first inhabitants of New Zealand are known as the Tini a Toi. They are descendants of the great ancestor Toi, who was in turn a descendant of the magical Maui-Potiki. Maui discovered New Zealand while out on a fishing trip with his brothers. Using a hook made from his grandmother's jawbone, the trickster hero snagged a sea monster and eventually, with the help of his brothers, hauled up the North Island of New Zealand. The first piece of land to break water was Mount Hikurangi, which is where the hook caught. And it is from there that the Maui people spread over New Zealand.*

*It's believed that Maui arrived on the East Coast of New Zealand about three hundred years before the fleet of canoes that brought the Maori here from their mysterious homeland in the east, Hawaiki.*

*Maui himself didn't stay in New Zealand. But he left his son Kui in charge. The people were therefore called Ngati-Kui. Today's Ngati Porou are mainly descended from the Toi element (or tangata whenua, people of the land), the Hawaiki (or Maori) immigrants and Pakeha (or European settlers).*

*Within a few generations of arrival, the Maori had asserted their "mana" or authority over the landowners by means both warlike and peaceful. They obtained a right to the land either by annihilation of the Toi-people or by marriage. But there is one Toi tribe that survives today, which has never been subserviant to even the greatest Ngati Porou chiefs. They have inherited the mana of one of their great warriors (Uamariki). They are Ngati Ue Pohatu, the Stone People.*

*I'll now quote some extracts from a thesis on the history of Ngati Porou that one of the librarians at Gisborne's HB Williams Memorial Library found for me. The late Robert John Hugh Drummond, of Lansdowne, Masterton, wrote the thesis. Drummond was a spitfire pilot who was killed when he was shot down over Tunisia on April 24, 1943. Most of the material in the thesis was gathered while he was teaching at Ruatoria, and Sir Apirana Ngata supplied much of it.*

"Something is known of three of the Toi-tribes that inhabited the East Coast region, and of these, two survive as tribes today and are included in Ngati Porou. They are Whanau-a-Rua-Waipu, Ngati-Ue-Pohatu, and Nga-Oho, of whom, the latter no longer exists as a tribe...

"...Ngati-Ue-Pohatu are an aboriginal, that is, Toi, tribe, renowned as warriors and still holding their ancestral lands which extend from Reporua to about Whareponga and inland to the mountains, including in their possessions Mount Hikurangi, on the top of which they say that Maui-Potiki's canoe, turned to stone, may be seen, and on whose slopes is buried their great ancestor himself...

"...This story, that (the Toi) population in New Zealand spread from the Hikurangi district in all directions is probably true, for the same tradition is handed down with respect to the (Hawaiki) canoes. These all made their landfall on the East Coast – at Whangara, Tikirau or Whareponga whither the direct sea-lines from Hawaiki, Rarotonga, Tahiti and America lead.

"...(W. E.) Gudgeon considers the Maui myths quite capable of explanation. Maui-Potiki was a real person, who lived many years ago, and the story of whose marvellous deeds must be taken as allegorical. For instance, the fishing up of the North Island means its discovery, while Maui's disappearance in the womb of Hine-Nui-Te-Po (the woman who brought death into the world) means that he sailed away on some voyage of exploration, and never returned...

"...What does seem clear is that there was a great Polynesian named Maui, through whose agency these islands, were, in the first place peopled, the population spreading from the Hikurangi district. Numbers increased and by the time of the well-known migration from Hawaiki there were distinct tribes living all along the East Coast in numbers great enough to over-awe the new arrivals, in many cases..."

**The following is rewritten from the book, Horouta, by Rongowhakaata Halbert:** The crew of the Horouta canoe were the first Maori inhabitants of the East Coast. They migrated from Hawaiki and, later, Ahuahu (or Great Mercury Island) after a dispute over the ownership of some trees used in the planting of kumara. Paoa led the migration in the early part of the fourteenth century. He was the grandson of Ngatoroirangi I of the first Arawa canoe. Paoa knew of the East Coast from his grandfather's favourable reports.

From Ahuahu, the voyagers sailed into the Bay of Plenty as far as the entrance to the Ohiwa estuary, where the canoe hit a sandbank or submerged rock and capsized.

47

One woman drowned but the rest of the crew reached the shore. The damaged canoe landed upside down on the beach with the headpiece ripped off and while some of the cargo floated ashore, the crew had to dive to retrieve the rest.

There was no suitable timber for repairs so Paoa sent the Horouta, with Kiwa in charge of a skeleton crew, further along the East Coast. He sent the women and children on an overland march to meet them. And he followed with the rest of the warriors, along with some additions from the local Tini a Toi people of Whakatane and Hapuoneone of Ohiwa. A special squad, carrying seven calabashes, containing seven gods and five sacred axes, traveled separately.

The Horouta's first stop was a few miles east of the Awatere River at Te Araroa, where a crop of kumara was planted. The next was at Muriwai, Poverty Bay, where one of Paoa's sisters and a few of her helpers decided to stay while Kiwa continued across the bay to inspect the land there. He decided the west bank of the Turanganui River (between Gladstone Road and the railway bridges in what is now Gisborne) would be ideal for the rendezvous of the Horouta people. He called the area Turanganui-a-Kiwa (the rendezvous selected by Kiwa). Meanwhile, Paoa and the overlanders marched from Ohiwa along the shores of the Bay of Plenty to a stream near Te Kaha. They took a short cut to the East Coast by going upstream, over the range and into the valley of the Tapuwaero Stream (on the northern side of what is now Ruatoria), and across to Tuparoa on the East Coast. After much searching, they eventually found the party carrying the calabashes at Whangara. They were lying around exhausted and starving. They'd had no one to prepare and serve them food and they couldn't do it themselves because they were carrying gods and had a great tapu on them. Paoa saw that his company fed and looked after them and, as food supplies again dwindled, he decided to leave the children and women with them. After telling them to travel along the coast until they met the Horouta crew, he went inland with his men.

## THE BLACK DIAMOND (3)

**Conversation with Joe Nepe (when I was still highly confused about the black diamond):** *What about the black diamond? What did you read into that? Because I've had so many interpretations of the black diamond, you know? Like* *they were saying that Chris was looking for the black diamond and Te Kooti was looking for the black diamond. Did you come across that much?*

Na. I didn't focus on what they were meaning by that at that time. But I knew Te Kooti was looking for it up there. I know he was looking for it up there. But I don't think he found it.

*That's right, yeah.*

It's supposed to be a cave up there, ay. But none of us have found that cave.

*Aw, there's supposed to be a cave up there with a black diamond in it?*

Yeah.

*See, cos some people say it's more of a spiritual thing, you know.*

If it's there, it's there. If it's not there, it's not there. That's all it is. But I've heard a lot of stories that say it's in that cave and that's where it is.

*And you've gotta find the cave?*

You've gotta find the cave. We don't know where it is.

*Although, I was talking to Hata's mum the other day.*

Aw yeah, Aunty Ga-ga.

*Yeah, and she was saying she believes it's like a spiritual thing, like Mount Hikurangi's the bottom part of the diamond and the top part is the star above Hikurangi. And then Hata's brother was saying he thought it was like, people. Like here's a woman at the top of the diamond, here's her children, and their children and then, in a small community, they're coming back to each other.*

Yeah.

*So I don't know.*

Yeah. Na, everybody's got their own interpretation, ay.

*That's right.*

But wherever that cave is, that's where that diamond is.

*Do you reckon it could be a physical diamond...*

Yeah.

*...or a spiritual diamond?*

Physical one. Like the one that Rua Kenana found.

*Yeah, yeah. Is there anything left there of that village that he built?*

Na, na, nothing.

*(That's not true. 3 News reporter Bob McNeil told me he's been up there and found a couple of old dwellings wallpapered with newspapers from the early 1900s).*

**Rasta leader John Heeney:** What about this one? King Solomon entertained the Queen of Sheba and then at the end of it he got her up the wop, ay, King Solomon. And then she departed back to her homeland. And he gave her a signet

49

ring. And he said to her, "I'll recognise the child when he come by this signet ring." And then many years went by and they all forgot about it. And then one day this boy turned up to King Solomon's court with the signet ring on that King Solomon had given the Queen of Sheba. He knew straight away, "This is my son. This is the heir to the kingdom."

And it's the same with the black diamond. He's the heir. He's gonna inherit all this, from the top of Hikurangi all the way to the sea, whether they like it or whether they do not like it.

*So the black diamond isn't something that you go looking for in the bush or anything?*

No.

*It's just someone you wait for. That's what it is isn't it?*

Donna: Yeah, he's already come.

*Who do you think it is?*

John: No, it's not a think. You don't think. We're telling you.

*Who is it?*

It's the Rasta-man. It's the Rasta-man.

Donna: Jah Rastafari, Haile Selassie, the black man.


**Ed Te Rauna, a former Rasta, interviewed in Gisborne in late 2000:** I'm twenty-six years old. I suppose I was part of the second generation of Rastas. Across my forehead is Ariki au te Rangi. It's actually, Ariki, it's got a diamond here in the middle with au te, then Rangi. Ariki au te Rangi. It just means Lord of the Heavens. It's a title, really.

John Heeney did my moko. He called the process the baptism of fire.

But they told us quite a convincing story about that, about these people who will be sealed on their foreheads. Those quotes came from The Bible. That's why the Rastas all got their names, like King Glory and all that.

That diamond in the middle of my forehead is supposed to be the black diamond. I was led to believe that the black diamond that was prophesised about were a people. Apparently, Te Kooti saw into the future and said something like, when God's people are on the earth you'll know because of these things that they'll do. And those things were what we did. But we were just jumping in there, you know, and following the prophesies. This name on my head actually has something to do with that prophecy, I think. The name Ariki Rangi, because Te Kooti's full name was Te Kooti Arikirangi Te Turuki. You see, I wasn't aware of the black diamond or the name at the time.

I used to camp up on Whakaahu mountain with the Rastafarians and do all those out in the bush Rastafarian things. And that's when I learnt about all the

50

scriptures pertaining to the sealing of your forehead and stuff. So I did a bit of soul searching and I looked for the name myself. And when I approached John Heeney he freaked out. Like I say, I was only sixteen. I was still in school. It was actually a school holidays. But I'd been staying up at Whakaahu with the Rastas every chance I got. This was after Chris Campbell had been killed and John Heeney had been released.

I went down to see John at this flat he was staying in with his missus. When I get there, Saint Christopher was there, Chris Thompson. He's got a little star on his head. He was feeling the same way, I believe. Neither of us wanted to miss out. To us it was like the days when Noah was going around, saying, "Come on, you gotta get on now or you're gonna miss out." And that's how it was put to us.

## HAILE SELASSIE

*The basis of all Rastafarian theology is the divine supremacy of the late Haile Selassie. He is regarded as the Second Coming of Christ So why do the Rastas put so much stock in this man?*

*His crowning as Emperor of Ethiopia in 1930 signified the realisation of several Biblical prophecies. Among those, one from Revelations, a book in which the author looks into the future to paint a picture of Armageddon and God's day of judgment: chapter 5, verses 2 and 5. "Then I saw a mighty angel who proclaimed in a loud voice: 'Who is worthy to open the scroll and break its seals?'" Then: "One of the elders said to me: 'Do not weep. The Lion of the Tribe of Judah, the Root of David, has conquered, so that he can open the scroll and its seven seals.'"*

*Then there's this from Revelations, chapter 19, verse 1: "The heavens were opened and as I looked on, a white horse appeared; its rider was called 'The Faithful and True'." And this, verse 16: "A name was written on the part of the cloak that covered his thigh: 'King of kings and Lord of lords'." As Joseph Owens notes in his book Dread: "Sufficient proof to the Rastas for the Messianic status of Selassie is the string of titles which he officially bears: King of kings, Lord of lords, Conquering Lion of the Tribe of Judah. As the brethren read the Book of Revelations, they observe that precisely those titles are reserved for the Messiah in his Return."*

*Haile Selassie maintained he was a direct descendent from King David. He was 225$^{th}$ in the line of Ethiopian kings, in unbroken succession from the time of*

*King Solomon and the Queen of Sheba. He was descended from the most ancient
and sacred of royal lineages. This was made clear in the first article of the
Ethiopian Constitution. "The imperial dignity shall remain perpetually attached
to the line of Haile Selassie I, descendant of King Sahle Selassie whose line
descends without interruption from the dynasty of Menelik I, son of the Queen of
Ethiopia, the Queen of Sheba, and King Solomon of Jerusalem."*

**Joseph Owens, Dread:** "The messianic status of Selassie is founded firmly,
the Rastas claim, on his Davidic descent. Just as Jesus was Messiah by virtue of
being in King David's line, so also is the Emperor. In Haile Selassie, in fact, we
see a definitive manifestation of the same Messiah that walked the earth two
thousand years ago...

"...The brethren maintain, then, that a real identity exists between Jesus and
Selassie, since Selassie is the Messiah returned. Recalling that Jesus proclaimed
that he would appear once again in history for a final judgment of the nations, the
Rastas see clearly that the appearance has already taken place in the person of
Selassie."

*The Rastas believe that Haile Selassie is the superhuman manifestation of
Jah, which was the name for God used in England before the King James version
of the Bible changed it to Jehovah.*

*Rastas often refer to themselves as "I and I". The other "I" is the Haile
Selassie element. He is in everyone who believes in him. For a Rasta, eternal life
means being inseparably linked to Haile Selassie. "I and I" also includes the
brethren, the other Rastafarians.*

*In Amharic, the ancient language of Ethiopia, the name Haile Selassie means
"Power of the Trinity", the trinity being the father, the son and the holy ghost,
and the emperor's original name, Ras Tafari, means "Head Creator".*

*So what sort of leader was Selassie? He started out as a reformer of
equalities in Ethiopia, giving attention to education, forbidding slavery and
venturing towards the modernisation of his Third World country. But ninety
percent of the population was poor and the majority illiterate. He also took care
not to disturb the traditional community patterns of Ethiopian society. He
asserted his authority in a balanced manner and there were no uprisings from
his people. But he was deposed by the defence force in 1974 and accused of
corruption. He died on August 27, 1975.*

*For the Rastafarians, however, he remained the returned messiah in the flesh
and, in spirit, he became even more powerful. Rastas still believe in his divinity.*

*Haile Selassie and his family denied the Rastas' claims that he was the Second Coming of Christ. The emperor was not a Rastafarian, but a devout Christian, coming from a long line of kings who belonged to the Ethiopian Orthodox Church.*

*Interestingly, Bob Marley, the Rastafarian reggae singer revered as a visionary by Rastas, converted to the Ethiopian Orthodox Church, taking the name Berhane Selassie (meaning Light of Trinity), in New York shortly before his death on May 11, 1981.*

## WHERE THERE'S SMOKE

**Excerpt from an interview in late 2002 with former Sergeant Alex Hope, who spent time in charge of the Ruatoria police and is now a partner in a legal firm:** *As far as the spiritual side of it goes, did you ever get a handle on where they were coming from there?*

Ah, it was all bullshit. There was no spiritual side to it.

*They talk about a black diamond and following prophecies.*

They were just smoking too much herb.

*Ha ha ha.*

No they were. I mean, those guys, they were gang members who became gang members under another label. Their gang had political and Maori sovereignty and messianic overtones, but it was still a gang. John Heeney got into reading The Bible and quoting this and that. Chris did, too. I don't think Chris was a believer in anything except... John Heeney might have, with his head full of smoke.

They smoked day in and day out. Barney Campbell told me they'd come into the station and you'd lock one of them up or a group of them up and they'd be ranting. And they were difficult. And they would be yelling abuse.

Now I don't know the physiological basis for this, but their blood sugar from all their dope smoking would be down. And we used to keep barley sugars in the watch house. You'd give them a barley sugar and they'd be as quiet as a lamb. It would work every time. And it was Barney who told me about it. He said, "These guys, if you give them something sweet to eat, they quieten down." And it worked. The other peculiar physical thing that happened when these guys were really stoned was they'd froth at the mouth, all of them would. Their saliva would become thick and there'd be strings of saliva between their lips that were thick and viscous and elastic. And they'd have froth around their lips. But that wasn't through being nutty. That was because they were just smoking so much dacc. They just had herb coming out of their ears. They were just stoked up with it completely.

**Barney Campbell, Ruatoria policeman and Rasta Chris Campbell's brother:** The fires were some way down the track, but a whole lot of other stuff went down: confrontations, pinching, horses going missing, saddle gear. It was going on quite a while before I realised, "These blokes are out to get rid of some people." You didn't like to think like that but that's how it started to look. We weren't brought up like that so it took me a while to catch on. I was just a policeman doing my job and someone rang up and said, "My horse has been pinched." Well, you went out to see them and took it from there. It didn't occur really that there might be another reason for anything.

**Beau Tuhura, one of the early Rasta leaders:** During that time a whole lot of other concepts that Maori had done away with, like utu (revenge), came back. And actually the Rasta movement went dreader and dreader, they were true to their philosophies, hence the fires and people being threatened, and going so far as to say, "If you're not one of us, then you're against us." Those were the hard messages.

Now you might ask, "Are they worthwhile messages to be following?" But you've got to look at it like David and Goliath. There's the system and the Government and the might and the power. And in our beliefs we're up against it all, whether it be trying to set up a parliament for ourselves, and determining things for ourselves or even exercising our *own* tino rangatiratanga (Maori sovereignty).

The kingi tanga movement came here in setting up their equivalent to the Queen of England. The kingi tanga movement believed that there should be one sovereign for the Maori people. Well they came here and they asked Te Kania-Takirau if he would become the figurehead for the movement. Te Kania was a chief here at the time (he died in 1856). His reply to them was, "No matter what titles you bestow upon me, by my birthright I am a king." So everyone in Ngati Porou adopted that philosophy. He was a chief anyway. He didn't need to join a movement to know he was a chief.

# CHAPTER 4

## THE FIRST FIRE

**Jacquie Williams, farmer Colin Williams' wife:** The Rastas had been cutting fences over on Taitai. And they'd been stealing horses. They were stirring up trouble. We were getting ready for the bull sale and I said to Colin, "I've got a funny feeling. I don't know what it's about but something's going to happen. Something big is going to happen." And sure enough...

*Monday, July 1, 1985 (three weeks after Operation Whareponga): Six Rastafarians are arrested in a police operation at Ruatoria. One of them is Gallace Hongara. I remember coming into contact with Gallace on two occasions some time between 1982, when I was seventeen, and 1987. The first time I walked around to his flat in Gisborne one night with my good friends Steve and Mick Simmonds to smoke dope. They knew Gallace and Tiger Hongara after playing rugby against them for years. Mick got upset this night because Gallace kicked his dog.*

*The second time was at the Tatapouri pub, up the coast from Gisborne, one Tuesday night. I was with Steve and Mick and our old school friend John Solvander. We were stoned and Mick and Steve got into a fight with Gallace and a friend of his. Thankfully, the barman broke it up before Solly and I had to get involved (we were both too paranoid to fight).*

*So those were my two meetings with Gallace Hongara.*

*The other five Rastas arrested are Gallace's brother Tika (Tiger), Daryl Te Hau, Cody Haua, Barney Wharepapa, and Jano Kirikino. Three of them – Tiger Hongara, Te Hau and Wharepapa – have been out on bail following Operation Whareponga last month.*

*Tiger and Gallace Hongara and Kirikino are all charged with threatening behaviour. Ian Sykes, the husband of Te Aowera Marae secretary Sarah Sykes, was driving his truck to gather metal when he was forced to the opposite side of the road by a group of men who abused him as he passed. On his way back he encountered the group again. He saw stones picked up and had abuse yelled at him. He says he feared violence and was concerned for his young daughter.*

*Cody Haua is charged with fourteen offences: twelve of theft and two of
burglary.*

*Gallace Hongara and Te Hau are jointly charged with stealing over two
thousand dollars worth of horse-riding gear from Ihungia Station, near
Tokomaru Bay.*

*That same night the first arson is committed.*

*Colin Williams is the target. The fire's in a hay barn on his Kaharau Stud
farm. It's lit at around 8.45pm. Two thousand bales of hay, set out in the L-
shaped barn to provide tiered seating for a bull sale the following day, go up in
flames. It's the first example of the incredibly cruel timing of some of the arsons
in Ruatoria.*

**Ken McKinnon, Ruatoria fire chief (now retired):** We soon realise it's an
arson. Round the back of the hay barn we find bits of newspaper that have been
screwed up and poked in and lit, but gone out again. The fire's actually started at
the two front corners. We ring up the local cop. But he says he can't come. He's
babysitting. But the cop from Tokomaru Bay comes up.

**Tom Heeney, Ruatoria deputy fire chief (now retired):** Colin Williams
lives just next door to us. It's a hay barn, his fire, and you can't put hay out once
it gets going. The barn's down on the flats. And it's well alight when we get
there. Luckily, we have a chap in the fire brigade who works for Waiapu Metal
Supplies. He gets their front-end loader, gets in and brings out all the hay and we
salvage the building pretty well.

**Farmer Colin Williams:** It's an open barn, all poles inside. The fire
brigade's there in two ticks. There's a creek handy and they hose the barn all
down. But we've set up all these hay bales inside as seating for the bull sale. And
pretty soon the hay's just a black, soggy, steaming, hot mess.

People in Ruatoria have heard the siren and they can probably see the fire. At
about 9.30 they all start turning up to help out. It's a real cross-section of the
community, but mostly Maori. They've obviously changed after work and
they've finished their dinner and are all in their good clothes. The driver of the
front-end loader manages to attack the hay through the big double doors at the
back of the shed. But he can't get right in. And we have to get all this stuff out.
We have to get all this rotten, stinking, black, burnt, soggy hay out of the barn.
They're bales. But all the strings are burnt. It's all just loose rubbish. And these
people are into it up to their armpits and loading it into this bucket.

It's four o'clock in the morning before they've finished cleaning it all out and made a big heap of it behind the shed. It's a terrible job and God knows what it's done to all their good clothes. But first thing the next morning, at daylight, most of them are there again to help us put all the fresh hay in for the people to sit on.

We can't cancel the sale. Everybody's either there already, staying at the hotel, or on their way up. People are coming from all over New Zealand, about three or four hundred of them. The power's off so the locals bring their barbecues and we're able to provide a meal down there at the barn. The community really gets behind us. And we sell all the bulls.

**Ruatoria deputy fire chief Tom Heeney:** We don't know who started the fire at Colin Williams' place. But then we get some information from a Williams and Kettle stock agent. He says he'd been to a sale way down the line somewhere. He'd come back and dropped off his clients and was on his way home. And he passed a group on horses going hell for leather. And he recognised some of the Rastafarians. We'd heard the horses galloping past our place up towards Colin's a bit before that so we put two and two together. But we've got no evidence. And the police can't touch them.

## THE WILLIAMS FAMILY

**As explained by Rasta Cody Haua and Sonny Brown:** They reckon Colin Williams had sold Pakihiroa Station back to the Crown just before his haybarns were burnt. Of course, the sale infuriated the Rastas, who thought it should be returned to the original owners, the local Maori. Cody and Sonny said Colin Williams was always going to leave the district because he'd made his millions, but he was keen to sell the land back to the Crown and make some more money.

**Colin Williams:** Samuel Williams took over the lease of a huge block of land up near Ruatoria from Sir George Whitmore, who was in the British Army. It was all scrub and swamp and useless stuff when Samuel took it on. K.S., Jeremy's great grandfather, and T.S., my grandfather, broke in a lot of country: Matahiia, Kaharau.

**Jeremy Williams:** Henry and William Williams were brothers. The other side of the family come from William Williams, the first Bishop of Waiapu. We come from Henry Williams.

Henry arrived in Paihia in 1823. He was the guy who stopped those inter-tribal battles by walking out in the middle of fights with his hands up, saying, "Woo, woo, woo," while the spears were flying all around.

And they used to call him Four Eyes. He had a lot of personal mana. He was the guy who translated the Treaty of Waitangi for the Maori. Some people say he translated it wrongly. But he did his best. And he lived in Paihea.

His son Sam Williams, Archdeacon Sam Williams, founded Te Aute College in Hawke's Bay. And he was a very able administrator and able stock farmer - he had the first short horn stud in the country - as well as being a man of the cloth. He was a self-taught engineer. He started the drainage of the Te Aute swamp. And he also got involved in land up the East Coast. This is separate to the J. N. Williams family.

J.N. Williams and Sam Williams were first cousins.

So Sam Williams, most of his empire was in Hawke's Bay. But he got into financial strife in the 1880s.

So he called up two nephews who were living in the Bay of Islands. One was his brother Edward's son Thomas, Colin's grandfather. The other nephew was his bother John's son Ken, my great grandfather. And Sam Williams said to them, "You boys go down to the East Coast. I'll give you ten years to see if you can do something with my land down there."

So Thomas Sydney Williams went down to the coast in his thirties. And Ken Williams went down when he was twenty in 1890.

Sam told them, "Things are a mess down there. I've incurred a lot of debt. If you can pay the debt off before ten years is up you can keep the profit."

So what they did was Thomas Sydney took all that area where they're harvesting logs now: Hikurangi and all that. And he lived at Kaharau and leased Maori land going over to the sea at Whareponga. So he had two sections.

Ken Williams went to Matahiia and he also leased Maori land which went from Pakihiroa right down to the junction between the two rivers.

They virtually had all the land from Ruatoria right back to Hikurangi. It wasn't all freehold. There was a lot of Maori lease in there.

I'm not sure about Thomas Sydney, but it took Ken Williams eight years to pay his share of the debt off. And from 1898 to 1900 he made a hundred thousand pounds. That was an absolutely astronomical amount of money back then. These days it would be worth millions and millions. So aged thirty he had a whole pocketful of money. And he continued to make money right through. Even in the Great War he made a lot of money. And what did he do with his money? He lent it to other people up the coast. And he joint-guaranteed a lot of the loans as well. And there were a number of families - A.B. Williams, H.B. Williams,

T.S. Williams and K.S. Williams – they all lent a whole lot of money to people. In our particular case, Ken Williams actually over-committed himself and then when the depression in the '30s hit he knew they couldn't pay and he didn't ask for interest and they become null and void after a few years if you don't send someone a bill. So he lost everything. In fact by 1935 my branch of the family was broke. And Ken died in 1935 as well. Ken's estate was owed eighty eight thousand pounds. Or was it eighty two? All the papers got burnt, you see. So I'm going on memory. But it was over eighty thousand pounds. See, there was no income tax until 1926 so you could keep most of what you made.

So my grandfather, Charlie, and my uncle and aunt went to the bank and the bank virtually said to them, Well, we may as well leave you there as put another broke farmer on the land.

So they boxed on and it took until 1968 to wipe those family debts. So my father was paying off his grandfather's debts.

So that's sort of how we came along.

And then in my time I personally only had to pay my sisters, not other members of the family. I pay my sisters because I bought their shares out of the family business. If you're going to run a family farm somebody has to consolidate every generation. Otherwise it becomes an incorporation. Why bust your arse for just a percentage? I've got an aunt in North Canterbury. Do I want to be ringing her up to get permission to buy a new Toyota?

So that's how we came to be at Matahiia.

**Colin Williams:** My grandfather Thomas Sydney's aim was to promote farming and to help local farmers, Maori and Pakeha, and to build a strong farming community around Ruatoria and further up, too. He helped out so many people on the coast with personal loans it's incredible. On top of that, he also stood as guarantor for people's loans with the bank. So when these people couldn't pay back the bank Thomas Sydney paid the bank instead. So these people now became indebted to him instead of the bank and, unfortunately for the family, these debts became recognised as assets on which the Government calculated death duties.

So when he died in 1930 it left the family in deep financial strife. All this money he'd lent and the bank loans he'd guaranteed were all considered to be death dutiable assets. But there was no money in the bank to pay the duties. So my father and uncle and aunt had to go to the bank and borrow the money to pay the death duties, which was a bloody fortune in those days. Then the slump came. Most of the people who had loaned money off my grandfather went bust and a lot of them never paid anything back. But I must say that I remember my father saying that most of the *Maori* people if not all *did* pay the money back eventually. But there were quite a lot of Europeans that he'd helped who didn't pay. They just shot through. My father paid that debt off until just a few years before he died, in about 1985.

My grandfather was too jolly kind. And there are a lot of families up there still who remember what he did to help them get started. And K.S Williams, Jeremy's great granfather, did pretty much the same thing.

**Tom Heeney, John's dad:** The Rastas had this grudge about the Williamses and the owning of the land. I don't think the Williamses had ripped off the land. They're big benefactors to the community.

**Colin Williams**: One of the most valuable things grandfather contributed to all those early Maori farmers was just his knowledge and his advice. And on Sundays they used to come and sit around in a circle talking to him after church. And he could talk Maori just like they could. And he'd share his knowledge of farming and tell them how they should go about working their land. And it was a regular thing. Every Sunday they all came to his home in Ruatoria there, about a dozen of them.

**Jeremy Williams:** My great grandfather, Ken Williams, was a fluent Maori speaker. The old fulla that worked for our family - both my mother's and my father's families - he used to tell me that the locals all used to say how beautifully he spoke Maori. Ken was a minister of Parliament. He's the only man ever to be elected unopposed three times, which must say something for his standing. And he used to walk along the shearing board, teaching the locals how to shear sheep.

Evidently after the First World War a lot of the locals came home. There was no work. So he cut a whole lot of scrub. He had forty men working for him, over and above the normal staff for three years, from 1918 to 1921, just to give them a bit of work. He said, "Well, righto, I've got some fencing here, some scrub-cutting, we'll take you on." He was very civic minded and aware that he himself had been fortunate and given a start.

**Beau Tuhura, early Rasta leader:** Our philosophy about the missionaires who came here is how can you bring the word of God to a people created by God? We believe the Creator made all of us, all the different nations, each with their own tongue, and their own customs and culture. It's a bit rude to say to one nation, you fullas have got a heathen sort of culture and heathen beliefs and this

60

is what you should be believing in. And quite frankly Maori have become so converted that they've forsaken their Maoritanga for their religious beliefs. Why you see churches and marae together is because those that were converted started practising their Christian beliefs on the marae. And the people who weren't converted said, if you want to practise your beliefs then build a church and practise in that so you don't trample on the Maori beliefs. And for a time those churches were filled. But if you go to a church here on Sunday, because I did, I started attending the church up here, just to see who the converted were, and there were only one or two and they were old people.

The young people all went to Rastafari. Young people were chanting down Babylon, talking about their beliefs, the White Man philosophy, the oppressor, all the things that we were identifying with that were impacting on us as a nation and as a people, as Ngati Porou.

Here we are, we have ninety per cent of our whenua, our land, and yet we've only got control of about three per cent of it because of these perpetual leases.

I think they still pay something like thruppence a hectare for the land.

I suppose it came down to the Maori Trust as well. When they came through the Native Land Courts and made every Maori an owner of the land, even down to children, the shares eventually became minute. The system was set up so that the shares *would* decrease by generation until the shares of every person in a family *would* be minute. And it was set up so that if you didn't have a certain percentage of shares then the moneys from your shares went straight into the Maori Trust, also known as Te Puni Kokiri. That's where money went to Te Puni Kokiri coffers and they wondered how they could disperse it amongst iwi and that sort of thing. It never came back to the land-owners because of those dwindling shareholders with each generation.

I only have to look at my own family to think how at one time where my great grandfather had eighty shares, the shareholders today have point something of a share each.


## THE HORSE-DRAGGING INCIDENT


***Friday, July 5, 1985:*** *The Rastas have been struggling to break in a willful horse. In a last-ditch effort to "break in" the horse they tie it to the back of their black Wolseley car and tow it along Waiomatatini Road.*

**Saturday, July 6:** *The horse dies.*

**Monday, July 8:** *John Heeney and Cody and Aperahama Haua appear in court on a joint charge of aggravated cruelty to a horse. (Heeney and Cody Haua are already on bail for charges of horse theft.)*

*When Heeney stands to face his charge, he tells Judge Hole, "The horse we handled is still alive."*

*Judge Hole says he's not interested in hearing from Heeney at this stage.*

*"You should be interested," Heeney replies. "That is why we are here."*

*All three plead not guilty. Judge Hole refuses Heeney and Cody Haua bail and remands them in custody until July 10. Twenty five year old Aperahama Haua is remanded on bail to July 10.*

**Former Detective Sergeant Laurie Naden:** Their main means of transport was by horse. They were bloody cruel to their animals. *But* they were rather possessive of them too.

The horse-dragging, that was basically a warning. Something had happened to one of their horses. So they took this horse belonging to someone else and they dragged it up and down the road and eventually killed it of course, just to show: "Hey, don't muck around with our horses," which was bloody ludicrous, but, again, that's what they did.

**Wednesday, July 10:** *The three Rastas are back in court on the horse cruelty charge. Witnesses identify Cody Haua and Heeney as being part of the group who towed the horse behind the car. Heeney was driving the vehicle while Haua was walking along the road near the horse. The animal was choking blood, had a bloodied mouth and head and at times was rearing while tethered to the car.*

*The following day the same grey horse was seen tied to a power pole near a house belonging to the Rastafarians.*

*Ruatoria traffic officer Bruce Laing says he saw the horse at 8.30am on Saturday in this position. Its face and nose were badly swollen and it was so weak its head was barely off the ground. Laing left to call a vet and while he was away a neighbour noticed the Rastafarians untie the horse and walk it along Waiomatatini Road.*

*When Laing returned at 11.45am he found the horse missing. He drove up Waiomatatini Road and saw the animal lying on the road with the Rastafarians' black Wolseley driving slowly towards him.*

*Laing says he saw Aperahama Haua crouched beside the horse and Cody Haua astride it. He admits he didn't see Aperahama Haua's face but says he's certain in his own mind it was him he saw.*

*Laing left the area but when he returned at 1.30pm with John Hewitt, the Tolaga Bay vet, they found the horse lying dead on Walkers Road.*

*Hewitt says it was the worst case of cruelty he's seen in thirteen years as a vet. The horse had gross tissue swelling around the head, muscle and neck and its top lip had been torn away, resulting in considerable blood about the mouth. The horse's right eyeball had also been removed from its socket. There was deep muscle and tissue bruising around the neck while there was severe hemorrhaging around the windpipe. Its brain was devoid of blood and its lungs had turned a dark purple.*

*Hewitt determined the horse had died of strangulation or asphyxiation and had been dead for around two hours. The gross swelling around the head and neck areas suggested the horse had been fighting ropes for some time.*

*Witnesses who saw the horse being towed on Friday afternoon say the horse was highly distressed, was shaking badly on its feet and was choking, with blood running out of its nose and mouth.*

*The canvas strop was seen tied tightly around the horse's throat and every now and again the animal would rear up.*

*Although the car was only being driven at walking pace, the horse was seen to fall to the ground and one witness says it was "just like jelly".*

*Aperahama Haua is acquitted of the cruelty charge. After hearing evidence from eleven prosecution witnesses, Judge J. D. Hole rules that he has no case to answer.*

*Aperahama Haua wasn't seen by any of the witnesses when the horse was being towed along Waiomatatini Road towards Ruatoria on Friday afternoon.*

*One witness says she saw Aperahama on the other side of Ruatoria just before the incident, and that he couldn't have been involved.*

*But the judge decides that Heeney and Cody Haua do have cases to answer.*

*The pair have been held in custody and the police oppose bail for them. The police say further offences are likely and they may not adhere to their reporting dates.*

*Prosecuting sergeant Bill Davidson says several other Rastas, already on bail and also believed to be involved in the horse cruelty incident, haven't been reporting to the Ruatoria police station, as ordered by the court. And extensive police inquiries have failed to turn up any trace of the men.*

*But Judge Hole points out that the men are supposed to be reporting over previous horse theft charges, which are entirely different to the horse cruelty charges. He considers them as separate matters.*

*Heeney and Cody Haua are remanded on bail until July 18.*


## COLIN WILLIAMS GETS HIT AGAIN


***Saturday, July 13, 1985:*** *There's a second fire at Colin Williams' farm today, just twelve days after the first. It's the other hay shed at Kaharau Stud, up on the hill. Another two thousand bales are burnt. The corrugated iron shed is over a hundred metres from the road up a steep farm track. And the firemen are unable to get their machines close to the fire.*

**Tom Heeney, Ruatoria deputy fire chief (retired):** The second fire happens in the afternoon, while the rugby's on. Colin says, "Don't put the fire out because if you do I'll have to clean up the whole mess." He just lets the whole damned barn go. We sit around and make sure it doesn't spread too far.

We've got this red-head traffic cop here, Bruce Laing. He turns up and runs around pulling out some of the newspaper that's been used to ignite the fire. Then we call the police. Well we wait for about two hours up on the hill. No one comes. So I send the boys back. I come down and stand at the gate just to keep guard. Gary Condon, the detective from Gisborne, eventually turns up and says, "Where's the police?"

"Haven't turned up," I say. "We've called for the local cop. We know it's arson. I believe Waho Tibble's crook and he's gone to the hospital. But I don't know where the other bloke is."

"Well hang on," he says. "He'll be here in two minutes."

He gets Sergeant Norm Gray to come out and the sergeant isn't too happy. His wife is away and he has these kids to look after. And now we're offside with him because he knows we've potted him.

***Wednesday, July 17:*** *Chris Campbell, Dick Maxwell and Hata Thompson appear in court and plead not guilty on a joint charge of aggravated cruelty to a horse. Police say they intended to arrest them straight after the incident (when they arrested Heeney and Cody and Aperahama Haua). But they couldn't find them.*

*Friday, July 21: Rastas and members of the Hiruharama community attend a meeting at Hiruharama Marae. It gets quite heated. Ngata Memorial College deputy principal Hopa Keelan demands that the Rastas apologise to Colin Williams (for the fires). He says that they should work for Williams as reparation for the damage. The Rastas speak about living as a whanau and sharing land. They refuse to accept responsibility for the fires.*

## "UNFORESEEN CIRCUMSTANCES" CAUSED DEATH

*Wednesday, July 31: The horse cruelty trial continues in the Gisborne court. And two major question marks arise. Margaret Mathieson and Sam Reedy were both occupants of a car that passed the horse. And they contradict each other on the number of people in the Rastas' Black Wolseley. Mathieson says four people, while Reedy's adamant there were only three.*

*The Rastafarians point out that if these witnesses can't remember how many people were in the car, how can they remember who was outside it.*

*Constable Waho Tibble says when he saw the horse being towed he wasn't aware an offence was occurring. The horse was distressed and it was being towed by a car. But he wasn't aware a crime was being committed. He did think though that something unusual was happening.*

*Thursday, August 22: Chris Campbell, Dick Maxwell and Hata Thompson are all in court facing the joint charge of aggravated cruelty to a horse.*

*They say a series of "unforeseen circumstances" led to the death of the horse, which had been towed behind the Rastas' black Wolseley car. While towing the horse in an attempt to break it in, the car's brakes jammed, it stuck in first gear and at the same time a knot slipped on a strop on the horse's neck – strangling the horse after it reared up.*

*In defending himself and his two friends, Campbell says the death of the horse was a "very, very bad accident", the result of a series of incidents, which did not normally occur together. "This thing was done by the Lord," he says. "Cars don't normally lock in first gear. Brakes don't normally jam at the same time. Unslippable knots don't normally slip."*

*He says the death of the horse was a big loss to the Rastafarians and retribution from the Lord for working on a Saturday – the Sabbath. "Being a* member of the Ringatu faith I do not believe in doing anything on Saturday because it's God's special day."

Campbell says he realised his mistake when the horse died after being towed along the road on a Saturday. The Rastafarians had learnt a hard lesson and lost a valuable horse.

The prosecution calls Arthur Dolan, a professional horse-breaker of ten years experience. Dolan says he's never head of breaking in a horse by towing it behind a car. He says the most difficult horses to break in are older entires. The dead horse was a seven to eight-year-old entire.

Campbell maintains towing is one of the methods he's been taught to break in difficult horses.

He says that before towing the horse on the Friday, the Rastafarians tried to break it in by using a rope and strop on it in a yard, tying it to a post and bagging it and tying it to another horse.

None of these methods worked on the "old horse who was full of crafty ideas". While in the yard the horse had temporarily escaped by smashing its way through two sets of stockyards. Campbell says that's when the horse injured its mouth.

He admits the horse was towed at a walking pace behind the car on Friday and at night was tied to a power pole beside the Rastafarians' house at the Crossroads "to rest and eat long grass". He says the horse was in very good condition at this time.

Campbell says the horse was towed for about three or four hours on Saturday. Although it was fighting the strop around its neck it was weakening – "not in strength but to the point of submitting". He says it was about this point the horse reared up and fell down on the road.

"At this time the black Wolseley locked in first gear," he says. "I put it down to the stress of the horse pulling on the car. The brakes locked and the bow-line knot slipped. I knew we had eight to twelve seconds to remove the strop from the horse's head or it would die of strangulation. Half of this time was taken up with removing the car from gear and un-jamming the brakes. We had a knife but it was too blunt and would not cut the strop. More time was taken to get the rope off. By the time we did get it off it was too late. The horse had died."

The horse was later towed by another man's tractor to Walker's Road, where it was later inspected by a vet.

Campbell says he's a horseman born and bred and loves horses. "There is no way we were purposely cruel to the animal."

*Tuesday, September 10: Campbell, Cody Haua, Thompson, Heeney and Maxwell are acquitted of aggravated cruelty to a horse causing death. Judge Hole says although tying the horse behind the car was cruel he's satisfied the defendants didn't intend to kill the horse. He says the act of willful intent is an essential ingredient of the charge and the prosecution hasn't proved beyond reasonable doubt that an act of aggravated cruelty was committed.*

*Judge Hole believes the Rastas were trying to break-in rather than kill the horse.*

**Sergeant Alex Hope's backgrounder on the Ruatoria troubles:** The Police appealed against the court's decision (on the horse cruelty charges). The appeal was allowed, however the matter has proceeded no further.

At about this time a deputation from Ruatoria of Federated Farmers members (I am told all Pakeha) approached the Gisborne District Commander and apparently expressed dissatisfaction at the performance of Constable Waho Tibble. Constable Tibble, a Maori, in his late 40s was from Ruatoria. He involved himself in community affairs, particularly Maori functions, with the full approval and encouragement of Superintendent Burrows (District Commander until mid 1985). It was apparently stated that he spent all his time at Maori hui (meetings) and was responsible for the existing situation because of inappropriate responses to earlier incidents.

Constable Tibble was transferred to Palmerston North (he did not actually shift until 6.12.85).

A large portion of the Maori community, and the Ruatoria Sub Area Police considered that Constable Tibble had been scapegoated. It was felt that Traffic Officer Laing played a part in Constable Tibble's transfer. Ruatoria Sub Area staff distrusted Laing from this time onwards.

The newly promoted Ruatoria Sergeant Norm Gray also came under criticism at this time because of alleged lack of leadership and inaction. (Gray arrived in Ruatoria in May 1985 from Palmerston North. He had never worked out of a city and had no experience amongst Maoris. He had never been to Ruatoria before applying for the position, and both he and his wife disliked living there).

**Rasta Hata Thompson (July 2001):** The horse incident happened. It *did* happen. But it just got blown out of hand by the Mathiesons. And that's how they became involved: getting involved in something that really didn't concern them.

It was a bit of a fight between, well, it was family feuding. Allan Mathieson was working for the fulla Chris was feuding with (Jeremy Williams). Allan became entangled in it and that's how it became a tangled web, ay. And once *he* got entangled, he put *his* nose in it and that started it. And then when they saw the horse get pinged they went straight down to the police station and got us charged for it. Fair enough, but we went to court for that. It was pretty rugged, that. And that was a lot of bad publicity.

So then we had Mathieson getting involved and we had Colin Williams and them getting involved, because we were stirring them up at the same time, telling them that they owe us, give us back our mountain.

# CHAPTER 5

## POP GAGE AND THE FOOTSTEPS OF FIRE

*Many people in and around Ruatoria, including the Rastafarians, believe in the prophecies of a late tohunga from Te Kaha, further up the coast. He was known as Pop Gage, Hori Gage or Hori Keeti and belonged to the sub-tribe Te Whanau a Apanui.*

*Hori Keeti's daughter was the first wife of Ruatoria resident Tom Te Maro. Tom's also said to be a gifted tohunga and Hori Keeti's said to have taught him a lot about Maori prophecy and the spiritual arts. Tom in turn passed on some nuggets of local wisdom to members of the Rastafarians. They looked up to him and were sponges for the old stories. But some say Tom may have shared historical information and prophecies with the Rastafarians that they weren't supposed to hear... and upon which they acted.*

*Anyway, Ngati Porou tradition includes prophecies of the birth of a new leader. And the tribe is always looking for signs.*

*One Ruatoria resident who asked not to be named said that Pop Gage came to Te Aowera Marae in the 1950s. He was standing at the gates when he saw the tiny footprints of a child. The footprints were on fire. And they led straight into the whare tipuna, the house of the ancestors.*

*Pop Gage said that they were the footsteps of a great spiritual leader. Many believed this person would have messianic qualities.*

*The story goes that when Pop Gage saw the fiery footsteps at Te Aowera, he wanted to follow them because he wanted that power, that knowledge that might come from following them. He wanted to find out who the promised child would be. But he wasn't allowed into the whare tipuna. He couldn't follow the footsteps in there and he realised that. He held back. The tipuna wouldn't let him go any further. They wouldn't let him on to the marae. He never went on to the marae at Te Aowera.*

**Beau Tuhura, one of the early Rasta leaders:** The Second Coming of Man will be reflective of what's prophesied in Maoridom. When you have a look at the rest of the world you'd have to acknowledge the Muslims, who face east every day in their millions, and pray. Why face east? Why not face the north, west or south? But they feel that *this* is where the Son of Man will come.

Years ago there were men who came around who were considered to be men of God. People like Hori Keeti came to lift the tapu on the maraes and to make it noa, so it couldn't be consecrated or trampled. They could see that the generations to come weren't going to be able to honour the tapu because of the new technology and education and everything that was coming along with the Pakeha. They could see that the Maori were already adapting and forsaking some of their tikanga or their concepts and assimilating with the Pakeha. And a lot of the older people felt that it was good, that it was progress. But a lot of them felt that there was also a danger in doing so that they would forsake their Maori beliefs and customs and culture in preference for the Pakeha ways.

So they lifted the tapu with the intention that, one day the tapu would be restored on the land. The land would become a tapu place again and the people would honour the tapu, just as the tipuna (the ancestors) observed all the tapu of all the living things, the trees, the animals, everything. That way people could again live in harmony with the whenua (the land) and the seasons.

Well this fulla Hori Keeti went to Te Aowera. This would have been in the mid-50s. A woman who was there revealed this to me. She said you couldn't come into the marae. The reason why was because Hori saw the footprints of the child. They magically appeared. Hori said the child was there, but still but a child in the midst of them. And that child would become the leader of Ngati Porou.

Obviously the chosen one is in the midst of the people. The person was at Te Aowera Marae that day. But no one's saying anything. No one's mentioning any names or putting anybody in the frame.

*Q: Were you there that day?*
I was one of the children there.
*Do you think it could be you?*

I don't profess to be different from anyone else or to have any special talent over anyone else. I haven't been brought up in a special way. We're all equals as far as I know. I don't perceive any visions...

...Chris didn't think that he was the chosen one of the Ngati Porou. But he believed that he was the closest to the chosen one. He believed that whomever that man was going to be that he would reveal himself to him. Chris more or less saw himself as the right hand man.

But I think because of everything that went down, the man became reluctant to reveal himself because a lot of things that were happening weren't how he planned it, how he saw it happening. And instead the dread more or less took over the reins and said, "If he comes well he's gonna come in a blaze of fire." They saw it as a very physical thing.

Ngati Porou is a bit of a hard case iwi because as far as they're concerned they're *all* leaders, they're *all* chosen. And you could say that in Ngati Porou every family thinks that one of their own is the one to lead the iwi. And if the chosen one were to spring up he'd have a lot of competition from other people thinking *they* were the chosen. But I suppose Chris in a way was a forerunner to the chosen one coming. He had to come first.

## DEATH

**Beau Tuhura:** I had this dream. I was strolling along this road and there were all these white fences and white buildings. And what I saw was that there were people inside these houses. They were celebrating weddings and birthdays and drinking and they were having a good time. Life was continuing as normal.

And then I looked up and there was an image of Haile Selassie in the heavens. And around it were all the star constellations of the twelve tribes of Israel.

But no one in the houses had seen this image in the sky. Life was continuing like normal for them. I looked around and I was the only one on the road and I was the only one who could see Him.

And so I went down to the pa and I told the others who were there - and Tom Te Maro (a Maori elder and tohunga) was one of them - to look up because He was revealing Himself.

To me the start of the dream signified that there would be a gathering of the nations to acknowledge one God. The image in the middle was Haile Selassie but it could have been anyone. It was more significant that there was the one God than who was in the image. The people celebrating in their houses suggests that when He comes the majority won't notice. He will come quietly. And I believe that Tom Te Maro and the other people in the dream have a part to play in my life in some way.

But the dream hadn't finished there.

I looked around and I saw the marae, and there was this blind fulla with dark glasses on, singing a song and playing a guitar. I went down and I heard him singing this song Old Black Jack. I'd never heard this song before but that's what he was singing about, Old Black Jack. Well, hello, it was revealed to me that Black Jack's a card game and if you have the Black Jack you're the winner, it was *the* card to have.

*Compare the second half of Tuhura's dream to the following one collected in psychologist Dr Wilhelm Stekel's book "Die Sprache des Traumes". "I was on a bridge where I met a blind fiddler. Everyone was tossing coins into his hat. I came closer and perceived that the musician was not blind. He had a squint, and was looking at me with a crooked glance from the side. Suddenly, there was a little old woman sitting at the side of a road. It was dark and I was afraid. 'Where does this road lead?' I thought. A young peasant came along the road and took me by the hand. 'Do you want to come home,' he said, 'and drink coffee?' 'Let me go! You are holding too tight!' I cried, and awoke."*

*It is a dream about death. Dr Stekel observes that death here appears in four symbols: the Blind Fiddler, the Squinting One, the Old Woman and the Young Peasant.*

**Monday, July 22, 1985:** *A terrible thing happens today. A twenty-two-year-old man named Joe Nepe takes a twenty-year-old man named Lance Kupenga up to a sacred hillside at Whakaahu, near Ruatoria, and makes him kneel before him on the ground. Kupenga does not struggle in his final moment. He accepts the inevitable as the much bigger and stronger Nepe swings the axe. It takes three swings for Nepe to remove Lance Kupenga's head. There are two deep holes nearby. He puts the head down one hole and the body down the other. Two boys in their early teens are with the pair and witness the murder.*

**Beau Tuhura, one of the early Rasta leaders:** At Lance's tangi (on Wednesday, August 10) I saw that guy who'd been in my dream. It was the blind man with the dark glasses on and he was singing and playing the guitar just like he'd been doing in my dream. I'm not sure if he played that same song about Old

Black Jack. But I freaked out. I'd never seen this guy before, except in my dream. I didn't know who he was. But I didn't get an opportunity to speak to him. And he left that same day. He didn't stay for the whole tangi. He wasn't someone that the locals knew. He wasn't talking to anyone. And I didn't bother to inquire about who he was either. I just figured there would be another time when I'd probably see him. I thought, "We're probably on the same path." And I haven't seen him since.

Then something else strange happened at Lance's tangi. It was during a karakia, at night when they have a prayer, and I got up to offer mine. And my karakia acknowledged his Imperial Majesty Haile Selassie I the first, the Ruler of David and Lion of the tribe of Judah. And one of my aunties started going into a trance. I went to stop what I was saying. But my mother urged me to carry on. And my aunty was whispering something. She was trying to tell my mother something. And when I asked my mother what it was she just said that she saw a white horse. Now in the Ringatu faith the white horse signifies that the prayers have been heard and that the prayers will be answered. Now in Ringatu they karakia and karakia right around the house until someone sees the sign of the white horse. Well I freaked out about that. It came before I even got into the theme of my prayer, just after I mentioned Haile Selassie.

In the community our Rastafarian group was something that had provoked fear and dread for a while. People daren't mention their opposition to it or displeasure. Otherwise their house could be next. And some people mightn't have liked me mentioning Haile Selassie in my karakia. But I wasn't about to jump ship from my beliefs. I still hold on to the philosophy of what the Rastafarianism was about.

*There are the official theories as to why Joe Nepe killed Lance Kupenga, those that came out in court. And there are the unofficial ones that are discussed behind closed doors in Ruatoria. I've read the crime reports in the newspaper and the court notes from the trial. I've interviewed Joe and various people involved in the case. I was asked by locals not to approach Lance's father, Paetene Kupenga, and I acceded to that request until instructed by Te Aowera Marae secretary Sarah Sykes in 2007 that I had to talk to Paetene before I could get any support from the Ngati Porou heirarchy. But I'm still not sure what was going on in Joe's mind and why he **really** did what he did. Maybe the reason is included in one of the following possibilities, or maybe in a combination of them. The official theories include:*

*1: Joe was insane.*

*2: Joe was punishing Lance for messing with the grave of one of Joe's ancestors who died in the First World War.*

*3: Joe was carrying out an utu or revenge for the killing of one of his ancestors by one of Lance's ancestors in the 1700s.*

*The unofficial theories include:*

*1: Joe was punishing Lance for raiding a dope plantation he shouldn't have.*

*2: Joe was consciously or unconsciously repeating a ritual beheading that happened at the same place, Whakaahu, in the same way about a hundred years earlier. Te Aowera marae secretary Sarah Sykes and Joe's brother were among those who'd heard about this possible incident. Joe's brother told me on the phone that one of the marae in Ruatoria had a small clipping from an old Maori newspaper about the earlier incident. But most people I talked to hadn't heard about it and if they had, they weren't telling. I found it hard to get details. And I'm still not sure if it happened.*

*3: The child the Rastas are claimed to have wanted to sacrifice was actually Lance's and, when the mother fled town with the child, Lance either offered himself or was chosen as a replacement.*

*4: Lance Kupenga may have been killed as a sacrifice to Haile Selassie, the late Emperor of Ethiopia, on his birthday. The Rastas held a party at Te Aowera marae to commemorate Selassie's birthday. Lance was killed on July 22, 1985. Haile Selassie's birthdate is July 23 1892: around the world it is one of the holiest days in the Rastafarian religious calendar.*

*5: The Rastas thought Lance Kupenga could be a significant figure in the realisation of Hori Gage's prophecy about a new spiritual leader for Ngati Porou. The Rastas had been told by older Maori that, in earlier times, one way of getting a person's mana was by beheading them (another way was to eat them). So they acted on that information for their own ends. Lance was beheaded for his mana, to help steer the course of the prophecy towards other members of the Ruatoria Rastafarians. It seems to me that if there was any credence to this last theory, then there would need to have been collusion with Joe or persuasion of him by other Rastas. Some police privately suspect that Joe, being vulnerable, was put up to the killing by other hardcore members of the Rastas, known among themselves as The Twelve.*

*While talking to Joe about Junior Paul, whom the Rastas believed was cursed or possessed prior to their assault on him, I wondered at one point whether Joe had inadvertently admitted to some persuasion from his fellow-Rastas. We had been talking earlier about the killing of Lance Kupenga. Part of the conversation about Junior went like this:*

"So what was the feeling there? Junior was a bit out-there as soon as he turned up wasn't he?"

"Mmm."

"He was already under the influence of whatever had him wasn't he?"

"Mmm."

"And, um, what was there, a council to decide how to deal with it?"

"Same thing. The Twelve."

I just about fell off my seat. Same thing as what? It seemed obvious. Same thing as Lance. "The Twelve."

We continued talking. And eventually, I returned to the subject. "Now when you were saying that the twelve had decided about Junior Paul, had there been any talk about Lance before..."

"Na. Lance wasn't even thought of."

"So the group hadn't got together and decided anything about Lance or anything like that?"

"No. No. No."

So maybe there was collusion or persuasion. And maybe there wasn't. My conclusion is that **no** conclusion can be drawn from Joe's "slip" of the tongue about The Twelve. It seems to me that Joe Nepe might have been better off if he'd served time in prison for his crime, instead of in the high security wing of Kingseat Mental Hospital in South Auckland. His face twitches a lot and when he speaks he seems to search for words as if in a fog. Sometimes he laughs and it sounds like it's coming from far away. It sounds like Vincent Price's fake evil laugh from the old Hammer Horror movies being played in the next room. Joe seems to be suffering the side-effects of some heavy and prolonged medication.

Joe's method of conversation is to immediately agree with everything you suggest, and then only slowly, from that initial point of agreement, actually make clear what he really feels or what really happened. Later, as I quote Joe more fully, that will become obvious to the reader.

I should add here that Paetene, Lance's father, gave me a completely different reason for the beheading of his son, one that I'd never imagined or heard put forward before. We'll come to that later.

# SARAH SYKES

*Sarah Sykes is the secretary of Te Aowera marae at the base of Mt
Hikurangi. She is a very spiritual person, perhaps psychic, and is a firm believer
in the prophecies handed down about a new spiritual leader for Ngati Porou.
She also believes her father possessed unique insight into how the prophecy
would unfold.*

*The following is from tape recorded notes made after a conversation my
father, Iain Gillies, and I had with Sarah Sykes, sitting at one of the wooden
table and benches at the side of the main road in Ruatoria on a sunny morning,
November 20, 2000. I'd seen her in her little red car as I came out of the dairy
with a couple of pies and I'd introduced her to Dad.*

**Iain Gillies:** It was very interesting when we asked about herself, just to get
her own background. She said that she had been in Kawerau when she left
school. She stayed at school until she was eighteen to fulfill her dad's wishes.
Then she married her husband in Kawerau. He worked at the mill there. And the
children were born in Kawerau. Before all these troubles in Ruatoria broke she
had this feeling that she was the one who should come back to the East Coast
because there was unfinished work there and she had a part to play in this.

So there was just this inward feeling that she was the one who would have to
come back, not anyone else in her family. She was the youngest and outwardly
the least likely candidate to do this because she, as she said herself, was just a
little teeny-bopper in high heeled shoes and lipstick, looking like the young
women of the times. But she came back and had a role to play in as much that
she was not a great doer of outward actions but she listened, watched and, when
she was asked, could provide answers to people who were looking for them. But
all the time she knew that there was this leader that would come along and she is
still waiting for that leader.

And it was quite interesting that basically she is talking about a spiritual
person and a leader who was more or less coming out of the blue that no one
would expect. And she actually fills this bill remarkably well herself without
realising it. Angus and I both realised that here she is and at the moment they've
got lots of community problems in Ruatoria. They've got problems with water
supply, septic tanks, things like that. There was one specific instance of a woman
whose septic tank was just a mess. She was told it would cost about $15,000 or
so to get it sorted out. And this woman had been to all authorities around. She'd
tried councils, district councils, but nobody could do anything about it. Sarah has

actually got the programme moving like a rocket. She's met with people from the Government. She's short-circuited the Government wheels. She's got things moving. It looks very much like Ruatoria will get the benefit of a septic tank clean-out pool, which basically she's done without any great fuss or bother. Nobody knows about it at this stage. But she took the woman's case, took it through the channels. And it looks as though this could go ahead and that other septic tanks giving trouble could be made functional again, which is a very big thing in Ruatoria. And who knows, it could be the start of a better water scheme for them up there. If they can sort out the sewerage problem, then they might be able to fix up the water shortage problem that they have in the summer. And that is not bad leadership.

**The following is from a tape recording of myself trying to remember details of a conversation I had with Sarah Sykes at her house one morning in early December, 2000:** Sarah believes that whoever was behind the killing of Lance Kupenga may have got the wrong person when they got Lance.

She says people have heard different parts of the prophecy concerning the chosen one or the so-called golden child. But they don't understand the prophecy in its entirety. And they all want to bring the prophecy or the kaupapa forward. They want to speed it up because they believe they are the golden child. Maybe John Heeney believes he is the promised child. Chris Campbell probably believed he was the promised child. And Beau probably believed he was the promised child because his family has the royal blood.

Sarah believes Joe Nepe beheaded Lance because the Rastas thought his mana would help speed up the prophecies. But the person who actually had the power and the mana and the "pearls of wisdom" that these guys wanted, according to Sarah, wasn't Lance; it was Sarah's father.

This, according to Sarah, is how it worked. Chris Campbell and Sarah Sykes had the same grandfather from different marriages. Chris's line of the family came from the first marriage. Sarah's line (and Lance Kupenga's) came from the second marriage. Now there were prophecies that a leader would come from Te Aowera marae going way back before what Pop Gage had said, and these had been passed down.

And Chris thought that because his side of the family was the tuakana or more senior line that the prophecy would be dealing with them.

But Sarah believes the prophecy was actually dealing with her family, the younger line from the second marriage. And Sarah's father passed on to her that it would be down their line. (I mentioned to Sarah that if her father was the person who had been passed down the wisdom, then it was like Jacob and Esau receiving their blessings from their father Isaac in the Bible. Esau missed out on his blessing even though he was the older one. Sarah said it was very similar to that. Sarah also said that her father told her that, while watching the prophecy unfold, she should look for parallels in the scriptures because it would unfold in accordance with the scriptures.)

Sarah says her father knew that he was just a part of the kaupapa. It was bigger than him. And he would even say, "It wants me to close my eyes. It can't wait for me to close my eyes so that it can get started."

But the reason he took a while to close his eyes was because he was saying, "I won't close my eyes until I see that one walk," meaning Sarah's youngest daughter, the youngest of three kids (Sarah didn't tell me her name). And it wasn't just that he wanted to see his grand daughter walk. He wanted to see the footsteps (a reference, I think, to the footsteps of fire seen by the visionary Hori Gage).

And he wanted to see not just the footsteps, but the next step of the kaupapa, what would happen after Sarah, the next step of it.

Lance's father is called Paetene Kupenga. Apparently, the Kupengas thought they had the promised child in their family. They thought it was Paetene's brother. And apparently they suffered for that because it wasn't the brother.

Then Kate Walker (John Heeney's aunty) announced at a hui in Auckland that Selwyn Parata was the new leader of Ngati Porou. (At the time of writing, Selwyn Parata is a public servant for the Ministry of Maori Development, Te Puni Kokiri, and is a respected expert in Ngati Porou reo and tikanga, or language and culture). But Sarah said, "No, no, he's not the one. We don't need an announcement when this person comes." And her father had told her that she'd be there and the person would cross her path. She wouldn't have to move to find the person. She'd just have to go about her daily business and the person would cross her path. And it wouldn't be anything great. It would be from a humble family, probably not a family like the Ngatas or the Mahuikas, but one of the lesser-known families. And what would be significant about them would be what came out of their mouth. They would be very spiritual.

Now a similar thing has happened to what happened with Lance except not as dramatically. And that is where a member of the family, from another branch, has tried to gain the mana of Sarah and Chris's grandfather.

What happened was these people took a stone from Mt Hikurangi and took it to Wellington, where they hoped to use the stone to somehow invoke the mana of this grandfather. And this woman got sick. She suffered from mate Maori and they took her to a physician and they couldn't find anything wrong with her. Then they took her to a tohunga. By this time the stone was starting to cry. What happened was she'd go out and look at the stone and it was all wet. And she'd say to her husband, "What have you done to the stone?"

"I ain't done nothing to the stone."

So anyway the next day the stone's wet. "What have you done with the stone?"

"I've done nothing to the stone." The stone's all wet. This carried on until eventually she realised that he was doing nothing to the stone. And the stone was just becoming wet of its own accord. According to Sarah, it was crying.

And anyway this woman told the tohunga that this stone was crying and he said, "Well you've gotta take the stone back to Te Aowera." And they brought the stone back and Sarah said, "What's the hidden agenda here?"

Well apparently she was out when they arrived. But she must have talked to them at some stage. And she said to the woman: "What's the hidden agenda?" because they weren't going to tell her. They were just going to make up some good story. But Sarah said, "No, no, I'm sensing a hidden agenda. You may as well tell it now. Otherwise I'll just find it out later from the tipuna (the ancestors)." And it turned out that the agenda was that they were trying to invoke the mana of this common grandfather with the stone. So the stone had to be returned and hopefully the woman has recovered. But Sarah didn't know that at the time of telling me. This had just happened in the last few weeks (December, 2000).

So this whole idea of trying to force the kaupapa, to play with the kaupapa, to change the kaupapa, to quicken the kaupapa, to try and make the kaupapa bend to their will is still happening. People still want that power. She said that one person has even gone so far as to give his grandson a certain special name, as if they were the promised child...

...Sarah was brought up in Gisborne. Her father was what they call whakatoaed, I think. His father had a Ringatu ritual performed. Now what that means is that they perform a ritual so that the mother can have a boy. Sarah's father was an only child from that marriage, or an only son at least. The father wasn't having any luck having a son. And they needed a son to keep the kaupapa going, I suppose.

So it was agreed that the Ringatu tohunga would perform a whakatoa, I think it's called.

After that Sarah's father was born and as he grew up he had lots of friends around him. There's a Maori word for them. Basically, they're what Europeans would call an imaginary friend.

As a whakatoaed child he was very spiritual as he was brought forth through spiritual means. And he had these little friends around him. People have seen them occasionally around Te Aowera, as in ghosts. And Sarah believes that she will find them somewhere, that she will come across them somewhere. Even though he was an only child, he was surrounded by these imaginary friends, which no one else could see. And he grew up with these kids and talked to them, all these little people. Now when he was grown up and had his own family, he was blessed with sons. Because he was a spiritual child it was one of his blessings that he would have all these sons. He was brought forth from a blessing to be a son himself so he ended up getting married to Sarah's mum and then ended up having ten boys and four girls and Sarah was the youngest.

Now the mother wanted to know who was going to stay in the house next to the marae because their family was meant to be the caretakers of the marae, or the gate of the marae anyway. And the house stood empty for twenty-three years apparently when the family went to Gisborne to live and to grow up there. That's where Sarah grew up and went to high school.

Some of her brothers tried to live in the house next to the marae. And they'd all last about six months before spiritual happenings would drive them out. One brother would see one of the tipuna as big as the world outside the door, standing really huge outside the house. Another, his son had a small stone fall on his foot and the brother couldn't believe how this small stone could do so much damage. So Sarah believed that these things happened to drive them away, to drive them out because she was the one who was meant to stay there.

Anyway one day she was living with Ian in Kawerau – I think she was working at the paper mill – and she heard a rustling of leaves through the window. She could tell it was the poplar tree at Te Aowera Marae calling to her. She believes it was the poplar tree calling her home.

Now the poplar tree was a memorial tree and I'll digress here and tell this story. Apparently not many people know this but the tree is a memorial to the moment when Ropata Wahawaha and Tuta Nihoniho realised that Te Kooti was a man called of God. And it was the last time they confronted him. And what happened was they chased him down into a gulley somewhere up the coast and they slept for the night. They thought there was no escape for Te Kooti and his men. But when they woke up in the morning somehow Te Kooti had disappeared. And that's when they realised they were actually chasing a ghost or a man actually who was called of God. He was on a divine path. And they decided then that they would give up chasing Te Kooti and return home. And they took from that gulley a little poplar sapling. And that grew into the poplar tree that's at the marae today and it would be over a hundred years old.

And by the way, around Te Aowera, Ropata is not a well-liked tipuna. They won't have a bar of him. Sarah says they won't allow him back on to the marae.

He is buried at Matiatia along with Paratene Ngata, who was Apirana Ngata's father. They believe Ropata was responsible for a lot of deaths in the family and that he shouldn't have been going against Te Kooti. And they weren't that keen to go with him, but he dragged them along.

Anyway, so Sarah's mum was dying. And she was waiting to see the next phase of the kaupapa. She'd been trying to figure it out and waiting for things to happen. But now she'd got to the end of her life and she was running out of time. And she wanted to see, at least see who would end up back in the house to live next to the marae.

Every morning and afternoon she'd be praying, "Please let me see, let me hear from their own mouth who is going to live back at the house, who is going to take over the house."

And eventually after Sarah had heard the poplar calling her back home she went to her mother and said, "It's me, Mother. I'm the one who's been called back home."

And her mother couldn't believe it. Sarah was the youngest one. She was brought up in Gisborne. She was a bit of a townie. She had her Cutex fingernails, lipstick, high heels and mini skirts. But Sarah believed that she was the one who was going back.

Of course her husband, Ian Sykes, is from a reasonably well-off Pakeha family in the Bay of Plenty. They're all pretty good at doing well for themselves. And here he is being dragged off to Ruatoria as well. But she believes that that's why she was with him: because he allowed her to trust her instincts and her intuition. And perhaps it was to her benefit that she was with a Pakeha as well: to keep her grounded.

Anyway, she went back to the coast. And after her mother died her father came and stayed with them for twelve months. And when her father died things started happening at Te Aowera Marae. The Rastas moved into the marae. And she was busy trying to clean the rats and the possums and all the rest of it out of the house and trying to make it an inhabitable house. Her mother had only two wishes. One was that she'd put new carpet on the floors and the other was that she would look after her roses, which Sarah did...

**Former Detective Sergeant Laurie Naden:** The Rastas took over the marae. They committed some terrible bloody transgressions there. They allowed dogs into the whare nui. They allowed pigs to graze the graveyard and things like that.

That became quite a major standoff between the elders and the Rastas.

**Tape recording of myself trying to remember details of a conversation I had with Sarah Sykes at her house one morning in early December, 2000:** Sarah said that in the early days Chris and Beau Tuhura were always coming around to her place, picking her brains, trying to get information out of her about the prophecy, what she'd heard. But her father had schooled her up in the last twelve months of his life. He told her different people would come along thinking they were the leaders. But she was to ignore them. He told her people would come looking to her, but that she had to guard her pearls and that she would know when to let them drop, pearls being the prophecies.

She wasn't so worried about Chris coming to see her because he was family. But she did wonder what Beau was doing there because he wasn't such close family. She soon realised that he also thought he was the promised child.

But she told Chris that he wasn't the one. This is one thing she was worried about because she realised Chris and Beau were trying to find out as much as they could. They wanted to force whatever it was, the kaupapa, into action when it wasn't ready. They weren't prepared to sit and watch and wait. They wanted to nudge it into life so that they could imprint themselves upon it.

With John and Chris and Beau each suspecting that they were the promised child, moves were afoot to try and find out as much as they could and to mould the prophecies to suit their circumstances.

Sarah knew that it couldn't be them because she was still working on the house and still working through things. She still had to get the house ready, to get the flowers done and to get the carpet laid for her deceased mum, to see her father off, and things like that. So she said to Chris, "You aren't the one. It's not the time. There's no use in trying to make it come too soon. This is bigger. You are in it, Chris. But you're just a small part of it. And I'm just a small part of it." And she now believes her youngest daughter is a part of it, but once again, just a part of it, paving the way for the promised child.

And Sarah talks about a knowing inside her. She said she knew that Chris wasn't the prophesied child because her father had said that she would know who this promised child was by what came out of their mouth. And there would be no great fanfare. The chosen one would be a very simple person from a simple background. In fact the background would be so simple that people wouldn't recognise it or believe it. But then it would make itself clear.

Another reason that Sarah felt Chris and them were off the track a bit was that they got right into the Ringatu faith and took it to Te Aowera. But Sarah's father had told her before he died that the Ringatu faith wasn't for his children. He opened it up for them. He said it's all right for other people but it's not for you, not for your generation. So it seemed strange that the Rastas were bringing it back to the marae. Although the Rastas would probably argue that it needed to go back.

Sarah said she knew of only two children who were whakatoaed and they were her father and Sir Apirana Ngata. She said Sir Apirana Ngata was more of a human influence whereas her father was spiritual. She said her father was a lot like Paetene Kupenga. People thought he was a bit peculiar. Her father spoke in parables. He didn't really speak to a lot of people. But people felt honoured if he spoke to them. He said to her that she would have to be strong, that trouble was coming to Te Aowera and that it was very sad, but that she would need to be strong.


## BAD OMENS


*Friday, July 26, 1985: Gisborne mayor Hink Healey declares a Civil Defence emergency at 6.30am. Torrential rain has left huge areas of the city and the Poverty Bay Flats flooded and has forced homes to be abandoned.*

*Civil Defence offices have been open all night and staff have been busy directing rescue operations and anxiously watching the Taraheru and Waimata rivers. Their worst fears are realised this morning. The rivers have burst their banks and over one hundred and fifty people have been evacuated.*

*Prime Minister David Lange flies over the devastated farmland of Gisborne's hinterland and acknowledges that the Government must come up with some money to help.*

**Maori Myth and Legend, Margaret Orbell, Tama-i-waho, A god in the sky:** This powerful atua in the sky was a war god of a number of Bay of Plenty and east coast peoples. His visible form was a star, which has not been identified. Before a battle he would be asked to foretell the outcome, and would reply by taking possession of a tohunga and speaking through him. He also warned of approaching enemies. Some say he flew from Hawaiiki, the mythical homeland from which the Maori ancestors made the voyage to New Zealand, and landed on the peak of Mount Hikurangi. There he remained, a dangerous ogre known sometimes as Tama-ki-Hikurangi (Tama on Hikurangi).

**Former Rasta Beau Tuhura:** I had this dream when I was at Hiruharama Marae and I just happened to reveal it to some aunties who were there. I could see balls of fire like explosions, all these great big balls of fire, and uniformed men - they looked Chinese - and there were thousands of them. It looked like we were being invaded. They were coming from the East and marching inland. I was in the midst of them and they were just going past me. And there was this weapon like a nuclear war-head. It came from out at sea and it was heading towards Mount Hikurangi. And that was it.

The aunties asked me, "Did it land on the mountain?"And I said, "No." And they were relieved to hear that.

They saw the balls of fire as being Te Aowera, the sub-tribe and the marae. They saw all this trouble and conflict there. And they saw the invaders as Nga Tama Toa. That was the name we had taken for our Rasta group. They said the nuclear war-head that threatened the mountain was a star of destruction and doom. They knew the name of the star but I can't remember it now. So you could say the dream was about trouble and conflict at Te Aowera as the Rasta group moved in, and a threat to the mountain.

**Witi Ihimaera, from his novel The Dream Swimmer:** Maoripeople believe that you travel in your dreams most often when your yearnings of aroha, of mokemoke, one for another, need to be expressed. Even in these great days of change, when nobody believes in these things, they still travel in dreams to talk with whanaunga about old ancestral matters that need to be resolved, about breaches that must be healed, or to tell of taonga, family heirlooms, that still must be found. When they are dying they travel to embrace, mingle tears and say farewell to all those they have loved. Or they travel to protect or warn a loved one of some malignant star or malevolent sign...

...Whatever the travel, all must be achieved within the space of the dream. So if they are in a hurry, or must travel far, Maori people will call upon their family protector, their kaitiaki, to help them.

**Tape recorded notes following a conversation with Sarah Sykes:** Sarah lives next door to Te Aowera Marae. She says her father told her: "There is trouble coming. And though it will start well away from you, it will end up on your doorstep."

And that's pretty much what happened when the Rastas came and took over Te Aowera Marae.

Sarah believes the tipuna weren't happy with the Rastas showing disrespect to them. She said that John Heeney was going to hit her once. She said some of the police wouldn't have minded if old John had hit her because then they'd have been able to put him away.

She said she's seen John Heeney give his wife, Donna, a thrashing at the front of the tipuna whare. And she went up to John and said, "That's an insult to our tipuna. How dare you insult the tipuna like that."

She said to John's wife, "You don't have to stay with him. You can go back to Te Teko." That's where she's from, Te Teko, in the Bay of Plenty. "But if you do want to stay with him, he can give you a thrashing *behind* the marae where no one has to see it."...

...When the Rastas moved into Te Aowera marae, they had a big post in the middle and they put a picture of Haile Selassie on it. And they had a little shrine to Haile Selassie, where the women would make up flower arrangements, which would include marijuana leaves. And they had marijuana seedlings growing and things like that. Sarah thought it was an insult to the tipuna.

Anyway, Sarah went around to see them. She wasn't very happy that the Rastas had taken over the marae with this Haile Selassie. So she went over there with a picture of Jesus Christ. And she said, "All right." She was standing in the middle of all the Rastas. Ian, her husband, was away this day and she went over there on her own. And there were about twelve of them and they were all around her. She said to Chris, "Okay, Chris, you can have the centre post. But I'll have the second post." So she stuck a picture of Jesus Christ on the second post in the marae. She said, "And I'll tell you, tomorrow my picture of Jesus Christ will still be there and your picture of Haile Selassie will be gone."

She says the next day the picture of Haile Selassie was gone and the picture of Jesus Christ is still hanging in there today...

...Another thing Sarah Sykes' father told her was that the people had always been there. He actually said, "We have always been here." It ties in with a few other comments I heard or discovered while researching this book. John Heeney at one stage said that the Ngati Porou had started on the coast, then travelled around the world and come back. It ties in with what Joe Nepe told me about Whakaahu being the Garden of Eden and what Laura Thompson, Hata's mum, said about the Stone People or Ngati Ue Pohatu and the Tini a Toi.

It also ties in with what Canon Hone Kaa said during the trial of Joe Nepe for the murder of Lance Kupenga.

Peter Williams (for the defence): I want to come to another topic that concerns the place or the hill or mountain where the homicide took place. The Whakaahu Block and trig at Otuaru. What are the Maori beliefs in relation to that mountain?

Canon Hone Kaa: It was I understand originally the pa site.

Williams: Was that pa taken by conquest?

Kaa: Well the people of that place have always lived there. There is of course a belief among Ngati Porou that we have always been here.

Williams: Always been in New Zealand?

Kaa: Yes, we did not come on canoe, we have always been here.

# CHAPTER 6

## ARSON, INTIMIDATION AND A BATTLE WITH POLICE

*Saturday, July 27, 1985: Another fire. Constable Geoffrey Mills sees the flames as he's driving from Ruatoria to Tokomaru Bay in his patrol car at 11.20pm. The fire's on Kevin Brown's Horehore farm, just south of Hiruharama Marae. It's a haybarn about a hundred metres off the main road. Constable Mills stops at two houses. At the second he finds someone to call the volunteer fire service. By the time the brigade arrives, the barn is well alight. It burns to the ground, taking about two thousand bales of hay with it. The firemen are at the scene until 4am. When they leave, only smouldering ruins are left.*

*Sunday, July 28: The Gisborne CIB and Fire Brigade are sifting through the ashes of Kevin Brown's haybarn. Detective Rex Harrison says it appears some accelerant was used to start the fire. He reckons the offender, or offenders, may have walked across several paddocks to reach the barn after leaving a car parked nearby. But despite extensive inquiries there is little evidence to suggest who may be responsible.*

*Later, a police party turns up at Te Aowera Marae to arrest John Heeney for failing to appear in court on the horse cruelty charge. The Rastafarians have been staying at the marae. Some people in the community don't want them there. But the Rastas say it's their right as they belong to the marae. When police try to arrest Heeney, they're told to get off the marae by a group of Rastas threatening to fight any police who enter.*

*Marae officials are contacted to negotiate with the group and after an hour the police are invited on to the marae.*

*Alan (Jano) Kirikino's arrested for trying to stop the police entering at the gate. The others try to stop the police arresting Heeney, who's been brandishing a piece of wood and threatening to use it as a weapon. The tension explodes into a brawl between Rastas and police. A detective wrestles with Gallace Hongara, dodges a few punches and finally, after the Rasta escapes a headlock, manages to handcuff him. Hongara spits in his face.*

*Daryl Te Hau comes at Constable Robert Mills, inviting him to fight. Mills punches him in the head. And so on.*

**Monday, July 29:** *Daryl Te Hau and Barney Rangi Wharepapa are arrested in connection with the fight against police at Te Aowera Marae yesterday. The police waited a day to arrest them to avoid more violence.*

*Meanwhile, three Rastas who were on bail – Heeney, Gallace Hongara and Alan Kirikino – appear in the Gisborne District Court.*

*Heeney's charged with assaulting a policeman and failing to appear in court. He's remanded in custody until Thursday. Hongara's charged with assault, resisting arrest and obstructing a constable, while Kirikino's charged with obstructing a constable. They're remanded in custody to August 5.*

**Sue Nikora, early influence on the Rastas:** The instigators of the gang began with Hone Heeney. John Heeney is one of the most intelligent persons I've ever known. He has a brilliant mind and is not to be under-estimated in any way. I've seen him perform very well in the courts... excellent, ay. And he was really the leader of it all. He was more the leader than Chris. Then Chris came back from Wellington or somewhere down the line and fell in love with John's sister. But John was the one who was most upset about the alienation of the lands. He wasn't there to make trouble but he was there as the instigator of the movement. And the movement was simply to make everybody aware of what was happening and how they were feeling about this. Both Chris and John are mukupuna to me. They're grand-nephews of mine. And when they first brought it to our attention, Hone was very much to the front of it. He's a very deep thinker and very verbal and well mannered. And he was very much the leader of the pack. But as I say, Chris linked up with John's sister, they became whanau and of course their leadership came out. There was never a struggle between them to be in charge. They complemented each other. There was never an internal struggle in the movement. There was a lot of love there. I'm saying that because they'd invite us over and we'd go and sleep at Te Aowera Marae. And maybe it was because of our presence that nothing sinister happened. But they'd have their children there. The children would cry and all the women were mothers to the child. A woman would pick up a baby, it might not be hers, but if she was producing milk, she'd give it a breast. All the men were fathers to the children. We owned a lot of land that they were occupying. I don't know whether you understand Maori protocol, but they used to come to me and my two brothers. They'd come to us and say, "Right, we haven't got anywhere to go. Can we occupy this house?" What could we do? We'd say, "Kei te pai."

The Rastas were talking to us a lot. We were there in the capacity of elders. We never, ever interfered unless they came to us for advice. They'd ask us, "Is this the right thing as far as Maori culture is concerned? Is that the right thing? Should we do this? Should we do that?" And that's Maori protocol. And we never really over-stepped our mark with them and they didn't over-step the mark with us. We never directed them although it has been said that we influenced them. In what way?

The young ones would call a meeting. They expected us to be there. If we went missing, they'd be here. "Why didn't you come to our meeting? What have we done wrong to you?" What could I do? "Aw well, we just wanted you to be there."

It wasn't just John and Chris talking to us. It was the whole lot of them. Each and every one of them had their own sovereignty, or own tino rangatiratanga. They didn't try to suppress anyone. There was a whole lot of love there. In fact, too much love. But love for one another. A baby would cry; they'd suckle the baby. The mother would go somewhere and if the baby cried again someone else would suckle the baby. I never saw such love in my life than with them. Because that was how we nurtured our children in the old days. The emphasis was always on the calmness of the child. When my eldest daughter was born my uncle and aunt said, "Right, I'm taking your child. This is our privilege to do that." I doubt the Scottish is like that. But we lay a lot of emphasis on the upbringing of the child. That's why we're really hurting when we see pictures of how children have been abused. I would say that much. It did foster a lot of caring, sharing and happiness during that time.

**Thursday, August 1:** *Chris Campbell tells Judge Hole that he's fed up of being remanded in custody.*

*He says he's been told by a jailer that his twenty-one consecutive days in the Gisborne Police Station cells is a record.*

*"I'm sick of it," Campbell says in court. "It is becoming ludicrous."*

*Campbell's in court for the joint charge of aggravated cruelty to a horse. He's also appearing on charges of trespass, resisting a constable and escaping from custody.*

"I'm quite sick of being remanded in custody," he says. "Twenty one days is a long time. We are led to believe that one is not guilty in this country until he is proven guilty. But we are being put off and put off. We don't sort of enjoy breaking records."

The judge asks Campbell if he has any objection to being remanded until tomorrow for his trespass hearing. And Campbell says he's strongly opposed to it.

"I have subpoenaed witnesses to be here today," he says. "I was informed by the court that the matter would be heard today so it should go ahead."

John Heeney decides to follow Campbell's lead. He says he also strongly objects to being remanded in custody. While in the dock, he says charges should be laid against the police for trespassing on a marae. He asks Judge Hole how to go about laying charges. When Judge Hole asks him who his solicitor is, Heeney replies, "God."

"You should see your solicitor about it."

**Monday, August 5:** *Gallace Hongara and Daryl Te Hau appear in court today and are remanded to Friday on obstruction and assault charges arising from their scrap with police.*

**Thursday, August 8, 1985:** *Hone Heeney and Chris Campbell appear in court in Gisborne.*

Heeney's charged with damaging a traffic officer's car and behaving in a threatening manner. Campbell's charged with threatening to injure. Both have pleaded not guilty.

The charges arise from an incident at night after a group of Rastafarians on horseback surrounded a patrol car.

The court hears evidence from Sergeant Norman Gray and Traffic Officer Bruce Laing regarding an incident on Whareponga Road, near the intersection with the main highway.

As the sergeant tried to speak to the group about riding horses on the road in the dark, the five horsemen surrounded the patrol car and started to abuse and threaten the officers. Both officers accuse Campbell of thrusting a Rasta flag through the window at the sergeant's face. They say Campbell accused him of trespassing on their road and ordered him to leave.

Sergeant Gray was in some doubt it was Campbell, as he did not know him personally. But the traffic officer told him later that it was Campbell and Gray identifies Campbell in court as the man who attacked him.

*The sergeant describes how they decided to leave a situation that was becoming dangerous. He saw Heeney pick up a rock and throw it at the car. It struck the boot lid and bounced off.*

*Under cross examination, Sergeant Gray admits it was dark but maintains the man he saw was Campbell, though he can't say he's one hundred per cent sure.*

*Traffic Officer Laing identifies Heeney and Campbell. He says he saw Campbell thrust the flag at Sergeant Gray and strike the roof of the car with it.*

*Heeney rode up to him, abused him and said if they did not get off the road he would put the traffic officer "down the hole". Heeney said the road was private.*

*The traffic officer said he would leave, then heard a thump against the car. Heeney began to repeat his threats. The traffic officer looked in his rear vision mirror and saw him dismount and throw a rock at the car (the area was well lit by the red flashing lights, often used to light up accident scenes).*

*Neither defence counsel calls evidence. Neil Weatherhead and John Matheson submit there's no case to answer. They claim there's doubt as to whether it was Campbell who thrust the flag.*

*The judge agrees. He says it's obvious from the way the sergeant gave evidence that he didn't have the faintest idea who it was holding the flag. The traffic officer couldn't see the face of the man holding the flag as it was thrust through the window. Furthermore, Bruce Laing's sighting of someone throwing a stone at the car was in a mirror in the light of red lights on top of the car.*

*Events appear confused and although Judge J. D. Hole accepts that men on horseback **did** surround the car, that a flag **was** thrust through the window at Sergeant Gray's face and words **were** said, he's not satisfied beyond reasonable doubt that Heeney and Campbell are responsible.*

*The case against them is dismissed...*

**Bob Kaa, Ruatoria resident:** I can remember the last two traffic cops we had here. They were good guys. I knew them very well. The traffic department had a nice home down the road here.

And two of them came to the meeting when the problems had already happened. They said, "Yes, we'll stop these bastards. We'll stop them."

And I said to them: "Be careful with that statement." They'd brought these traffic cops in from the city. I said: "You don't know this community. We know this community. You be very, very careful. I'm warning you now, these people won't like your big talk." Well what happened is they deliberately baled them up on a one-way bridge on the main road. There's a lot of one-way bridges as you come up the coast. And they couldn't do a bloody thing. What do they do? Wrecked their car. See, the cops had been chasing them. They deliberately baited the traffic cops. They stopped at one end of the bridge. By the time the traffic cops got out of their car, whoosh, they came in behind. And the cops knew straight away they were in trouble. They got beaten up and their car was a write-off. One of them even had a nervous breakdown. And the other guy just left town. And they were bloody nice guys.

*...John Heeney also faces charges in connection to the brawl between police and Rastas at Te Aowera Marae. The judge decides these will be heard in October.*

*But Gallace Hongara, Daryl Te Hau, Barney Wharepapa, and Alan Kirikino are dealt with. They plead not guilty, but are convicted on all charges.*

*All four defendants appear for themselves. They give evidence that they saw the arrival of police at the marae as a violation of marae protocol. They say they tried to stop the police from "bringing their brutality" on to the marae.*

*Judge Hole jails Hongara for fourteen days for assaulting a police officer. On the obstruction charges faced by all defendants, he takes their mistaken belief that the policemen weren't allowed on the marae into account and places them under suspended sentence for one year.*

*But there's extra bad news for Wharepapa. Judge Hole sends him to youth prison for twenty-one days for breach of probation and periodic detention orders.*

*Friday, August 9: Chris Campbell is fined $65 for escaping from custody, a charge arising from an incident in which he broke away from a constable attempting to detain him.*

*And he's ordered to pay costs on charges of resisting arrest and offensive behaviour (he spat at a police sergeant in Ruatoria).*

*A charge of willful damage to a police tunic is dismissed after a defended hearing. The jacket was torn when he grabbed an officer in the police cells. The court hears police evidence of Campbell refusing to go into his cell. During a struggle with two officers he ripped a tunic from top to bottom. Campbell remembers struggling with them but says he can't remember ripping the jacket and says he had no intention of doing so.*

*Saturday, August 10, 1985: It's announced that Ruatoria's manual telephone exchange will be replaced by a modern electronic automatic system. That's good news for police investigating the Rastafarians. People are often too*

*scared to ring the police with information because there are party lines, which
neighbours can listen into, and operators, who can hear every call. No one
wants to be known as someone who snitches on family.*

*Ruatoria has less than five hundred subscribers and they're all used to every
call being connected by hand. The operators are used to questions like: "What
time does the 6 o'clock bus go to town?" Or: "I'm having trouble with my TV
set. What are you gonna do about it?" The operators know when something big
has happened locally. The phones run hot. And the place goes mad if Ruatoria
features in the news, as it has so often lately.*

*__Wednesday, September 4:__ A group of police from Ruatoria, Te Araroa and
Tokomaru Bay go to Te Aowera Marae. Their intention is to evict the Rastas
from the marae. But there are doubts about the legality of this action because of
the traditional rights some of the Rastas have to the marae.*

*There are heated discussions and full-blown arguments on the road outside
the marae. Eventually, the police party withdraws. The marae trustees are
advised to pursue the matter through the civil court. As a result of this a High
Court injunction is obtained preventing the Rastas from going on to the marae.*

## COMES THE DAWN

**Excerpt from Comes The Dawn, a previously unpublished memoir by
Paetene Kupenga, father of Lance Kupenga (who was beheaded by Joe
Nepe) written in 2002:** During these months the people of Hiruharama,
especially Te Aowera, were having trouble removing some of our own sons and
daughters from Te Aowera marae. The chairman of the marae, Hopa Keelan, had
had a dozen or so huis with the Rastas but to no avail. They were determined to
use the free power, cooking and sleeping facilities available, soil the mattresses
and linen and just throw them out. When we finally got them out weeks later, Ian
Sykes and I, with the help of others, heaped up the remains of 50 mattresses, 100
sheets, pillows and pillow cases, poured petrol on them and burnt the lot. Many
dishes were missing, especially the kai dishes with lids. We learnt later that these
dishes were excellent for nurturing young marijuana plants.

Prior to the Rastas commandeering the marae, we had grown corn and
bagged 150 sacks into a dam we had created behind Te Aowera. Well we found
out that the Rastas were eating our corn again. Ian Sykes and I borrowed a tractor

and shifted the leftover 20 bags to a secret site. These corn were grown to sell to our whanau to make money for our marae.

After being threatened one time too many our chairman Hopa Keelan came to Te Puia Springs and asked if I could take over. I told him it was up to the people.

So a few days later a meeting was held at Rongohaere, for obvious reasons. The uncles and aunties and cousins voted me in not just chairman but also chairman of trustees. So my first job was to find out how to remove the Rastas out of Te Aowera with as little ruckus as possible, hopefully without hurting anyone.

Tom Fox brought in a law expert he knew. This man explained the right way! The Te Aowera records will show that Te Aowera Marae had 21 meetings with the Police and the Rastas were still laughing at everybody who tried to remove them.

The expert explained that we had to get the signature of every trustee on a paper with our intentions clearly spelt out and delivered to every known Rasta in the area, after which we were all to meet at the courthouse in Gisborne on a set date. Some whanau atended the court but only the solicitor turned up for the Rastas. The judge ruled that it was breaking the law if the Rastas stepped on to Te Aowera grounds and this time the law could put them away indefinitely. Only the trustees can let them back on the marae if they thought that they were behaving individually or otherwise.

Although this whole episode only took a few lines in this book, it hurt a lot of people at the time. I remember clearly the tears in Uncle Charlie's eyes as he signed the trustee paper in his sitting room. Behind his and Auntie's TV was a loaded rifle: protection against the riff-raff that were living just down the road. I also feel that he was thinking about the three sons he sent to war to make this a better world, our cousins Parekura and Moss Ferris and their brother, cousin Toss Cooper.

During this time I was rung and told that The General, Lance's old horse, was at Te Aowera, starving on the fence. So I planned to deliver the trustee notices and collect The General in one move. So after work I loaded the bridle and saddle in the car, picked up a cuzzie to ride the horse back, but not to Te Puia Springs, to a secret location. We didn't want trouble brought toTe Puia Springs.

On our way to Te Aowera we met a very favourite cousin. After explaining what was going to happen he got in the car. We arrived at Sarah and Ian Sykes' house. We were given a cup of tea then we went to face the lions. We took a bridle for The General. As soon as we reached him I unsaddled him and Cuzzie changed the bridle. I lifted him on and he galloped away.

Meanwhile, the Rastas had circled us. Back to back we served them with the prepared notices. There were curses, swearing, you name it, we were getting told what to do with our notices, egging us to start a fight. I don't know to this day what my mates were thinking because it was very lopsided, about 30 to 3. I know what I was feeling, at least my pants did. It was very damp. I knew if it came to a showdown, as brave as Rongo and Ian were, we had no show. Then I remembered that before I left Te Puia Springs I had rung Ruatoria and was told that VJ (Victor Takarangi) was in Te Araroa. I told his daughter to send him to Te Aowera as soon as he arrived.

As the Rastas were tightening the noose around our necks, out of the corner of my eye, I saw VJ's car coming at full pace from the road gate to where we were. Everyone jumped out of the way. Ian, cousin Rongo and I jumped in quickly. VJ turned the car and we went off to Sarah's to cool down with a cuppa. Have never been so happy to see Victor, even though we don't see eye to eye now, I still thank him from the bottom of my heart.

As was stated earlier, only their lawyer turned up at the courthouse. He tried all the tricks lawyers try but I told him to get out. We the trustees and the people of Te Aowera had appointed us a lawyer about a month before all this. We found out he was two-timing us so we finished him off. It was a very trying time. You couldn't trust anyone. So it was best to just keep to yourself until it was all over.

A very strange thing happened on the night of the court case. I went to cousin Alf's place before coming home. His children told me he had gone to the shop and wouldn't be long. So I waited and waited. No Alf. I was about to leave when this man walked in. We got talking. He turned out to be an evangelist, Muru Thompson. I asked him to come to Te Aowera to have a karakia. He couldn't because of prior engagements but he told me Te Aowera like the great phoenix will rise out of the ashes. I came home feeling quite happy.

About ten years ago Dick Maxwell told me all through the serving the trustee notices episode, he had a .303 aimed at my head with his finger on the trigger. I'm very glad that he was not the nervous type. I told him. We both laughed. But deep down it was anything but a joke.

It's 20 years since all of this happened. A lot of our elders have gone on. They were the ones I felt sorry for. They didn't deserve this. They had brothers, uncles, aunties, cousins, sons and daughters who had gone to both world wars to keep this kind of rubbish from our shores.

People like Jack Ferris, who served in both the Boer and First World Wars. Iopa and his son Rua Te Puni, who both went to the First World War. Watene and Jim Pahai, Tutu Maraki and Gullas Hongara, who went to fight in every theatre of the Second World War. Tom, Joe and Sid Campbell. Their sister Pera.

Their many cousins, the Keelans Tom and Paddy, the Parkers Raki and Abraham, Tuhoro Haua, Pani Haereroa, Karauria Kirena, Rutene Ngaranoa, Pani Miromiro, who with others went to the First World War. I mention these papas, uncles and cousins because they all lived within the Te Aowera or Puhunga area.

A few weeks ago we had a rare and beautiful double wedding at Te Aowera, the first time I had witnessed one. Just last weekend we opened our new toilets, the very latest design, etc. Yes, Te Aowera has come a long way from the 1980s when a lot of us were waiting for the news that it was burnt to the ground. I travelled from Gisborne to Auckland to insure Te Aowera Marae in 1986. No insurance company would touch us with a thousand foot pole. That may give you an idea of how Te Aowera was in those years. No one wanted to know. Our present committee and trustees are the very best we can get. Their next move I believe is reroofing our dining room. I am rapt. The committee, etc are led by a more than capable couple. Since they have taken over everything has just blossomed, should I say, arrestingly. Is it any wonder as the couple are Edward and Edith Keelan, Ed being the senior policeman on the East Coast. Yes I think back to those days when everyone was terrified of the burnings, etc, when a stranger said to me at cousin Alf's place in Gisborne, "Like the great phoenix Te Aowera will rise from the ashes and the flowers will bloom." Well the roses were certainly blooming today.


## RASTA CHARGED WITH ARSON


***Monday, December 3, 1985:*** *Seventeen-year-old Rastafarian Eruera Ranfurly Morice appears in Gisborne District Court charged with willfully setting fire to Kevin Brown's haybarn on Horehore Station. "Tuck" Morice is granted interim name suppression and remanded in custody until December 18.*

***Friday, December 13:*** *John Heeney is found guilty of threatening grievous bodily harm and possessing an offensive weapon. This is for the incident at Te Aowera Marae when he brandished a piece of wood at police before a brawl erupted.*

***Saturday, December 21:*** *It's announced that traffic officer Bruce Laing is transferring out of Ruatoria because of the ongoing trouble with the Rastas. Laing was one of the officers hassled and threatened by Rastafarians on the road one night.*

**Genevieve Westcott, on the Close Up current affairs programme:** Local traffic officer Bruce Laing lived here for eleven months until the Rastas forced him out of town.

Bruce: One night I was bailed up in my patrol car on a public road. The patrol car was damaged intentionally by a group of the local Rastafarians. I was threatened, told never to go back onto their land or I'd be put down the hole at Whareponga.

Genevieve: Put down the hole, what does that mean to you?

Bruce: Well, as far as I'm concerned there's no doubt it meant that I'd be put down a hole which they have up there to dispose of bodies.

Genevieve: Your wife and your children were also terrorised

Bruce: My children at school were constantly called white maggots which, in my book, no kid should have to put up with. My nine-year-old son was held by each arm and driven head-first into a wall. We've taken problems to the court and made no headway there whatsoever and I've felt that it was time to either get out or go beneath the law and fight it that way.

*Wednesday, July 2, 1986: Tuck Morice is in court charged with arson. The Crown says he burned down a haybarn on the Hiruharama Straight on July 27 last year.*

*Kevin Brown owns Horehore Station in partnership with his wife Roberta. He says their barn was worth $1500, and the hay inside it (about two thousand bales) about $8000.*

*Detective Hemi Hikawai tells the court that he spoke to Morice at the Ruatoria Police Station at 12.25am on December 13 last year, five months after the fire. This is his version of what happened.*

*Hikawai asks Morice how many fires he's lit.*

*"None."*

*"What about the haybarn?"*

*Morice is silent for a few seconds. "Yeah, I lit that fire." He tells Hikawai how he used a lighter to ignite the fire "at the front" of the barn.*

*"Why?"*

*Morice says the land belonged to his grandmother. The boundary was the river. When a road was put through it, the kuia, or female elders, "did not worry about it". "That was years back," he says, "but this is today and I **am** worrying about it."*

*"How do you know the land belongs to you?"*

*Morice says he's "heard rumours" from a few people, but doesn't want to name them. He goes on to admit that another person was with him when the fire was lit. But, once again, he doesn't want to identify that person.*

*He says it took "just a few seconds" to get the fire started. He lit the hay, which was dry, and it "just went up". Morice says he then walked across the main road, over a hill and back to Te Aowera Marae, where the Rastas were staying.*

*He says he wasn't encouraged by anyone to light the fire and doesn't regret doing it. "They were on my land. They have no right to be there and if they won't get off then I will make them get off."*

*At 2.30am Detective Hikawai arrests Morice and charges him with arson...*

**Sergeant Alex Hope's backgrounder on Ruatoria (written for Police involved in the situation):** The offenders for this incident came to notice later during enquiries into the Kupenga homicide. A young Rasta named Eruera "Tuck" Morice admitted setting the fire with John Heeney. He later refused to implicate Heeney. He was subsequently charged with arson and eventually sentenced to one year in prison.

*...Eruera Morice's lawyer Tony Adeane sets about undermining the prosecution's case. The evidence against his client is "very limited", he says. There's a verbal statement by the accused to a detective, and the rest of the evidence proves nothing more than that a barn caught fire and burned down. The statement wasn't signed by the accused as being correct. And it was **not** made one or two days after the fire when the accused would be "very careful" in making a statement on a serious question. Adeane can't help wondering whether, five months after the fire, Morice might have made his admission out of sheer bravado. "I think there are a number of reasons why you might treat the verbal admission with a great deal of caution," says Adeane. "If you can't rely on that there is no other evidence against the accused on which you can rely at all."*

*The jury of seven men and five women takes just twenty minutes to reach their verdict: guilty.*

**Thursday, July 17, 1986:** *Eruera "Tuck" Morice is sentenced to one year in prison for burning down Kevin Brown's haybarn on Horehore Station.*

**Former Detective Sergeant Laurie Naden:** They were quite frightening. They'd get on their gear, get their balaclavas on. And they had this bloody sickle attached to a broomstick. And they would ride around. Like if you'd pissed them off they would ride and ride around and round your house. A whole group of them. Could be up to a dozen. And one of them would be holding this broomstick with this sickle on the end out in front of them. They had a name for this broomstick. But I can't remember what it was. But if this happened you could almost guarantee that something was going to happen to your house. And if you left your house you could guarantee it was going to get burnt. And that's why we used to have to send cops up there. People would say, "I've gotta go to a wedding and these bastards have just gone and done a circuit of my house." So we'd have to put cops in there to baby-sit the house so it wouldn't get burnt. So meanwhile they'd go somewhere else and burn that down. They actually held that area in bloody terror for a long time.

# CHAPTER 7

## DREAMS LEAD POLICE TO LANCE KUPENGA

**Former Detective Sergeant Laurie Naden:** I remember when we had staff come in from Hawke's Bay. I gave them their initial briefing. And I said, "When you start talking to these people you'll hear about the ghosts and the spirits and that." They all started to bloody laugh. And I said, "Don't do that cos they'll shut up on you. If you can keep a poker face and listen then you can take out of it what you want." And fortunately they did cos it's quite strong up there the old Maori beliefs. And the moment you take the piss out of them that's it. They won't talk to you.

I remember a woman up there, Sarah Sykes. She was the one that brought the Lance Kupenga homicide to our notice. That came about by a joker who'd not long been out of prison. I can't remember his name. And they were all living over at Te Aowera marae. And I don't know whether they'd been smoking and what have you. But *he* had a vision. And it worried him. And he went over and he saw Sarah, who's right into the spiritual stuff. And he related this story to her that he was in a cell, which he'd not long been out of actually – he'd been in Napier prison – and this cat came in and clawed him or some bloody thing. And then she got into the old, "ooh-ooh-ooh". She was communicating with the old spirits. So she's bloody doing her thing. I'm not sure if she had a vision or what happened. But anyhow it all came to pass that there was a body on the hill and its head had been chopped off. That's how she interpreted what she'd seen.

It was bloody hard to sit down and take all this sort of thing in. Okay. I was brought up a Catholic. I don't practise my religion. But I don't have a *problem* with religion. And I'm sort of sitting there, thinking, "Yeah, well it's not quite right, this." So, "Come on, Sarah. Tell us how you know. Have you been up and had a look?" See, the scary thing is I think she worked it out from the signs. She'd never been up on that hill. This other joker that came along to her, he'd just got out of jail. And he denied emphatically ever having heard anything about the murder.

*Cody Haua reckons what happened was that an old tohunga told Sarah Sykes that there was a decapitated body in the hole up on the hill at Whakaahu. The tohunga hadn't been told what had happened, but knew psychically. Sarah told the police about the body but not about the old tohunga.*

*Detective Sergeant Hemi Hikawai told Cody that when **he** asked Sarah how she knew this body was up the hill, she apparently replied, "The more-porks told me." And when he asked, "What did they say?" she said, "Coo... coo."*

*Sometimes the police must have felt like the locals were having a little joke at their expense.*

*This is Sarah's version of what happened. She says she had a dream that told her she had to go to a certain house. When she got there she told them about her dream (she didn't say what that dream was). And then, she says, she did hear the more-porks giving her a message. And after that she had another dream. She saw her father and he was cut in half. There was nothing from the waist down, just his body and his head and arms. And she thought, "Father, why have you come to me like this? You always said that when you came to me you would be whole." She knew Lance was missing and then she realised that she had to work fast because something had happened to Lance and that he could have been cut or chopped. And it went from there.*

*Sarah says she had to find a couple of weak links within the group once she realised how urgent it was to find Lance. And she found those links in Sammy Keelan and Tiger Hongara. And she said that the group was so tight that they needed those two if they were going to find out what had happened to Lance. If they'd got one of the others perhaps they might have done away with the body further. The body was hidden in a hole in a way which suggested it was not meant to be found. Sarah believes that if Lance hadn't been found there may have been other beheadings, or murders, because the Rastas were riding high at* that time. She believes that the finding of Lance's body was the first crack in their kaupapa. Up until that time they believed the body wouldn't be found because they were on the right kaupapa. They were on the right path and God was behind them and helping them.

She believes they had a hit list, a piece of paper with names written on it and Lance was on that piece of paper. So was the Government, she said. They wanted to destroy a lot of people and they needed a lot of power to do it. They believed there were a lot of people in the system who were evil. And, according to Maori custom, you could acquire another person's power or mana by beheading them.

**Tape recorded note to myself after a conversation with Rasta Cody Haua:** Cody was saying that when Sergeant Norm Gray was questioning Joe Nepe about what had happened, the light bulb in the room was spinning around and around. And he had to stick his hand up in the air and physically stop it.

People were beginning to think that Norm Gray had been freaked out by the killing. He'd been left guarding the scene at Whakaahu overnight. And he said, "Once and once only." Apparently it really freaked him out.

*Joe Nepe's murder trial in June 1986 is the source for this next section. It's been pieced together from evidence given by Lance's uncle Jacob Kauhamu Kupenga, Senior Constable Eric Winter (now retired), Whakarau Henare Ngarimu, and brothers and (then) Rastafarians Sammy Keelan and Tiger Hongara.*

*Jacob Kupenga received a call from his nephew Lance at about 9am on July 22. Lance wanted Jacob to bring him some of his stuff. He met Lance by a small takeaway bar in Ruatoria. Lance was with Joe Nepe and a boy named Jason Keelan. Jacob handed Lance a bag, which had inside some clothing, a bridle and a bankbook. Lance looked through the bag to see if it was all there. Jacob asked Lance what he needed the bridle for. Lance said he wanted it to catch his horse, but didn't need it after all. He handed it back along with the bag.*

*Later that morning, Joe and Jason were using a red and black Swann Dri of Lance's as a saddle. They hadn't found Lance's horse. But they'd found another and were riding it up Whakaahu Hill. Lance was walking in front of the horse. Joe snapped a broomstick over Lance's head. He dismounted the horse to grab an old fence post with which to beat Lance again and the Swann Dri fell off. Joe ordered Jason to, "Leave it there."*

*About a week later, Whakarau Henare Ngarimu and a friend, Steve Rangiwai, were "looking for horses" in the Whakaahu area. They found Lance's red and black Swann Dri. They said they didn't know whose it was, but knew it* had been there a few days because the grass underneath was yellow. They looked through the pockets and found a bankbook and chequebook. They were both in Lance's name. Whakarau put them back in the pocket and took the Swann Dri further up to the hut, often used by the Rastas. He left it there, thinking "the owner might pick it up".

Later Whakarau told his Rastafarian friend Sammy Keelan about the red and black Swann Dri and the bank and cheque books in Lance's name. Sammy knew Lance had been missing for a while. He talked about what he'd heard with his brother and fellow Rasta Tiger Hongara. They knew the hut well and the holes further up the hill, known by the group as "the pits of hell". Sammy used to muster sheep in the area. They had a feeling they knew where to find Lance.

Sammy and Tiger set off for Whakaahu about 6.30 on the morning of August 16, 1985. They went part of the way by car, and then borrowed a couple of horses to get up to the hut. They noticed the "bach" was messy, when normally it was pretty well kept. They spent ten to fifteen minutes looking around, but didn't find the Swann Dri. They decided to head up to the two holes. On the way they passed a dead grey horse that was decomposing. They tied their horses up about five metres from the hole. The first thing they would have seen was an axe, with Rasta colours taped to the handle, embedded in a tree. Sammy walked over to the holes first. "I looked into the hole and saw a body lying down there. There were trees in the hole and I told Tiger that our presumptions were right."

Tiger came up. He went down into the hole a bit to have a better look at the body, staying long enough to notice its head was missing, and then climbing straight back out. It was not a nice place to be. He and Sammy said a prayer together and then headed back down the hill. They never looked down the other hole. It was about midday by the time they got to their car. They drove to Te Aowera to see the marae secretary, Sarah Sykes. After discussing what they'd found with her, Sammy and Tiger went to the Ruatoria Police Station. They told police what they'd found and went back up to Whakaahu with them to show where the body was. Senior Constable Eric Winter went up to the homicide scene the next day. His task was to act as exhibits officer. He was in charge of all the exhibits he either received or found during the course of the investigation. Senior Constable Winter found the red and black Swann Dri with the bank and chequebooks in the pocket, lying on top of a bunk in the hut. Soon after, Sammy and Tiger cut off their dreadlocks and left the Rastafarians.

**The Gisborne Herald, Saturday, August 17, 1985:** Police have mounted a major homicide inquiry in hill country east of Ruatoria after the discovery late yesterday of a man's body in a hole.

An axe has been found at the scene and police say early indications show the body has received injuries "consistent" with the use of an axe.

The man's body is about four metres down in a hole that is roughly six metres across. The hole is on land on Whakaahu Station, not far from a hut that had been used by the Rastafarian group.

Two Rastafarians walking in the hill country found the dead man, thought to have had links with the Rastafarians, late yesterday. The body was flown out from the scene this morning and then driven to Gisborne for an immediate post mortem. The state of the body has made identification difficult and fingerprints and dental records are under study.

**Detective Sergeant Gary Condon:** I was the officer in charge of the scene where Lance Kupenga was beheaded and the body was dumped in a hole on the top of Whakaahu. That was all over dope. Joe Nepe warned him a couple of times about pinching cannabis seeds. So he marched him up the top of the hill. We still don't know how he got him up the hill. We know that they went on horseback up the river towards Whareponga. And he was on horseback and he had Lance tied with an axe held behind him. He got him up to the top and he got to a disused sheep pen about eight hundred metres from the Whakaahu Hill. And then they moved on to the hut at Whakaahu. He actually sat him down and went into the hut for a while. Then he started marching him up the hill. At one stage Kupenga managed to escape and ran into the bushes but Joe Nepe actually managed to get him back out of the bushes, tie him up again and march him up the cliff. Now *we* couldn't get up the cliff. So how a guy could get up there with an axe at his back, I don't know. We looked at a couple of tracks that he may have gone up but by gee it was pretty hard. And he took Lance Kupenga up the top and chopped his head off.

**Lyn Hillock, Gisborne Deputy Fire Chief (now living in Australia):** Anyway, we go up to look for Lance's body. There's Laurie Naden, myself, Danny Batchelor, who's the police photographer, and quite a few other members of the CIB. We're walking around the hill. We do an area search and it's all manuka and the hill's quite steep. There's a place at the bottom of these cliffs, which is one of their bases. And they've just been lambing there. So everyone's searching around in the undergrowth and Danny comes up with something. "Aah, Jesus!" he cries. "Somebody's guts!" He's on the radio: "Yeah, yeah, we've got something here." A whole lot of us descend.

I look at it. "Aw fuck, Danny. It's the afterbirth of a lamb for Chris' sake. It's the birth sac and the umbilical cord of a baby lamb."

Eventually, we locate the body. There are two holes; the head's in one and the body's in the other. First we grab the head and put it in a bag ready to go in the body bag. Then I put Danny Batchelor in his harness and I put on mine and extend out about ten metres of line. I lie down on the ground with my feet braced so Danny can take his full body weight looking down into this hole to photograph the torso.

So Danny's moving around the hole and he gets to the front of it. But he hasn't told me or given me any warning that he's shifting his position, so I haven't taken up any slack for him, like I would normally, to keep him firm. So he leaps around the front of the hole, thinking I'm holding him firm. And he leans backwards and just falls straight back. He ends up sitting right across the chest of Lance Kupenga. As he sits down I hear this, "Whoomf," of air being pushed out the top of the body. And the smell! All of a sudden the smell wafting from the hole is phenomenal. And of course the body's been there a while and the maggots are crawling around.

The hole isn't that terribly deep, a couple of metres maybe. But it's still a mission to leap out in one bound. I guess Danny's just got that big a fright because it's absolutely incredible. All I see of Danny are his eyes. They're about the size of saucers. And he takes off and he runs straight towards me, the line between his legs, camera still clutched in his hand. And this freight train is coming at me, not even seeing me. And all I can see is this big set of eyes. And he runs right over the top of me - stomps on my knees, my stomach - and he's gone. And when he gets to the end of the harness line he comes jerking to a stop and just about drags me along the ground behind him.

That was a bit of a laugh. It took us another quarter of an hour to get the body and the head in the body bag and load it on to Bob Torr's chopper and take it back down to Ruatoria, behind the old police station there.

When you look back it was really comical; a bit sadistic, I suppose, but...


## ONE HOMICIDE INVESTIGATION, MANY MEMORIES


*Sunday, August 18, 1985: Police are studying fingerprints and dental records in a bid to positively identify the young man found beheaded in two holes on the hillside near Ruatoria. Police know that Rastafarian Lance Kupenga has been missing for almost a month but it may be two days before they can link him with the murder.*

**David Conway, The Gisborne Herald, Monday, August 19:** Lance Kupenga was a tall, friendly, rather intelligent boy – something of an under-achiever, perhaps a little easily led, but a young man with his own potential.

That's the way they knew the missing Te Puia lad as a teenager in the early '80s. But "Ku" was also a young man in search of his destiny. He does not appear to have been a hardcore member of the Rasta group, though arrested during the police operation at Whareponga on June 11.

Lance Owen Huataki Kupenga is the son of Paetene and Kathleen Kupenga of McKenzie Street, Te Puia. He grew up in the small Coast township where his parents worked for the hospital.

From a primary education at Te Puia, Lance went on to Ngata College where he is remembered as a good student. He spent four years there, two of them in the fifth form and, although he achieved no great heights as a scholar, he left his quiet mark on Ngata.

They remember Lance there as a likeable kid, no hassles, courteous, a boy who never lifted his finger against anyone, a "good type of lad" with a clean sheet... a boy his teachers and principal say had considerable potential like other members of his family who have been through the school.

He was a member of the Maori culture group and a useful back in the rugby 2$^{nd}$ XV.

**The Gisborne Herald (back page), Monday August 19:** LATE NEWS: No Second Body: There is no suggestion that a second body has been found in Ruatoria. Police say rumours of two deaths have been flying around since the weekend and appear based on confusion over the existence of a body and a missing man.

**Former Detective Sergeant Laurie Naden:** When we did the luminol testing it was quite interesting. The first one didn't actually kill him. The first whack got him between the shoulder blades, which probably would've just about knocked him out. It took about three chops to get the head off.

There were two little tomo, little limestone caves, in the ground. And the body went down one and they flipped the head down the other.

But you actually see in the luminol, which is a thing that reacts in the light, where the head had been kicked along like a football. And you could actually see in the ground that they didn't put him on a tree or anything. They just locked him down and whopped him. His head would-a been free when they chopped it. And you could actually see with the luminol where the v's were in the ground where they'd hit'm. Then they just calmly bloody put the axe in a tree and fucked off.

*The killing has ritualistic hallmarks, but the inquiry has uncovered nothing to suggest there was a ritualistic motive. The inquiry is centred on the Rastafarians. But the police are no closer to discovering what led to the slaying.*

**David Conway, The Gisborne Herald:** The boy, whose bushy hairstyle pinpointed him in school magazine photographs, left Ngata College en route for a trade training course in Hamilton to become a fitter and turner.

That was late 1982. Between then and 1985 something changed for Lance Kupenga as he fell into the "fringe" of Ruatoria's controversial Rastafarians. He had been unemployed apart from apparently some time with a shearing gang and at the hospital.

He rode with the brethren and played rugby for the Rastas' self-styled football club, Nga Tama Toa (the Warriors) in the East Coast competition.Was he led astray? Dick Maxwell, former Mongrel Mob and Black Power gang member, now a Rastafarian, says the community turned its back on Lance Kupenga.

But the man who says he spent the eleven best years of his life behind bars turns now to his faith when he says the killing is the work of Jah and is fated.

"Ku was a man searching for his destiny, trying to walk the path of righteousness."

Mr Maxwell refutes rumbles in the community that the grisly slaying might be the work of members of his own group. He shakes his head at the talk of thrashings for members of the faith. Killing would go against their beliefs.

He was only two days out of jail on bail when he learned of the murder.Whoever did the killing, he believes, could have aimed to frame the Rastamen. "But when it would have happened a lot of us were in jail."

*Wednesday, August 21, 1985: There are now more than forty in the murder inquiry team in Ruatoria. Fifteen extra policemen and two DSIR scientists arrived today. The policemen are sweep-searching the scrub-covered hillsides of Whakaahu and Koura stations looking for anything unusual that might tie in with the killing. The scientists are looking for blood or other traces that could establish whether or not Lance Kupenga died where his body was found.*

*One of the most vital exhibits is the axe found embedded in a cleft of a manuka tree near one of the holes. It bears the Rastafarian colours of yellow,*

*green and red on the handle. Police are hopeful that forensic examination at the
DSIR's Lower Hutt laboratories will link it with the killing.*

*Another useful piece of evidence is the Swann Dri, which has been found.*

*Lance Kupenga is buried today at 1pm. The tangi is at Hiruharama Marae.*

**David Conway:** What about the murder scene itself? Do Dick Maxwell and
other Rastafarians know the hillside high on the ridge overlooking Koura Station,
with deep holes in it? Yes, they know it well. They had a meeting place not far
away.

Does it have any special significance? Yes it is known for its legend.

Dick Maxwell says pits in the area are final resting places for slaves who
were killed for murdering a tipuna (ancestor).

Those who were cast in the holes were the bad ones. It could be a big
graveyard and there is talk of the area having its own tapu.

There is also talk of one exceptionally deep hole in that area.

There was talk during a recent court hearing of a policeman being threatened
with being put "down the hole". Has that any significance to the Rastaman? Yes,
says the Rastafarian. That would refer to the bottomless pit talked of in The
Bible, a "place where bad people go".

Will the Rastaman help the police catch the killer? "I have nothing to say to
the police. But if they get the man, good on them.

"Whoever did it will be punished more severely by Jah than we could do."

**Detective Rex Harrison (retired):** My nephew was there when Lance
Kupenga was beheaded. Jason Keelan saw the whole thing. And he's a direct
nephew. He's my sister's son. He was pretty shattered after that. It wasn't until
Lance's tangi that it really sunk home for him. I ended up speaking to him. And
subsequently the whole story came out.

*Thursday, August 22: Joe Nepe is arrested in connection with the murder of
fellow Rastafarian Lance Kupenga. No one else is being sought for any part of
the murder.*

*Police now believe the killing took place on July 22. Officer in charge
Detective Inspector Barry Hunter says the inquiry team has established a motive
for the killing and the movements of the two men and events leading up to the
murder.*

*Friday, August 23: Joe Nepe appears in the Gisborne District Court charged
with murdering Lance Kupenga. Nepe's dressed in denim and has Rastafarian*

*dreadlocks. He enters no plea and stands silently in the dock during the brief remand appearance. He's granted interim name suppression by Judge J. D. Hole. Crown prosecutor Terry Stapleton seeks a remand in custody to September 6 so that Nepe can undergo a psychiatric examination.*

# CHAPTER 8

## JO-JO & THE GARDEN OF EDEN

**Interview with Joe Nepe in November 2000:** *Why is there such a tie-up with Israel around that area, like you've got Hiruharama, Jerusalem, and that's the star of David there isn't it (pointing at Joe's moko, the tattoo on his face).*
Well I believe that this is the Israel they're looking for, ay.
*Aw, that this is like Israel for the lost tribe?*
Well, they're all looking for the lost tribe but nobody knows where it is and I believe the Maori people are the lost tribe.
*Yeah. A lot of people have said that, haven't they?*
Yeah.
*That's the lost tribe of Dan is it?*
Yeah.
*Yeah. And where did Chris fit in?*
He was our leader.
*He was the leader of the Rastas.*
He was the leader of the Rastas.
*Was there a belief that he was like the Christ or the...*
The coming of the new Christ?
*Yeah, yeah.*
I reckon in a way he was.
*Yeah, he was like the Second Coming?*
He was a prophet anyway.
*Yeah.*
And he had the ways and things that were passed on down to him from his tipuna.

*He just hadn't, um…*

He just hadn't revealed it then. I think he was still young, too, at that time.

*Did he say to you guys though that he believed he was the Christ?*

Na, not that I know of. He didn't actually come out and say it to us.

*Cos Bob Kaa (the leader of the neighbourhood watch group) reckoned he came and said it to him one time.*

Aw yeah. Aw yeah.

*You know, he said, "Bob, I am the Christ."*

Ha ha ha ha ha ha ha ha.

*And, you know, Bob said, "You're all **shet**."*

Ha ha ha ha ha ha ha ha.

*And then he said, "Certain things are gonna happen and I'll be in the middle of them." That was just before the kidnapping of Laurie and everything. See cos one thing that's come clear to me is that there's a belief around Ruatoria that the Second Coming, whoever it may be, is gonna come from that area isn't it?*

Yeah.

*That's the feeling.*

That's the whole idea. That was the whole idea of our get-together.

*To pave the way or…*

To pave the way for the coming of Christ.

*The Second Coming.*

Yeah. No matter what religion you are. It was coming from that area. That's where the sun rises.

*And that's tied up with the prophecies of Pop Gage or Hori Keeti?*

Yeah, Hori Keeti. His prophecies are direct to that place. And Tuta Nihoniho, too. (Tuta Nihoniho is one of the most important ancestors from Te Aowera marae).

*Aw, did he make prophecies?*

Yeah.

*Gees. How would I get my hands on those?*

Ooh. Very hard, very hard, very hard. Actually, not very many of them speak of it now.

*It's been forgotten?*

It's tapu.

*Aw, is that right?*

It's sacred.

*Oh. But he had alluded to the same thing, had he?*

Yeah.

*In a nutshell, what was the basis of it, just that the Second Coming would come from…*

Would come from there.

*From where? Te Aowera? Mangahanea?*

Hiruharama.

*Aw, from that area.*

That area.

*He didn't specify one marae?*

No it didn't say which marae. They're all one. They're all one.

*Yeah, cos Mangahanea believe it's…*

Yeah, it's got the star there, ay, Mangahanea.

*Yeah, now, the six-sided star. Is it like that one? (I nod to the Star of David on Joe's moko).*

Yeah.

*Aw, is that why they believe that um…*

Well they believe it's them.

*Yeah. And then Te Aowera believe it's them.*

Ha ha ha ha ha ha ha ha.

*I bet Hiruharama believe it's them and Ngati Porou Marae believe it's them.*

Ha ha ha.

*That's one thing I've noticed as I've wandered around the coast. Everyone seems to quietly say to you, "It could be my son."*

Ha ha ha ha.

*You know what I mean? Like, there's a lot of people who think it'll sort of end up coming from their family. And if the Second Coming comes, he's gonna have a lot of competition out there.*

Yeah.

*Plus, there's that other belief in Ngati Porou that everyone's a leader.*

Yeah.

*So it kind of fosters that, I suppose. Everyone believes they're Christ-like.*

Yeah. There only can be one though.

*There only can be one, yeah. Are there any signs to look for when that comes about?*

Well I believe the Garden of Eden.

*Yeah, in what way?*

That's where he came from.

*Aw, what? The original?*

The original. So wherever the Garden of Eden is, that's where the man is heading to.

*And you reckon the Garden of Eden is around the East Coast?*
Has to be.
*Yeah, yeah. **Aw!** So you reckon that the **Garden of Eden** was originally on
the East Coast!*
Ha ha ha ha ha ha ha ha. Well they got Mount Hikurangi there so that's
Mount Zion so the Garden must be there somewhere.
*Yeah, yeah. It's amazing stuff when you get into it, ay.*
Mmm.
*So is there any time frame or anything like that?*
Na.

*Joe was born on a farm in Ruatoria in 1963. He was his mother's second son
and was brought up as a whangai child by her parents. (A whangai child is not
legally adopted. But in Maori custom the adults are expected to raise the child as
one of their own, while the child, in turn, is expected to look after the adults
when they grow old.) Joe's grandparents were fluent Maori speakers. Because of
his upbringing, Joe was well versed in local history and custom and was also a
fluent speaker of Maori. "My grandparents' name was Moeke," Joe told me.
"He used to run Whakaahu Mountain. He was the shepherd there and I grew up
on the mountain. It's a very sacred place. My grandparents told me that
Whakaahu was the Garden of Eden. And I was thinking that if the Rastas are
gonna grow their herb up there it must be the Garden of Eden."*

*Talk of Whakaahu being the Garden of Eden ties in with another local belief,
which I've already mentioned. The Toi descendants, Ngati Ue Pohatu, the stone
people, are adamant they did not come to New Zealand on canoe. They claim
they've always been here. How long? Well, if you're a human and you believe
the Old Testament, then it doesn't go any further back than Adam and Eve, or
whatever your culture has decided to call the first man and woman.*

**Rasta John Heeney, interviewed in Ruatoria in early 2000 (this was my
second interview in this whole project, which may explain some of my
responses to his answers):** Ethiopia is the oldest throne in the whole world.
*Oldest language and everything isn't it?*
Ethiopia is mentioned in Chapter Two of The Bible.
*Was it Amharic or something?*
That's right, Amharic. Now you look how they do their whakapapa. The next
people who got a whakapapa equivalent to the Ethiopians is the Maori, and he
don't need no book. He don't need no book to recite and trace his ancestry back

to his offspring. He can just stand there and recite it like a poem all the way back.

*How far can the Maori go back?*

Right back to God.

*Can they?*

Yeah. Right back through every tree in the bush.

*Yeah.*

The father and mother of every tree in the bush, the father and mother of every kind of creek and water, of everything living, the Maoris can put that into their family tree and check it right back to God.

Donna (John's partner): They can go right back to Maui.

John: Past it. Past it before there was no men. Right back to where the trees came from. And there was no human beings on the Earth when the trees were being born and made. And the fish. This is nothing new. It's an old thing.

*Can they do it right back to before Maori people come to New Zealand?*

Maori people were always here.

Donna: That's why they say we might come from Egypt, you see? Because we're a sea-faring people?

John: No we came from here. We were always here. When we got created God made us from the dirt of this land. He never bought us from a handful of dirt from that land and bucked us over here and reckoned, "Yeah, this is your fullas." We got made from the dirt here. See? Cos when we go back to our last human being ancestor, then we go back into our gods and the ancestors of our gods and they go back into trees because there was no man on this Earth, yet the family tree goes back. I got told by my old kaua that we were always here. The thing was, the Maori people started from here, sailed right around the world and came back. Because why wouldn't we? Why would we start at half-way then come to the beginning? We started from the beginning and came back round. We've conquered the whole world. We have conquered the whole world. And why is that? Well, come to the millennium, which was the first little insignificant place that kicked this whole millennium off. And you ask yourself, "Ruatoria, what good has ever come out-a you? Hikurangi, what good has ever come out-a you? We've heard weeping and we've heard fires burning." And yet... this is the beginning. We got a saying amongst us: "The Lord loveth the gates of Zion more than all the other dwellings of Jacob." And Zion is the mountain in the east. Not the Middle East. Not the Far East. The East. And we know...

*Aw, Zion.*

Yeah.

*You reckon Mount Hikurangi is Zion?*

110

Yeah, it is.

*Yeah? So what would be the equivalent of a Lion in Zion, you know? Who would that be? That's just anyone who's a Rasta-man is it?*

Yeah, yeah.

Donna: Rastafari is the lion. He came as the conquering lion because Christ came as a lamb to the slaughter and Rastafari came as a lion.

John showing a tattoo of a lion on his chest: We're lion-hearted men. We've got the hearts of lions. Fearless.

Donna: Because in the end day the lamb and the lion will sit in God's throne.

*Yeah, yeah, together.*

Donna: In the kingdom.

John: See? Jesus came to die for the people. When he comes again He's not gonna come to die. He's gonna come and (punches his fist), he's gonna come and do that to those who are not for him, ay, that are against him. Because in the end there are only two sides, ay: those that are with it and those that are trying to destroy it. And with us, we're at this stage now; they murder us and get away with it just like that.

**Interview with Joe Nepe in November 2000:** *When did you get the moko?*
I've only had it for three years.

*What inspired you to stick it on there in the end?*
John (Heeney) inspired me to stick it on.

*Did he do it?*
Yeah, he did it.

*What meaning does it have for you personally?*
Aw, it indicates the twelve tribes.

*Aw yeah.*
Tu-mata-uenga, god of war.

*Yeah, yeah, yeah. Why the god of war for yourself?*
Well it's for the soldiers that went away that fought for us.

*For the people who had to do the time and whatnot.*
Mmm.

*Is there any part of it that explains that.*
Na, just the whole thing. I've got Jah written across my forehead. My name is Jah Jobee. That comes from Job, the prophet in The Bible. In the Rastas' House of Israel I was the tribe of Benjamin because I was born in March, March 28.

*Yeah. Now what's the story with Whakaahu itself? The guys in Ruatoria reckon it's got no bottom to it. It's like a bottomless pit sort of thing?*
Yeah. Na, it goes right down. But over the years it's been covered, ay.

111

*What with?*
Filled in. They've filled it in, ay. It used to go right down before.
*Right down to where?*
Aw, nowhere.
*Just, just keep going...*
Just kept on going.
*And now people have what? Put stuff across?*
Aw, they've throwed trees in and, you know...
*So if you dug all that stuff out you'd probably get a clear hole through again...*
Yeah.
*Aw is that right? Far out. And why? Because it was dangerous? Kids could come along and fall in?*
No. That was there for a purpose, that hole. It was where they used to throw the slaves, ay.
*Yeah, I read that. And what was that like? A sacrifice?*
A sacrifice. Yeah.
*And was it a sacrifice to an underworld god or what?*
I wouldn't know. I don't know much about that place.


## ON TRIAL FOR MURDER


*The depositions hearing into whether Joseph McNab Nepe should stand trial for the murder of Lance Kupenga begins in the Gisborne District Court on Monday, January 20, 1986. Since his arrest Nepe has been in custody and undergoing medical examinations. Until now he's had interim name suppression. But a continuation of the order isn't sought.*

*After hearing the hesitant testimony of the only eyewitness, fifteen-year-old Jason Keelan, the court sends Nepe to trial.*

*The trial begins in the High Court in Gisborne on Monday, June 23. Defence counsel Peter Williams QC intends to prove Nepe not guilty by reason of insanity.*

*At the time of the trial, Joe's dad Puni is a prison officer at Mt Eden and his mum, Tuakana, a secondary teacher at a training college. They live in Hillsborough, Auckland.*

*Joe's mum is called by Peter Williams to give evidence. She says Joe went to school in Ruatoria until he was about eleven or twelve. Then he went up to Auckland and stayed with her and Puni, attending intermediate school, before becoming a boarder at (the now defunct) St Stephens, an Anglican Maori school south of Auckland. During his four years there, Joe took a normal interest in religious and Maori matters. But, during cross-examination, Mrs Nepe agrees with Peter Williams that later on Joe began to develop a morbid interest in these matters.*

Mrs Nepe: Going back about 1983 I think.

Williams: What happened then?

Mrs Nepe: Joseph's two daughters. I have them now, my husband and I. He broke up with his de facto wife when the baby was seven months old. We have legal custody of them. I don't think he was aware that was about to happen. I think from that time on - I know our mother verified that too, because she brought him up - there was a change in him, a withdrawal...

*Mrs Nepe says she noticed more dramatic changes in early 1984. She considered herself more fluent in Maori and more conversant with Maori history and custom than Joe, but he kept asking questions relating to land and ancestors that she wasn't even aware of.*

Mrs Nepe: "He went into great detail about things I was very, very surprised he understood."

Williams: Then, during 1984, did you notice him getting involved in the Rastafarian movement?

Mrs Nepe: Yes. It would be about the time a lot of our young people were out of work, hence a lot of them moving back home.

Williams: A lot of them couldn't find jobs in the town?

Mrs Nepe: Yes.

Mrs Nepe also noticed Joe was reading the Bible more than ever before. She found the only people able to make contact with Joe were his daughters and the only way to get through to him was through his daughters. Meanwhile, his interest in things Maori kept increasing.

Williams: You think it was reaching an obsession?

Mrs Nepe: I'm sure it was. As his mother, I believe he thought he might have had the kind of wairua (spirit). I, as his mother, was trying to appreciate where he was at and where he was trying to come from. It felt, for me... I felt that he was tampering and moving into an area that is strongly Maori and to do that those are the kind of areas that high priests and tohungas move into. He was my son, I knew in my heart, (he was) not really able to cope... and I mean cope in the Maori sense.

Williams: Do you think in lay language, he was out of his depth?

Mrs Nepe: Too much out of his depth.

*Joe became deeply interested in the Ringatu church, founded by Te Kooti. He attended the Apirana Ngata lectures on local history. He went to meetings of the Tino Rangatiratanga (Maori sovereignty) movement. He marched with Dame Whena Cooper from Ngaruawahia to Waitangi. And during all this he found the elders to be willing mines of information about things Maori.*

*The movie "Utu" came out in May 1985, two months before the killing. Two booklets on utu and patu (n. club, weapon; v. strike, beat, kill) were published separately from the film. Mrs Nepe noticed both booklets on the table in her mother's lounge. Joe was often unreachable and suffered violent mood swings. His mother began to get apprehensive vibes about Joseph.*

"I think at that point in time I realised that he was someone else... ...He wasn't the son I know."

*It seems Joe Nepe first became upset with Lance Kupenga in the weeks leading up to the killing. He believed Kupenga had stolen a knife and bayonet belonging to one of his ancestors from their grave.*

*During the murder trial, Crown prosecutor Geoff Rea explains that during Operation Whareponga (the raid on the top house at Koura Station on June 11, 1985) police recovered some property from the Ruatoria area and took it to the Ruatoria police station for identification. Among that property was a saddle, which had a knife belt and other items strapped to it. A knife in a scabbard and a bayonet were also among the property. (Nepe later told police that Kupenga had moved a knife, which had belonged to Nepe's grandfather and had been in the family's possession since around the time of the First World War.)*

*Nepe examined the property at the police station on June 20. He said the saddle, knife, scabbard and bayonet were all his.*

Bridget Coughlan (for the Crown): When the accused identified them what did he say to you?

Tamati Reedy (a Ruatoria man who was then a constable stationed in Gisborne): He said to me, "Those have to go back." I asked him why. He told me they were tapu. I asked him where they had to go back to. He didn't answer me.

Peter Williams: Is it sometimes the Maori custom to bury chattels with the deceased?

Reedy: Yes.

If that grave is later interfered with and somebody takes the chattel out of the grave do some Maoris believe that a tapu exists in relation to the chattel, in those circumstances?

Yes they do.

Does the tapu relate to the chattel itself does it, so if the chattel changes hands the tapu changes hands, the tapu would go with the chattel?

That is true.

So it wouldn't matter what the bearer of the chattel had actually stolen. He could still be affected by the tapu purely because he wasn't the true man in possession of the chattel?

Yes.

Do some people believe a person holding a chattel in that type of circumstance could be exposed to some of the spirits of the ancestors, in their malevolency?

Some people believe that.

*Joe Nepe left the station without taking any of the property he had said was his. The knife and bayonet were later taken to Gisborne Police Station.*

*On July 17, 1985, five days before Lance Kupenga was killed, Nepe was in a vehicle with Gisborne constable Peter Carroll. Nepe started talking in a loud voice about a knife he had to get back because it had a tapu on it.*

Carroll: After he repeated this a second time, I turned around and told him that (Constable Pani) Campbell had it, he is stationed in Ruatoria, and I told him the matter could be sorted out. The defendant carried on talking in a loud voice but I took no further part in the conversation.

**Glynn Walker Findlay (giving evidence at Nepe's trial):** I am a detective attached to the CIB in Hastings. On Monday, 19 August, I was a member of an inquiry team in the Ruatoria area investigating the death of Lance Kupenga. On this day I travelled to Tuparoa Beach, near Ruatoria, to speak to one of the residents there. One of the residents I spoke to was Sharon Te Purei and I showed her some photos of some Rasta members. The following day at approximately 3pm, I went to the address of 2 Holland Place, Ruatoria, with the expectation of locating a Mrs Bartlett. On going to the address I was met by a male person now known to me as Joseph Nepe... ...I introduced myself to Nepe and he introduced himself as a name, which I do not recall.

Geoff Rea (prosecution): It wasn't Joe Nepe?

Walker Findlay: That is correct. I told him that I believed his correct name to be Joe Nepe and with this he invited me into the house for a cup of tea. I took up his invitation and was sat at the dining table in the house for a period of approximately one and a half hours discussing various topics, including himself, the Rastafarians, and his relationships with the Rastafarians and Lance Kupenga. On the dining table where we were seated was a copy of a newspaper with the headlines of the homicide investigation visible. Nepe said that he had been reading about the death and that Lance's death had disturbed him. His demeanour was very subdued and quiet. I spoke further with him and asked him why he had not been to the marae where Lance's body was lying. He said that it was protocol that he could not go to the marae until the body was in the ground and the tapu had been lifted. I told him that the other Rastafarians were already at the marae and he repeated that he could not go to the marae until the tapu was lifted.

I showed him a series of photographs of the Rastafarians and he asked to view them privately. I gave him the photos and he took them to the hallway of the address to view them. When he came back to the dining room he held each photograph in front of him and touched his nose to each photograph. He then sat at the table and sorted the photos into two piles. I asked the significance of this and he told me that he was showing the hierarchy, the structure between the younger and older Rastafarians.

Rea: Was hierarchy your word or his?

Walker Findlay: My word... ...A short time later, approximately 4.45pm on that Tuesday, Nepe came with me to the Ruatoria Police Station... ...Just after 5pm myself and Detective (Hemi) Hikawai took Joe Nepe to the Government Offices in Ruatoria, which were being used for the purposes of interview... ...When he spoke of his daughters, one aged four, the other three, this was the only time he showed any form of emotion, and said that his children were being looked after by their mother, who was living with someone else...

...At approximately 7.40pm Nepe stopped answering verbally any questions put to him either by Detective Hikawai or myself. He acknowledged questions and began giving answers in the form of shrugs, shaking his head or moving his feet. Shortly after this I left the interview room...

...At approximately 8pm I returned to the interview room and found that Nepe was still not answering questions verbally. At approximately 8.50pm Detective Hikawai left the interview room and I sat with Nepe. Some twenty minutes later Nepe began to get aggressive. He began stalking about the room banging furniture, snorting and clearing his throat loudly...

...At approximately 9.30 the interview was recommenced at the Ruatoria Police Station by Detective Hikawai, in my presence... ...At around 10.30 Nepe again began to get aggressive, stalking the room, banging furniture...

*Hemi Hikawai is an imposing figure, about six foot three and strongly built. He looks like he's stared death in the face a few times and death turned away first. When I first met him at the Gisborne Police Station in, I think, 2001, he was deep in conversation with a middle-aged woman. Later, as we walked up to his office, he explained the woman was concerned about her son. From memory, I think her son was involved in the Mongrel Mob. Hemi told me he'd given her son a clip around the ear a few nights earlier. He's an old school cop. And, in Gisborne, he's the stuff of urban myth. Like the story about the night he made a troublemaker jog naked in front of his patrol car down the main street. True? If not, then probably pretty close. He reckons he's put more murderers away than any other cop in New Zealand. But he's probably been the subject of more internal police inquiries than any other cop in the country, too. And, having worked undercover for the drug squad, he's no stranger to scary situations with deranged people. Maybe it's just bravado, but he says there's only one time he's been really shaken, like as close to being scared as Hemi ever gets. And that was when he was in the interview room at Ruatoria Police Station when Joe Nepe started to get aggressive. He said he had the feeling that Joe, in his agitated state, was stronger and more unpredictably dangerous than anybody he'd ever met. To make his point, Hemi even stalked back and forth around his office, huffing and puffing and snorting the way Joe had. And the way Hemi told the story put me right there in that interview room with him and Glynn Walker Findlay and Joe Nepe. I'd quote it here, but I lost that tape soon afterwards. Interestingly, when I knocked on the door of Joe Nepe's father's house in Auckland, about a year later, I expected to be greeted by a muscle-bound giant. I'm six foot three and waited with my head instinctively cocked up. A female friend of the Rastas had described Joe to me as "The Terminator". But when the door opened there was no one there. Eventually, I heard a friendly voice, "Kia ora, bro." I looked down to see a friendly chubby East Coast face and a pot-belly stretching a black tee-shirt, tucked into blue jeans that were pulled up far too high. I reckon the years in Kingseat Mental Hospital had turned The Terminator into Happy from the Seven Dwarfs. And, hey, maybe that's not a bad thing.*

Geoff Rea (for the prosecution): I think at the request of Detective Hemi Hikawai of Gisborne you spoke to Mr. Nepe in the police station at Ruatoria, the morning of 20 August?

Sergeant Norm Gray: Yes, the evening.

Rea: Can you outline to us what the discussion was you had with Mr. Nepe?

Gray: Mr Nepe requested me to go to the police station to speak to him. I took him to my office. He sat down. He told me he had been questioned and wanted to know what was going to happen to him. I told him that another person had been spoken to in respect of the Kupenga death and now it was his turn. He became agitated and started walking around the office and said that he did not want to talk about what happened as the body was not down and spirits were around. At that stage I told him that the body would be buried the following morning at which time Mr. Nepe appeared to calm down. I asked him if he would be in a position to talk about what had happened the following day. He said he would. I then arranged with Detective Findlay and Detective Hikawai to transport him to Gisborne.

Can you confirm Lance Kupenga was buried on 21 August?

Yes he was.

**Glynn Walker Findlay:** ...Arrangements were made to transport Nepe to Gisborne. At approximately 11.15pm myself and Detective Hikawai accompanied Nepe to Gisborne and we were met a short distance out of Gisborne by a police patrol who took Nepe the rest of the journey.

The following day, Wednesday, 21 August, Detective Hikawai and myself travelled to Gisborne from Ruatoria and spoke to Nepe at the police station. Nepe again was refusing to talk about the death of Lance Kupenga and after some hours this interview was terminated. On Thursday morning, the following day, Nepe was again spoken to at the Gisborne Police Station, in my presence, by Senior Sergeant Bruce Davidson. During the course of this discussion with Senior Sergeant Davidson, Nepe made certain admissions relating to the death of Lance Kupenga.

**Ross Howard Pinkham (giving evidence at Nepe's trial):** I am a detective senior sergeant in charge of the New Plymouth CIB. On Wednesday, 21 August, 1985, I spoke to the accused... ...at the Gisborne Police Station...

...It was apparent that Nepe was reluctant to speak about the death of Lance Kupenga. He said that a curse had been placed on Lance and that, in Nepe's words, Lance had trodden on the bones of his ancestors.

Geoff Rea (for the prosecution): Meaning Joe Nepe's ancestors?

Detective Senior Sergeant Pinkham: Yes. Nepe tried to explain to me what this meant and he said it didn't mean actually walking on the grave of his family, but that he had done something to them which was very sacred.

Did he tell you what that something was?

Yes. He said that a knife that had been in the family since after the First World War had been moved and later taken by the police. The knife was at the whare and that Constable Reedy had the knife and that until the knife had been returned to the whare or from where Constable Reedy had taken it, he would not be able to discuss anything in relation to Lance's death.

Was there any discussion about how the curse could be lifted?

Yes. He said the curse would be lifted when the knife had been returned, and once that had been done, Nepe told me, he would go to his family and that the curse would be lifted then.

*In an interview on September 18, 1985, Joe Nepe revealed to Rotorua psychiatrist Dr Henry Bennett that he believed Lance Kupenga wasn't alone when he stole the bayonet from the grave. "There was a bayonet found in the whare where the group had been staying on Te Whakaahu. The bayonet came from a burial ground, taken by Lance and another person called Junior." Junior, of course, is Junior Paul, who was given a severe beating (that lasted a day, a night and into the following day) by several Rastafarians, including Joe Nepe.*

*I met Canon Hone Kaa in the early 1990s. I belonged to a group he used to occasionally join for a drink at the Pinnacle Club in St Benedicts Street in Eden Terrace, Auckland. It wasn't a formal arrangement. I was a sports reporter at the Sunday News and drank there with my workmates. Hone would occasionally pop in for a few pints and, seeing us there, join us, which was great because he was hilarious, wise and an excellent storyteller. He had been a priest for twenty-one years at the time of the trial. He was of Ngati Porou descent and at Joe Nepe's trial defence counsel Peter Williams called him as an expert on local Maori custom.*

*It should be noted here that this section was written before I had secured an interview with Lance Kupenga's father, Paetene. Paetene totally refutes Hone Kaa's theory that Joe killed Lance as part of an utu for something that happened hundreds of years ago. He says for Kaa's theory to work, Lance would have to be junior to Joe in the genealogical bloodlines. But Paetene says Lance was not junior to Joe, therefore Kaa's theory falls over. Paetene, as I mentioned in an earlier chapter, has his own theory as to why Joe beheaded his son, which we will get to in due course.*

Peter Williams: I come now to the bayonet. Can you comment on that bayonet and on the practice in relation to burying artefacts or chattels with the body in the Maori custom.

Hone Kaa: With some Maori even today there is a belief that personal possessions, often things of tremendous value and even weapons or tools like this, could become endowed with the spirit or the wairua of the owner of that article. When they die those very precious items are often buried with them. People felt afraid to come in contact with such articles and burial in a sense put them at rest.

Williams: What about the situation where the artifacts or chattels are taken from the grave. What significance would that have?

Hone Kaa: Because the article is tapu, when it is removed from the place of death the person who does that is then declared to be extremely tapu.

Could his personal mana overcome that?

No, because the wairua of the dead is much stronger than the wairua of the living.

What about the chattel itself? If it is passed by the thief or plunderer to a third person?

Whoever has it is in danger by the wairua which possesses the article.

According to Maori history, what attitude would be taken by the tribe towards the person who plundered a grave?

There are two ways to describe. One, they are mad; the other is that they are brave. But the madness is the first description.

You've told us that the tapu would continue to accompany the chattel even though it were passed to a third person. How would the tapu ultimately be extinguished, if ever?

By returning the article to its place of burial. Or there is a second method. That is to seek out a medium who would connect spiritually with the wairua within the article, talk to it and then either a tohunga would be used to lift the tapu or, as often happens now, someone like myself, a priest of Christian extraction, would be called upon.

You have a special ceremony for that?

Yes. But most often it is the former that is used.


Hone Kaa cross-examined by prosecutor Geoff Rea: Would it, in Maori terms, be normally expected that he would check out whether in fact the bayonet had been taken by Lance?

Hone Kaa: As I understand it, he knew that Lance had the bayonet and, in Maori terms, others would tell you if an article associated with you had been removed from a particular place.

So you would receive information that you would assume to be correct?

Yes.

You told us that it was and still is in some instances a custom to bury Maori people with articles, chattels and the like.

Yes.

I think you'll accept that is historically true of many cultures, Egyptians, and peoples like that.

Yes.

Are they buried right in the ground with the body or are they left as it were on the surface above the body?

Depends on the article. Something like this would be buried attached to the body.

So if it had in fact been buried with the body it must have been a case of grave robbing to get it from the body.

Yes. (Hone Kaa goes on to explain how Constable Tamati Reedy wouldn't have been in danger from the wairua because he had "taken a different course in life and his handling of the knife would be in a different manner to that of Kupenga and Nepe.")

Rea: At the end of the case I picked up that bayonet and took it back to Napier with me. How does that affect my position?

Hone Kaa: I would say you are a brave man. I say that in all seriousness because three years ago...

Rea: I'm not mocking.

Hone Kaa: Three years ago I had a Pakeha family, who could trace their descent from one of the missionaries, who brought to me the bone head-comb worn in the topknot of a chief who was killed by von Tempski and his raiders in Taranaki. That family, for two generations, had experienced nothing but hardship and disaster throughout. The women were often the seers in a whanau or family. They had seen this severed head with the comb in the topknot night after night. They came to me and asked me what I should do. It was then I discovered their descent from von Tempski's raiders and I told them to take the comb back and that the wairua of the comb would lead them to the point where they could either bury it or return it to the descendant. They took it back to New Plymouth and they buried it. This family, ten days after the incident, came to me and said: "Thank you for saving us." I, at that point, according to my mother, was commanded by another wairua to tell them what to do because even I, a sophisticated priest as I am, did not know how to deal with their question of mana. My mother told me there was a wairua directing my thoughts, actions, and that's how strong those things are.


## UTU?


*Utu is another motive for the killing of Lance Kupenga offered at Joe Nepe's trial. These days the average New Zealander translates the Maori word utu as revenge. It is perhaps more correct to call it payment. But it is a special kind of payment, a form of recompense, procured by the shedding of blood.*

**Interview with Joe Nepe, November 17, 2000 (this was before I'd read the trial notes and knew only vaguely about the utu theory):** *Your brother was mentioning on the phone and I've heard it mentioned in Rua, too, that there was some sort of weird connection with what happened in '85 with something that happened way back.*
Aaawww! I dunno, I dunno, I dunno.
*Have you heard that one?*
Yeah. I know what you mean.
*Well I don't know much about it. I've heard it mentioned, like there was something that happened and maybe there was some ah...*
Actually there was a few things that happened back in those back, back, way back then.
*Yeah, yeah.*
Not just that one.
*That were quite mysterious?*
Yeah, same sort of thing, ay, but in another world, like in a Maoridom world, like you had to be a Maori warrior.
*Yeah, yeah, I know what you mean: way back before colonisation and that. So what was the tie-up there between your case and this other incident?*
I dunno. I don't know what they were trying to get at. Actually I was surprised they even brought it up when it came to my trial.
*Did they bring it up at the trial?*
Yeah, they brought it up at the trial.
*Did you know anything about that?*
Yeah.

*Aw, you'd heard about this whole story?*
I'd heard about that story.
*Even before what happened with you and Lance?*
Well before me and Lance.
*Mmm. Now what was it? Was it someone from your family had done the same thing to someone from Lance's family or something like that?*
I was a elder brother. This time it was a elder brother who did it.
*Aw yeah. Okay.*
Cos last time our elder brother died from his younger brothers when they got there and knocked him off.
*Yeah, yeah, yeah, yeah. An elder brother?*
Yeah.
*So what would Lance be?*
He was a taina at the time, a younger brother.
*Not to you though was he?*
In my family ways, yeah, a younger brother.

*What Joe means is that in the original incident in the 1700s the younger brothers killed the elder brother, who represented the "elder" or senior line in the genealogy. More than two hundred years later Joe was back representing that older brother and his line. And Lance Kupenga was back representing one of the younger brothers and their younger or taina line in the genealogy.*

**Joe:** It was the same family link-up. Aw well, it wasn't Nepe. It was another name in those days.
*But it was still...*
It was still whanau, direct descendancy.
*Yeah, yeah. And on his side as well?*
On his side as well.
*So when you heard that, did it freak you out?*
Yeah, it came up in my trial.
*You'd heard it before though.*
I'd heard it before but I didn't think they'd bring it up, you see.
*Who brought it up?*
Aw, some fuckin' lawyer.

*In his book Horouta, Rongowhakaata Halbert mentions, under the heading Te Aitanga A Materoa (an East Coast hapu or sub-tribe), the incident that Joe Nepe is talking about. It happened in the 1700s when a warrior living at*

*Makarika, southwest of Ruatoria, was killed during a visit to his brothers, a few miles away.*

*"While visiting his brothers Kukuwai and Korohau at Whareponga, Te Atau was fatally speared by a slave, and was buried on the Ahioteatua block..."*

*Halbert says a slave killed Te Atau with a spear. But Joe believes the Warrior was beheaded. He says that's the story that had been passed down through Te Atau's line until it reached him. And why would Kukuwai and Korohau do that to their elder brother? Perhaps because Te Atau had the mana and tapu of the senior line and his brothers were jealous. It was believed that beheading a person was a way of taking over their mana and tapu. Utu was never taken against the brothers. Halbert continues: "...Because of their lawlessness, Te Atau's brothers Kukuwai (Kuku), Korohau and Rongotangatake were rudely referred to as 'Nga Kuri Paakaa a Uetuhiao' (the ruddy dogs of Uetuhiao), Uetuhiao being their mother. On one occasion they waylaid an innocent party of Ngati Ira... near Ruatoria, and according to Taniwha, the sole survivor, they swooped down, 'me he manu e pokai ana' (like a flock of birds)."*

*Roro of Ngati Pokai set out from a nearby pa and attacked the trio at three different places. They escaped every time but the land "was taken over by Roro, who placed his son Te Hukui in occupation."*

*But 'Nga kuri paakaa' eventually came to a sticky end. "The three brothers captured some hunters of Whanau a Apanui of Te Kaha at Korauwhakamoe... After cutting the straps of the hunters' packs, they allowed them to go without their loads. But they met them again at Punaruku, where the three were slain in the battle of Maniaroa by Whanau a Apanui, including the bird hunters, who cut off their hands saying, 'These are the hands which cut the straps of our loads of birds at Korauwhakamoe.'*

**Joe Nepe, November 17, 2000:** Te Aitanga A Mate: that's my hapu and it's basically a combination of John Heeney's and my families. It's the Ngarimu and Nepe families put together. It also includes names like Moeke, Keelan and Tamati: big families.Te Aowera's at Whakapaurangi. Te Aowera was on Taitai Maunga (mountain) until they were forced to move down. When the Kuripaakaas had it on Taitai Maunga it wasn't known as Te Aowera. Te Aowera's just a new name to our people.

Now the four marae in that area – Kapohonga (Hiruharama), Rongohaere, Rongoitakai and Te Aowera – all make up one family.

Te Aitanga A Mate is the beginning of the Maori people (it's believed they have always lived there, since the Garden of Eden, which is on Whakaahu Hill). Now Te Aitanga A Mate is around that Whareponga area. That's where the

Maori people come from, in that area. That's where Porourangi's people are from and Porourangi is the ancestor of the Ngati Porou. But, see, they've gone and put Porourangi in Waiomatatini, see. They didn't build the marae at Whareponga. They say he's from over there. And Ropata Wahawaha (a controversial ancestor who fought on the side of police, hunting the rebel Te Kooti) had the Porourangi Marae built there (in 1888). But Porourangi's not from over there.

Now there's a river called Waingakia. That means the avenging river. That's where Te Atau got killed. He was one of our Kuripaakaas. He was our dreadful tipuna. He had dreads. Our "dreadful" because he's a dread man. These fullas had dreadlocks. That's why they were called Kuripaakaas (the ruddy dogs). And it's all one family: Keelans, Moekes, Ngarimus, Nepes.

This was in the 1800s or 1700s. It goes right back at the beginning of the Maori people. This guy's name was Te Atau Te Rangi. Kuku, Korohau, they killed him. They killed their brother. There were four brothers.

*And was Te Atau beheaded?*

Same thing (as Lance).

*And was it the same as in the mate Maori? Did the brothers see the mate Maori in Te Atau?*

Aw, you wouldn't call it mate Maori in those days.

*It was just sickness in those days.*

Not even sickness.

*What was it then?*

I wouldn't have a clue.

*Why do you think they had the dreadlocks?*

They were the Rastamen from the Bible.

*And it's been passed down that these guys were dread?*

Yeah.

*And you guys had known these stories as you'd been growing up?*

They're our tipuna.

*And that's part of the reason why you guys got the dreadlocks?*

Could be! Could be! Could be just passed on down to us and that's why we have the dread and no one else has it.

*So those guys who killed Te Atau, their family came down to the Kupengas. Is that right?*

Could be, could be.

*And your family came down from Te Atau?*

Could be.

*Is that your reading of it or are you not sure?*

No, that's true. That's true. That's true direct descendancy. See, if you get all those families back together they're one whanau. They come back to the four brothers.

*We should note that Lance's father, Paetene, refutes this reasoning. While he acknowledges that the Nepe and Kupenga families are both descended from the four brothers, he maintains that the senior bloodline actually comes down to Lance, not to Joe Nepe.*

*Now Joe reckons the four marae in that area around Hiruharama all make up one family. And the different branches have been connected and re-connected again and again over the years by both love and violence.*

*In the book, Horouta, it says that Kukuwai, one of the kuri paakaa back in the 1700s, had a son called Rongoitekai. Now Rongoitekai's wife Wairere died and he wished to marry her sister. "But their mother Kapohanga objected, and in the following argument Rongoitekai killed her. For this crime he lost not only his life at the hands of his brothers-in-law… but also his rights to Aorangi Maunga (mountain), Aorangiwai, Taoroa and Hauahu blocks." Interestingly, Kapohanga was married to Te Aowera's son. So in that story alone are tied up the tipuna of three of those marae: Rongoitekai, Kapohanga and Te Aowera.*

**Hata Thompson:** Some of the things we did *were* wrong. But there was no way we could sidestep that. That was the way it was meant to be, and it happened. You couldn't sidestep something like one of our mates getting his head chopped off, you know. And that was between two of our own brethren. But it was their *own* thing. And then it was sensationalised like we all took part in it, like it was a ritual slaying. And that was *wrong* because it was really between those two.

It was to do with "nga kuri paakaa". They were four brothers. And the eldest brother, Te Atau, was killed by the other three. And when they found Lance, Te Atau's were supposed to be the other bones that were inside that hole. Because there were two sets of bones found there. When they found Lance, he was on top of another set of bones. And they wondered if it was someone who'd been killed earlier. Then when they checked it out they realised the bones underneath Lance were older. And then the old people were saying about Te Atau and that that's how *he* got killed. Jo-jo and me, we come off Te Atau. We're kind-a like the senior line. Lance came off one of the younger brothers. And a lot of the older people were saying it was like utu. It was payback for what happened to Te Atau.

But when Lance got killed, I wasn't there. I was in jail when it happened. I was actually down here in Gisborne locked up. And I heard while I was in there that Lance had been killed. I couldn't even get out to attend his funeral.

But when those brothers killed Te Atau, they became like outcasts. They were made to go and sleep with the dogs. They had to fight the dogs to feed.

That's why they were known as "nga kuri paakaa" (the ruddy dogs).

But because of this more recent incident between Joe and Lance, the whole movement got tarred with the same brush. What happened between them had nothing to do with our Rastafarian beliefs. It was just between Joe and Lance.

**Peter Williams (for the defence):** Going back to the family, many years ago did something occur in that family that is of significance?

Canon Hone Kaa: Yes. The two younger brothers killed the older brother and it was a battle that hinged on the mana.

Williams: The mana that would usually be associated with the older brother.

Kaa: Yes.

Is it usual the older brother takes the mana of the family?

Mana passes from father to son. In this instance the younger brothers wanted the mana for themselves.

So they disposed of the older brother?

Yes.

Did that situation according to Maori belief form the basis of an utu?

Yes.

Would there be some Maori people who would believe, because of the common genealogy, that utu had been transferred through to the defendant and Lance?

Yes. In fact the old people would say that now.

You mean the Maori elders?

Yes.

In that sense would the word utu be synonymous with the European word curse?

Only partly, yes, because the utu itself has a wairua (spirit) of its own. And the belief of some Maoris is that that wairua would move around the people and it could go through generation after generation and no one knows the time and the place when it will realise itself.

Would some people believe that that wairua would have been present at the time that the defendant killed Lance?

Yes.

I want to come now to another topic, that concerns the place or the hill or mountain where the homicide took place. The Whakaahu block and trig at Otuaru. What are the Maori beliefs in relation to that mountain?

It was I understand originally the pa site.

Was that pa taken by conquest?

Well, the people of that place have always lived there. There is, of course, a belief among Ngati Porou that we have always been here.

Always been in New Zealand?

Yes. We did not come on canoe, we have always been here.

In particular were there any burials in that particular area?

From what I can understand, at some point in the history of that hill there was a tragedy there. In an instance where there is a tragedy that leads to death the tapu of the place changes. It then becomes the residence of death and in order for the people to feel right and safe the place would then become a cemetery or a burial place.

And the pa would shift?

Yes.

Would there be a belief that the wairua or spirits would exist at that place?

Very strongly. So much so that even for strangers coming into the area there would be the belief that such places were out of bounds to them. They would not have to be told. They would just know.

Geoff Rea (for the prosecution): Does it (the utu) move on following what Joe Nepe has done?

Canon Hone Kaa: As I understand it, Joe Nepe has fulfilled the wairua of the utu.

So it is not a continuous form of queue where the last one to be injured can be expected to exact injury on another person?

It can operate that way, but in most of the instances that I know of it ceased at that point.

Honour was restored.

Balance was retained.

What about mana?

It's the mana, the corporate mana of the whanau that is also restored. As I understand it the whanau are now so much closer. In fact they have come back to being one.

My question is: is there any historical reason or any reason particularly to Maori belief why it has taken that length of time for things, my word again, for things to be satisfied?

The old people would put it this way. There is no historical reason. It just proved to be the place and the time for this to happen.

For satisfaction of the utu to be completed is it necessary for violent retribution or can it be done by degradation and humiliation or some other way?

No, according to tradition there must be blood.

That's what utu involves, it involves blood?

Yes.

In your view, would a deep and abiding interest in ancient Maori tradition, beliefs and genealogy lead to an incident we have heard of in this court in the last three days?

Yes. Especially in connection with one so young.

Could that be accurately described in your view as a form of fanaticism?

No.

You don't believe that somebody could be so imbued with tradition and past conduct, which is not currently practised, to believe that the old ways were better than the new, and revert to them?

That is not necessarily to me a description of a fanatic. In Maori terms such a person would have been chosen by the wairua to become the vehicle.

# CHAPTER 9

## THE HOMICIDE

**Interview with Joe Nepe:** *Obviously the thing that sort of made big news as far as you were concerned was what happened with Lance, you know. How do you feel about that now?*

Aw no, I've still got no regrets about that.

*Aw yeah, well what was the sort of story there?*

No, there actually was a *big* story there. Johnny Too Bad had stepped in.

*Yeah.*

Yeah.

*Now when you say Johnny Too Bad, do you mean that from a Rasta perspective?*

Yeah, from a Rasta perspective.

*Not a...*

Well how can a bal'head say something else towards me, you know, like, what I'm saying, ay.

*Yeah, yeah. Now Johnny Too Bad is the devil, ay?*

Yeah. If I say Johnny Too Bad, what's the bal'head gonna say. What's he gonna believe? You know?

*Yeah, I know whatcha mean. It's like someone who doesn't believe in Rasta, they're not gonna understand where you're comin' from.*

No, they're not gonna understand.

*But was it tied up with mate Maori?*

Yes, mate Maori.

*A similar sort of thing?*

Similar thing. A spiritual thing.

*Did he have a curse on him or something?*

I wouldn't know.

*Aw yeah.*

At the time, he was playing up, at the time.

*So what was the sort of build-up to that?*

Aw it was a big build-up to that actually. Smoking marijuana and looting and, you know.

*He was?*

Both of us were. We were all looting at that time. Actually, that was the thick of it. We were right in the thick of it then.

*Stealing horses and all that?*

Stealing horses and all that, cutting fences.

*There was something to do with a bayonet or something on a gravestone that he'd taken or something like that?*

Oh, I don't know about that.

*Was that really part of it or...*

Could-a been. Could-a been when we went to the cemetery, something might-a gone missing. Something might-a gone missing from the cemetery I think. I'm not too sure what it was.

*Yeah. Would he have been nicking some dope or...*

Aw, I don't know. Young fullas, ay, these days, don't know what they're doing.

*Yeah. At that time do you think you'd been smoking too much dope?*

No. Dope had nothing to do with it. People just want to blame the dope because it's there, ay. They don't want to see the whole story to it.

*What was the story from your perspective?*

Johnny Too Bad. That's all there was to it.

*Is that right? How did you see him in Lance?*

It was through my mate kite, ay.

*Mate kite? Sorry.*

Visual sighting.

*Oh, just through sight. You could see him?*

Yeah, you could see him through sight.

*Just like normal sight?*

Normal sight.

*And what was he sort of transforming in front of you?*

Fuck, he was bigger than me.

*He was what?*

Fuck, he was bigger than me, by the time I'd finished with him.

*And what, were you guys just hangin' out together?*

Yeah. No, we were just hanging out together.

*Yeah, yeah, and he just started to turn into Johnny Too Bad?*

No, you could see it inside him and he just turned like in what he was saying to me and all that, ay, how he was swearing at me and cursing at me.

*Do you think he seemed in control of himself, the way he was...*

In one way he was in control but after a while he lost it, ay. Every word I got from him was 'f', that sort of thing, ay. I couldn't quite get where he was coming from.

*So he just was totally away from everyone else?*

Yeah, I think he had lost it a bit there.

*Was he upsetting the other guys?*

Na, not really.

*It was just you?*

Just me. Just the way he was carrying on.

*Joe began to see Johnny Too Bad in Lance's face the night before the killing. They were playing cards at Joe's sisters place. His sister was in bed. A few of the other Rastas were there, too. But they were asleep in the sitting room. Joe and Lance were playing gin-rummy. Joe later told a psychiatrist, Dr Henry Bennett, that he saw someone else in Lance's face, Johnny Too Bad. He "looked like someone out of a spooky ghost comic". Joe could see only one side of Lance's face. The side he could see, he believed, was the devil. Once he saw the devil in Lance's face, Joe felt it was his mission to kill him.*

**Interview with Joe Nepe:** *So what happened that day? Do you remember much about that day?*

Na not much. I can't remember much from that day.

*But whatever he'd done he'd sort of pissed you off to the extent that, you know...*

Actually, I wasn't gonna kill him that day.

*Yeah.*

I was gonna wait 'til we have a council, ay, and let the council decide.

*Were the councils called like reckonings. Was that the word?*

Aw, you could say that.

*Aw yeah, so more like just a meeting. You call it a council?*

Yeah. The twelve get together and we have a korero (talk). That would be *the* twelve. And we'd just work it out from there.

*And he's either gotta sort his shit out or...*

Sort *his* shit out or else get out of town.

*And there was no council decision on Lance? Just you at that time?*

Just me at that time. I just took over from there. I didn't want to leave it too late, ay, or else it would have spread.

*So you thought there was a sickness like mate Maori?*

It *was* mate Maori.

*Is that right?*

No, it *was* mate Maori. You could see it on him.

*How would you see it?*

Oh you'd start seeing keihuas and everything.

*Keihuas?*

Ghosts.

*Aw yeah. When he's around, you'd start seeing them around him?*

You start seeing them around him.

*Like they're coming off him and that.*

Yeah.

*Far out.*

You start seeing and visualising everything, ay. If you're not too sure with mate Maori, well, it'll get you, ay.

*Were you scared that what he had could manifest in yourself?*

I reckon it would have. But I was a bit stronger than him at that time, strong enough to repel it away, ay. I didn't wanna get that mate Maori.

*Yeah, yeah.*

See, people thought I was sick at the time, ay, why I did it. I wasn't sick at that time. I was like how I am now.

*So you were quite lucid? Quite clear?*
Yeah.

*Joe Nepe started the morning of July 22 with a couple of joints. Auckland psychiatrist Dr Roger Culpan, a witness for the defence, testifies in court that he doesn't think the cannabis would have had any bearing on Joe's actions. People under the influence were more likely to be inhibited, he says.*

*So where was Joe's head at that morning? He'd had visual hallucinations since the night before, when he looked at Lance and saw Satan's face. He'd also been hearing voices, the voices of his ancestors and old people from his childhood who'd passed away. He says they helped him, guided and protected him.*

Dr Henry Bennett (for the defence): He was also suffering delusions, that is, false beliefs. And the main one was that he had this awful mission to carry out and nothing could have convinced him to the contrary, I believe, to desist from that path upon which he had set himself...

**Thursday, June 26, 1986:** *The Gisborne Herald runs a story headlined: Avenged ancestor with utu slaying. The intro reads: Joseph McNab Nepe thought he was a Maori warrior avenging an ancestor by slaying the devil in Lance Kupenga, the High Court in Gisborne heard yesterday.*

*It goes on to say: "At the start of yesterday's proceedings written evidence from Nepe for the prosecution was read out.*

*"Nepe said that on July 22, he had gone with Kupenga and another person to find Kupenga's horse near Tuparoa.*

*"Nepe and the other person rode the horse towards the hut on Whakaahu Station, while Kupenga walked. He said he was going up there to do utu, blood for blood."*

*It was said to me in Ruatoria that even the fact that Nepe and Jason Keelan rode the horse while Kupenga walked was significant: that's the way the slaves used to be led up Whakaahu before they were thrown into the holes.*

*Jason Keelan was fifteen years old when all this happened. He'd known Kupenga since he was five, but says he did nothing during the killing because there was nothing he could do. During the depositions hearing, he tells defence counsel Peter Williams that Joe Nepe was "really quite crazy" and acting like a sick man.*

*Some people have said that a fourth person made the trip up Whakaahu. But that person didn't tell their story in court and their presence on Whakaahu that* day was never acknowledged during the court case. I didn't know about the possibility of a fourth person when I interviewed Joe, so never asked him about it, and he never mentioned a fourth person himself. I have not included a fourth person in my re-enactment. The foundation of this re-enactment is Jason Keelan's testimonies in the depositions hearing and in the murder trial. The picture's filled in with extra details gleaned from Nepe's evidence (for the prosecution), which is read out in court, and the testimonies of Lance's uncle Jacob Kauhamu Kupenga and psychiatrist for the defence, Dr Henry Bennett, who interviewed Nepe twice while he was in custody.

On the morning of July 22, 1985, Jason Keelan and a friend, Tuck Morice, were having some difficulty trying to dig out a blocked sump. They decided to head into Ruatoria to get a pick. While there, they stopped at a shop and bought milkshakes and some food, which they ate at a nearby seat on the main street. Joe Nepe and Lance Kupenga approached. Joe asked Jason and Tuck if they wanted to help catch Kupenga's horse at the beach at Tuparoa. Jason said yes, but Tuck didn't want to. "He said he would come around the roadway" and meet them later. Tuck wandered away, totally unaware of what he had just escaped.

Lance's uncle Jacob turned up in his car. He had a bag full of stuff Lance had asked him to bring: some clothes, a bridle and his bankbook. Lance handed back the bridle and the bag, but took the clothes and the bankbook.

They set off. Kupenga was wearing jeans, gumboots and a red and black Swann Dri. Nepe was wearing jeans, a black coat, a hat and a red scarf, and carrying a broomstick without the broom on the end of it.

A man – "some fellow Campbell" - gave Jason, Joe and Lance a lift to the end of the road, at Tuparoa Creek, near the beach. They walked past the local marae to some yards, where it was thought the horse would be. Lance's horse wasn't there, but another horse was. They took it and set off for Whareponga and, ultimately, Whakaahu Hill. Lance walked in front, while Joe and Jason rode the horse, using Lance's red and black Swann Dri as a saddle. Joe told Jason that Johnny Toobad had got into Lance. Jason understood whom he meant. The Rastafarians had borrowed the term from the lyrics of reggae stars like Bob Marley. Johnny Toobad was the devil.

They called at the home of Zula Rehutai, an old man who lived on the track they were taking up to Whakaahu. Jason noticed that, under his black coat, and around his waist, Joe was wearing a knife belt that held about four knives. While they were riding the horse up the hill, Lance, still on foot, made a grab for the bridle. Joe reacted by breaking the broomstick over his head. Lance rubbed his head and asked, "What was that for?" Joe got off the horse. As he did so, Lance's Swann Dri fell to the ground. Lance asked Jason to pick up the Swann

Dri for him. Joe pointed the snapped broomstick and said, "Leave it there." This struck Jason as odd. Why would you want to leave a perfectly good Swann Dri on the ground where someone else could find it? But Joe was acting strangely. And Jason was worried. So he did as he was told. Joe picked up an old piece of fence post from the ground and struck Lance on the heel with it.

They carried on through a gate. Joe again hit Lance about his gumboots and legs, telling him to "get up the hill".

Joe told Jason that Kupenga "was stink" and that he could smell him. Stink was a term the Rastas used to describe someone who smelt like a rotting corpse. It meant they could smell death on them. Jason understood it to mean he was "rotten inside", that he had Johnny Toobad inside him. But he could smell nothing strange about Lance.

Joe threatened Kupenga: "Get back down to the river or I'll teach you not to play marbles with me when we get back up on the hill." Jason understood playing marbles to mean playing games with someone or, more specifically, mind-games. They continued: Jason on the horse, and Joe and Lance walking in front.

About two hours after they set off up the hill, they arrived at the hut on Whakaahu, known by the Rastas as "the bach" and used by the group when they wanted to get away from things. Joe told Lance to sit on a seat outside facing the ashes of an old fire. To the right was the hut, to the left an area with some scrim, propped up like a tent. Joe told Lance to look at a kit (a Maori flax woven bag), which was hanging on a post to the right. Lance did as ordered. Joe went inside the hut.

Soon after he came out with some black cord, a blanket and an axe with the Rasta colours of red, yellow and green taped to the handle. Joe slammed the axe into the seat, about a foot away and to the right of where Lance was sitting, hard enough for it to stick into the wood.

Kupenga started to cry and plead with Nepe: "Leave me alone."

Joe grabbed Lance's arms and tied his hands behind his back with the black cord. Lance didn't struggle.

"What are you doing?" asked Lance.

Joe replied: "I'm going to give you a hiding."

Jason was over by the tent by now, watching all this. He said nothing.

Joe told Lance that he (Joe) was a toa (warrior).

Lance responded that he (Joe) was mad.

Nepe openly called him Johnny Toobad. And Kupenga told him again, "You're mad. You're mad, Joe."

Nepe replied, "That's not my name. I'm a warrior, Te Atau."

Again, he told Kupenga he was going to give him a hiding. And Kupenga said, "Leave me alone."

Nepe said, "Who's your name? Who's your name?"

"My name is Lance."

"Your name is Johnny Toobad."

Kupenga asked Jason to tell Nepe to leave him alone.

Nepe cut a hole in the blanket with one of his knives and put it over Kupenga's head.

Joe told Lance to walk up the hill. Lance walked on ahead and Joe began to follow him. Jason was still standing by the tent. Jason told Joe he didn't want to go up any further. He was scared because he hadn't seen Nepe act like this before. Joe told him to come up so his tipuna (or ancestors) could see him. Jason said he didn't want to. Joe called to Jason to walk up to him. Begrudgingly, Jason obeyed. While Joe was waiting, Lance picked his moment. He freed his hands from the cord, kicked off his gumboots, took off the blanket and ran into the manuka bush.

Jason and Joe ran up to where Lance had left the cord, his gumboots and the blanket. "That's how quick Johnny Toobad is," Nepe told his young friend. He called out to Kupenga, saying that if he came back everything would be all right. He said that if he came back he was Lance, but if he didn't he was Johnny Toobad. He called out like this several times. He told Jason to join in. And he did. "Then I thought everything was going to be all right." Ten minutes later, Kupenga emerged, limping. But Nepe told him to keep going up the hill.

They came to a waterfall where there were two pools. Joe ordered Jason to wash his hair in one pool at the waterfall, and his face and hands in the other. Joe did the same, but Lance didn't. He was up the hill about thirty metres. Nepe had told Kupenga to go up a goat track where his tipuna could see him. Jason was scared and freaked out.

By now it was about 2pm. Even though it was winter, the weather was fine. They walked on up the steep, narrow track in single file, Lance first, then Joe, then Jason. No one spoke until eventually Nepe announced they would pray. He said they would face the sea, so their tipuna could see them. They were only about thirty metres away from the holes by now. They knelt towards the sea and chanted a karakia (or prayer) in Maori. It was an "old" prayer, led by Joe, a farewell prayer, known as a poroporoaki. Lance, in the karakia, was to depart in peace. They chanted for about fifteen minutes.

After that Lance and Jason sat down together. Joe told them to have a talk. He walked about twenty metres away, sat down and sharpened his axe for the next ten minutes or so.

SIGN OF THINGS TO COME: One of the early haybarn fires in 1985.

that's a start at least.

**WILLIAM GOLDSMITH**

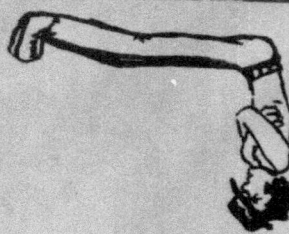

**THE JOB I WOULD LIKE TO DO WHEN I LEAVE SCHOOL**

When I leave school, hopefully with my U.E., I hope to be able to join the Air Force as an Officer Cadet.

The reason why I want to join the Air Force is because I find that our country needs to be protected from invasions from other countries, also we can keep fishing boats out of the 300 mile fishing zone. In the Air Force you get good wages.

I hope to become a Pilot and Navigator and maybe even do some engineering. But I'll have to wait until I am between the age of 17-19 years on entry, which is January each year.

Everytime I see a Strikemaster or Hawk fly over Ngata, I look up and start thinking that one of these days I'll be flying one of those babies. Maybe they might even have the F15 in New Zealand by then.

I've dreamed about driving trucks, car racing, lawyers or even becoming a doctor, but I have decided to join the Air Force, when I leave school and I am proud of it. I had a good think about joining the T.F. but I still want

**The Job I Would Like To Be When I Leave School**

The Job I am interested in doing at the moment is becoming a motor mechanic. I was almost born with a spanner in my hand. I have grown up in a mechanical family with my father being a motor mechanic. What are my reasons for wanting to do this trade? Well I have spent a lot of time helping my father with any little jobs ranging from fitting points and plugs to putting in new rings and valve grinds etc. Almost every Saturday I go with my father to the place where he does the repairs for the N.Z. Forest Service trucks. I have spent most of my life involved with cars and have totally enjoyed it so I have decided to spend the rest of my working days in the trade. Although it is not a very well paid job I feel I would rather be doing a job I enjoy for less money rather than a job I hate for more money.

**Robert Hayden 4F**

**THE JOB I WOULD LIKE TO DO WHEN I LEAVE SCHOOL**

When I leave school I would like to apply for a computing job. The reason for my choice, is that computers are becoming an ever increasing part of our lives. Many people need to have an understanding of computer technology as it relates to their spectual job. The computer field has a variety of jobs which cover a wide range of educational abilities. Some of the titles in computing are—

(1) Analysts
(2) Programmers
(3) Computer Operators
(4) Data Preparation Personnel
(5) Sales Representatives
(6) Systems Engineers
(7) Customer Engineers or
      Computer Servicepersons

There are four main employers of staff in the computer industry. They are — Commercial Users, Computer Bureaus, Computer Manufacturers, Government Depart-

BEHEADED: Lance Kupenga (left, with the afro) "a young man in search of his destiny".

138

THE WEAPON: The axe Joe Nepe used is found embedded in a tree on Whakaahu Hill. The tell-tale Rasta stripes can be seen on the handle.

THE HOMICIDE SCENE: A police cameraman tied to a rope was eased down one of the holes to photograph Lance Kupenga's body. The head was down another hole.

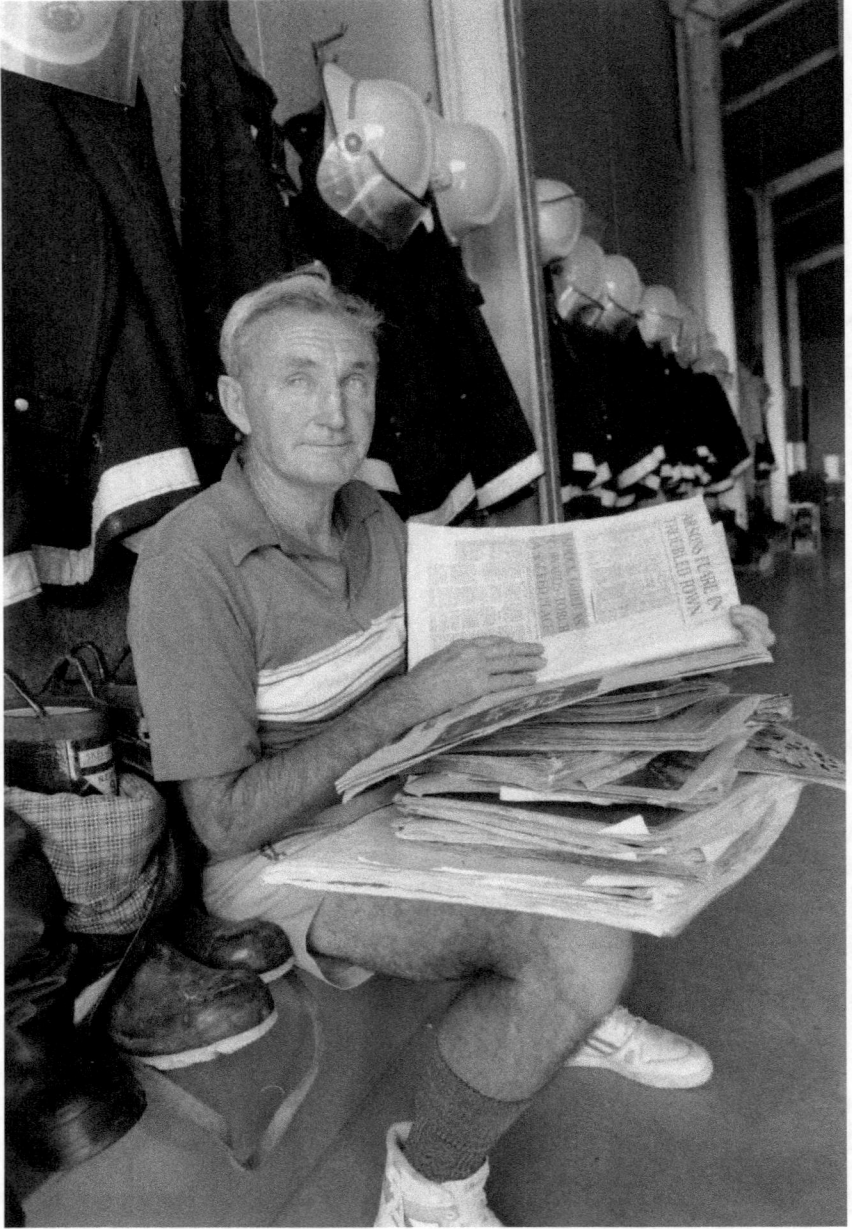

TOM HEENEY: The deputy chief of the Ruatoria Voluntary Fire Brigade and the father of co-leader of the Rastas John Heeney.

OCCUPATION: The Rastas occupied Tepoho-Te-Aowera Marae before fed-up members of their whanau gained a court order to have them removed.

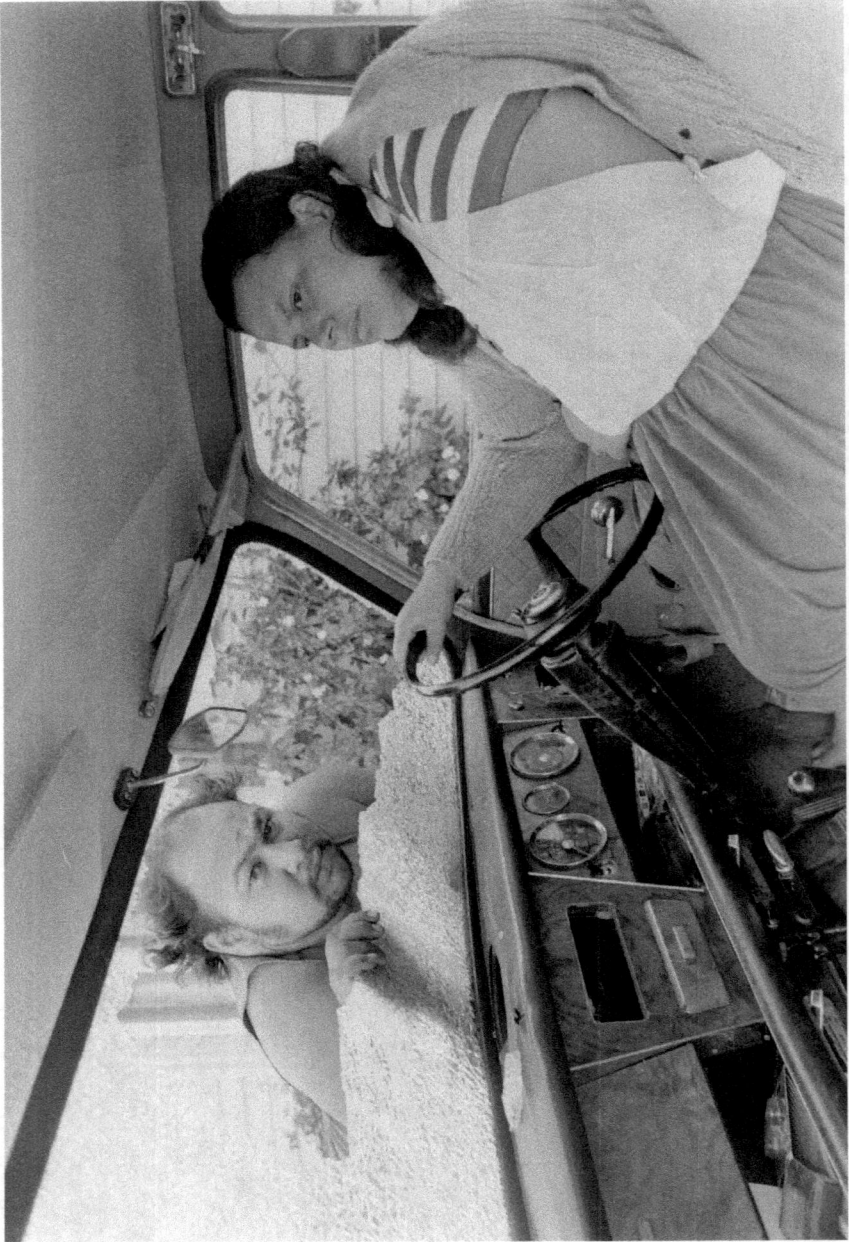

BACKLASH: Couple Paddy and Forli Brown were with Paddy's Rasta brother Hamana when they were attacked by fencepost-weilding "vigilantes". Forli suffered a broken collarbone.

"BALDHEADS" TARGETED: The burning of the Ruatoria courthouse-cum-police station was a direct attack on the establishment and many in the emergency services took it personally.

RASTA RETALIATION? The common theory is that the arson of the woolshed at Koura Station, managed by John Heeney's aunty, was in retaliation for the Rastas being charged for occupying the "top house".

MANHUNT: Armed police exit an RNZAF helicopter during the hunt for Chris Campbell, Hata Thompson and Cody Haua following the kidnapping of Detective Sergeant Laurie Naden.

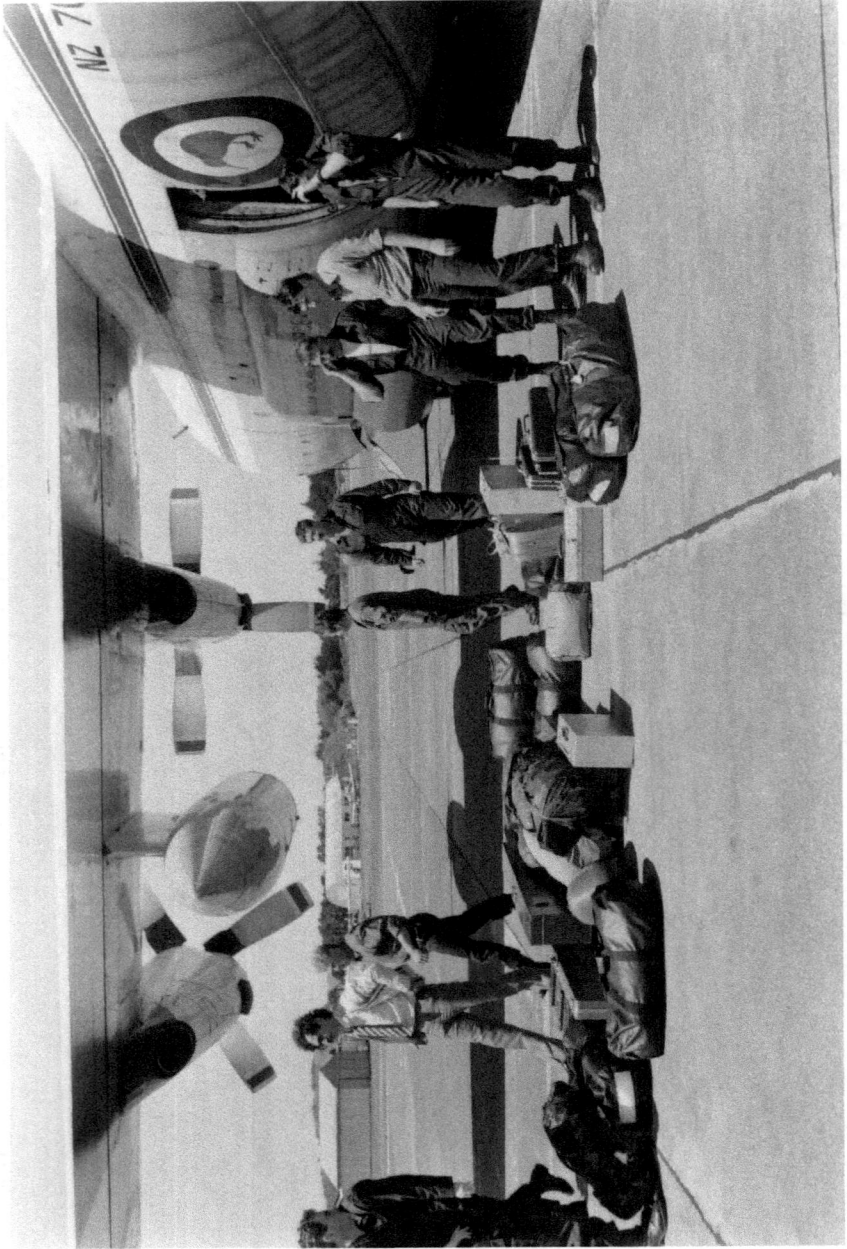

BIG OPERATION: Reinforcements and supplies arrive at Gisborne airport courtesy of the Air Force to join the search for the Rastafarian kidnappers.

TIMING IS EVERYTHING: This police house arson on February 12, 1986, indicated two trends: it happened on the 12th and it involved cruel timing (the day before the arrival of Constable Waho Tibble's replacement).

149

HATA (SAM) THOMPSON (middle): One of the original Rasta Twelve, Hata was jailed for his part in the kidnapping of Detective Sergeant Laurie Naden.

RASTA PAD: This tiny shed in Makarika, just south of Ruatoria, was the notorious hangout for the Rastas.

JOHN (HONE) HEENEY: Chris Campbell's right hand man in the
Ruatoria Rastafarians' original 12. These days he tattoos the moko for
the brethren. Photo courtesy of Maro Kouri.

CHRIS CAMPBELL: Seen by some as deluded, by
others as an outlaw prophet who would have been
more at home among his warrior tipuna.

Eventually, Joe got up and said he wanted to have a talk with Lance. Lance said that Nepe was bad and had something wrong with his head. Jason told Joe that Tuck Morice would be there soon.

Joe tied Lance's arms together with some orange twine and told him to lie on the ground on his chest. Lance complied. Jason reckons he could have run away. After all, he'd gotten away the last time, by the hut. But he complied. Joe used his knife to cut Kupenga's jersey sleeves, the legs of his jeans and to cut open his jersey from the neck to the middle of the back. He cut manuka branches and placed them over Kupenga's body. He kicked Kupenga in the head and the legs. He told Keelan to go up the hill. Jason did as he was told. Lance did nothing. Jason did nothing. He was terrified.

Joe pointed with the axe at the two holes, one after the other, and told Lance: "Your head is going into that one and your body's going into that one."

Lance shouted at him, "Wairangi!" meaning mentally disturbed.

But Joe didn't seem bothered. He was cool. He didn't show anything. It was as if what he was doing was nothing.

Then Jason Keelan saw "Jo-jo chopping with that axe at Lance" and Lance's head fall off. It took Joe Nepe two blows with the axe to sever Lance Kupenga's head. After that he cried, "Utu! Utu!"

He kicked Lance's head into one hole, and dragged his body over to the other, known as the bottomless pit. He threw the body down into the hole. Then he walked over to a tree and slammed the axe into it, leaving it embedded there. After this it started showering. The "bottomless pit" is also called the ua. Ua also means to rain. Joe knew by that, that he had concluded his mission.

Jason ran down the hill and waited. Joe followed in his own time.

They washed again, this time at a running stream. Jason washed his hands and splashed water on his chest and face. Joe washed the blood from his clothes and his boots. Nothing was said as they walked down the hill to Whareponga Road. But Jason had the feeling Joe was back, he'd returned to normal. On their way back to Ruatoria, Nepe and Keelan were given two rides: one by Ngahiraka Daisy Morice and the other by Judith Harrison. Neither noticed anything strange in their behaviour.

Although Joe told Jason not to tell anyone what had happened, Jason decided at Lance's tangi to go to the police.

There are a couple of discrepancies in the stories and evidence about what happened on Whakaahu Hill. They are perhaps only small details, but should be noted.

In the evidence from Nepe, which is read out in court, he says that after the killing, he and Jason rubbed noses, then walked to the creek, sprinkled water on their faces and hands and then walked home. Jason mentions nothing about rubbing noses. He says he just ran down the hill and waited.

In this written evidence, Nepe says he cried out "Utu! Utu!" and then struck Lance on the back of the neck twice. Jason says Joe cried out utu twice after he'd killed Lance. And pathologist Dr Michael Bottrill, who did the postmortem on Lance, says a minimum of three blows were used to sever Lance's head. (Also, as quoted earlier in this book, former policeman Laurie Naden said that luminol testing suggested there had been three blows from the axe).

An exchange during the trial between prosecutor Geoff Rea and Canon Hone Kaa gives a possible insight into the washing rituals performed by Joe and Jason on the ways up and down the hill. Kaa explains that in Maoridom it is common to wash oneself when entering a place associated with death (in this case a former pa site with a burial ground on the brow of the hill). Washing would have the function of putting the young men "at ease with the wairua (or spirit) that was there".

Rea: Is that why Lance was deliberately excluded from the washing?

Kaa: Yes or he could have chosen not to wash.

Rea: I think the evidence is there wasn't a great deal of choice in the sense that Jason washed because he was ordered to.

In his testimony, Canon Kaa is also able to offer some possible explanations behind some of the other ritualistic aspects of the homicide. (The questions are hypothetical).

1: Why did Joe beat Lance at the start of the tramp up the hill and kick his head and legs before killing him?

Kaa: "They are in a sense part of the initiation. And that was – if I understand our history correctly – one of the things that happened to people. They would be taken prisoner, especially those of noble descent... In fact, one of the known ways in my own tribe of humiliating people, especially male to male, was to rub the face with the penis of the victorious warrior."

2: Lance escaped but came back. Prosecutor Geoff Rea points out – and Canon Kaa agrees - that in some Maori communities it was considered unpardonable for a prisoner of war to attempt to escape. It just wasn't the right thing to do. Would that have any significance in this case?

Kaa: "I suppose it could, if you take the actions of Lance and in the whole of that ritual they are going through prior to decapitation, Maori history was being fulfilled at that particular point and he himself could not escape because the wairua itself was very strong. In fact, it surrounded all three of them."

*3: Why decapitation?*
*Kaa: "The head is a repository of all things sacred."*
*4: It's been suggested that Lance may have in the end lain down and accepted his fate. Is there an historical reference for this reaction to what most people would consider a terrifying prospect?*
*Kaa: "From what I understand of the history of my people there were specific places, rocks that were designated as decapitation points. The act of decapitation is known as hatepa and the idea of that was often people who were to be decapitated knew it was going to happen and accepted it because it was an honourable way of dying. It was preferable to being eaten."*

**From the murder trial:** Peter Williams: "Was Jo-jo in a strange mood?"
Keelan: "Yes."
"Jo-jo was really quite crazy wasn't he?"
"Yes."
"Lance was saying, 'That fellow is mad,' meaning Joe Nepe."
"Yes."
Williams: "You are a young man, but you saw something terrible."
"Yes."
"You'd agree with me that Jo-jo was a sick man at the time?"
"Yes."

*So how did the psychiatrists used in the trial diagnose Joe?*

**Dr Henry Bennett (defence):** Legally insane. Nepe's condition was of a paranoid-schizophrenic type. He had delusions, hallucinations and thought he had a special mission.

**Dr Roger Culpan (defence):** Legally insane. Nepe became psychotic on the eve of the tragedy and from that time his thinking was gravely disordered and deluded.

**Dr Una Watt Stephenson (prosecution):** Nepe said he had acted according to the beliefs of his group, the Ruatoria Rastafarians. She didn't think he could be diagnosed as a paranoid schizophrenic on the basis of the beliefs he shared with the group.

**Dr Patrick Savage (prosecution):** Available data did not show an obvious psychotic illness and Nepe seemed to have a fairly good insight into what he was about. But cultural factors loomed large for Nepe and some of the factors seemed disturbed in the mind due to mental illness hotted up by cannabis.

**Sergeant Alex Hope, former head of Ruatoria police, now a lawyer:**
Some of the Rastas on the fringes were known to talk. Joe Nepe was dobbed in
for killing Lance Kupenga. In the end the young Harrison boy – I can't
remember his name – Eddie Harrison's son admitted what had happened. Eddie's
the brother of Rex Harrison, the former cop. His son witnessed what happened
with Lance. There were actually two kids up there with Joe and Lance. They
were Jason Keelan, who gave evidence in court, and Eddie's son. They saw what
happened. They were shit scared. They ran all the way from Whakaahu down to
wherever.

**Former Detective Sergeant Laurie Naden:** Lance Kupenga was taken up
to Whakaahu by Joe Nepe and these two kids. And Nepe was going to beat the
devil out of him. The other two kids, they just sort of went along. They didn't
know where they were going.

**Phil Dreifuss, Gisborne lawyer (married to Storm, nee Dunn, one of the
author's best friends at school):** The Joe Nepe trial was my first job with this
law firm. I basically sat in as a spectator and after each day we'd have dinner
with Peter Williams. Doug Rishworth was junior with Peter. And we'd just have
a post-mortem basically. Peter kind of used me as a 13$^{th}$ juror. You know,
"How's it going from a spectator's point of view."

The main thing I remember of the Nepe trial was Hone Kaa's evidence. I
remembered Hone Kaa from university because he was a lecturer in Maori
studies at Auckland University. I remember his evidence because he had all that
historical stuff, which was great, about the three brothers, and their descendants.

I sat there during the Joe Nepe trial thinking that it would be good if there
was a defence of cultural appropriateness. I actually thought that the verdict of
insanity was an affront in a cultural sense. It's saying that what you are doing,
whilst it is culturally appropriate and you've been brought up to do it, it's insane
in a European sense.

But insanity was the only way Williams could run it. I actually discussed it
with Williams and he said, "Well there is no defence of cultural appropriateness
or cultural correctness. We have to work with what we've got."

Of course, it could also start a very dangerous precedent.

Nepe's grandmother sat in the trial the whole time. She was this very fine
looking Maori woman with white hair, tied back in a bun. Apparently she spoke
no English. She brought Joe Nepe up. And certainly the impression you got from
Hone Kaa was that he had been brought up knowing that there had been this
unavenged death, and that at some stage it had to be done. I suspect he thinks

he's leveled the playing field, that this thing was waiting to be done and had to be done, that there'd be a sickness in the community until it was done and that he's done the community a service. But in the European sense the only way you can prevent him from getting a life sentence for murder, was to prove to the jury that he was insane. And as I sat there I felt a little bit soiled by the process, because I was new to it. I wasn't indoctrinated in the law to such an extent that I probably am now. So I thought, "Yeah, this is an insult to Maoridom." But I can see that it was a very clever device to fit within our legal system we have here to ensure that his client was not put away for murder.

Joe probably feels that there was this festering sore and he's cleaned it out, disinfected this wound that's been there for centuries.

*Ike Campbell, Chris's brother, has a much more practical explanation for the killing. He reckons Lance Kupenga was killed because he kept ripping off the Rastafarians' marijuana patches. He'd been warned not to, and told he could be in deep trouble if he was caught again. But he kept on doing it. So he was killed.*

**Conversation with Joe Nepe:** *So, like the cops were saying that they couldn't understand how you got Lance up there, you know, cos it was like a huge cliff face. Do you remember much about that?*
Na. Can't remember much.
*Yeah, yeah.*
Got'm to where that hole was?
*Yeah.*
Aw na, it took me a long time to get him there. He knew where we were going, ay. But he didn't know why.
*Yeah, yeah. Was he resigned in the end?*
Aw, I wouldn't have a clue.
*But your feeling was it was a case of you or him sort of thing.*
Yeah.
*One of you had to go.*
One of us had to go.
*Yeah. And you were fighting for your own survival from this, this ah...*
I was protecting everyone else, ay, you know?
*Yeah, yeah.*
I didn't want them to catch the mate Maori that he had. It was a bad thing, ay.
*Had you seen it in action in the past or anything like that? In Rua and whatnot?*
I've seen it before.

*In what way?*
In my old people.
*Aw, in the kaumatua and that?*
Yeah.
*And what would happen then if someone caught it?*
That's when they'd start passing away. They used to pass away in threes before. Threes. Now they don't. They just have one here, one there, one here.
*Why in threes in the past, cos three's an important number isn't it?*
Yeah.
*Is that in Maoridom? Or just in Ngati Porou?*
Ah, believed to be in Ngati Porou.
*What's the significance of the three?*
I wouldn't know. I think it's a spiritual number, ay.
*Yeah. With what happened with Lance, what happened in the end? Because they found you not guilty, ay?*
Yeah.
*And said that you were mad at the time.*
Yeah.
*And dah-de-dah. What happened from there? Did you end up going away somewhere?*
I went away.
*Where'd you go to?*
Kingseat.
*That's South Auckland, ay?*
Yeah, Papakura.
*What was your experience like there?*
Good.
*How long were you there for?*
Ten years.
*Ten years?*
Ten years.
*And if you felt that you were okay, what was it like being in an institution?*
Nothing wrong, nothing wrong.
*You were okay with it?*
Yeah. Institution was all right.
*I mean what was the experience like?*
Aw, lot of friends, lot of friends around. There were a lot of good people around, you know, going through the same thing I was going through anyway.

*What were you going through, personally? Were you feeling a lot of remorse or...*

Na.

*Yeah... Did you feel that you **should** be feeling remorse? That people at home might have expected you to feel remorse?*

I think they wanted me to feel sorry for myself, ay.

*Yeah. They wanted you almost to punish yourself?*

Yeah.

*For what you did.*

For what I did. But I didn't.

*So you were being honest with yourself?*

Yeah.

*You didn't feel that...*

Na...

*so there's no point in saying, "I feel that."*

No, na.

*Yeah.*

Why should I feel the way they want me to feel?

*Exactly.*

Ay?

*Yeah, yeah, yeah. So did you feel quite comfortable?*

I was quite comfortable with that.

*Yeah, yeah. How hard was it coming out into the wide world again?*

Easy, easy.

*Aw yeah. Is that right?*

Easy. Just like another door had opened.

*Had things changed much?*

Yeah.

*What was the main changes you noticed?*

Oh!

*Did you go back to Rua?*

I went back to Rua and I just found that the people there, what I did, they learnt something from it.

*Yeah? Whadya think they learned from it?*

Like how to look after themselves in a way that they don't get affected by mate Maori.

*Yeah, yeah, yeah, yeah.*

So they started looking after their kids, their children, you know, things like that, ay.

159

*Just taking it more seriously?*

Yeah.

*Yeah.*

Cos in our days, man!

*What did you think about that story about the bayonet?*

All that stuff about the bayonet didn't mean much to me at the time. It was all about Johnny Toobad when I was working with it.

*What was the moment when it became critical for you like, "Shit, I've gotta get rid of this guy for my own safety."*

It wasn't until we got to the holes that it all started coming out of his mouth.

*Coming out of his mouth?*

Well I called him Johnny Toobad and he said, "I'm not fuckin' Johnny Toobad! Why should I be Johnny Toobad?" Now why should he say that? You know, that sort of thing, ay. I said, Aw, I just *called* you Johnny Toobad. I didn't say you *were* Johnny Toobad." He started swearing at me and cursing at me. He said, "What the fuck you gonna do now?" I said, "I'm gonna chop your head off cos you're Johnny Toobad." And he just freaked. I couldn't get a word out of him after that.

*Like you couldn't get any words out of him?*

I couldn't get anything out of him. Everything was f this, f that, you cunt this, you cunt that. Even Jason got a bit upset at him. He started calling Jason names. And Jason wasn't doing anything to him.

*What was Jason doing there?*

He was just coming along for the ride.

# CHAPTER 10

## PAETENE KUPENGA, LANCE'S FATHER

**Excerpt from Comes The Dawn, memoir by Paetene Kupenga, written in 2002:** "Boy, they have found The General." Jacob, one of my younger brothers, who was living in our old home in Puhunga near Hiruharama at the time, may or may not know, even now seventeen years later, but those six words changed my

160

family's life forever. It was J's way of telling me that someone had found Lance's body because The General was his stallion and they were seldom apart. Nevertheless a great weight which I had been carrying for weeks suddenly slid off my shoulders. I can say it now because I have no hate in my heart for anyone any more. But at the time... some people will never know, I suppose, how cruel they can be by spreading stories that my son was camped at Hikurangi one week and another story the next.

I'd be trying to borrow a horse and spend a weekend at Hikurangi looking, knowing full well that it would be like looking for a needle in a haystack and I suppose just trying to believe that he was still alive when everything Maori told me he was dead. Even cousin Jean Harrison was relieved. She said she could see it on me for quite some time, what the Maori call the wai mate.

I suppose I kept denying the truth that our son was dead because of how much it will hurt Kath. God knows she didn't deserve this. Her life since we've been married has been dedicated solely to her children and now her mokos have never asked for much and have made do with whatever little we could afford.

Life for my family at this time, early 1985, was cruising along beautifully - steady job, fair wages, excellent conditions, no need to work in the rain, you could always find somewhere dry. Not like my previous work, contract fencing. Once you got up the hill you carried on working. There was also a lot of shearing on weekends and holidays, which suited me down to the ground. I was working with excellent farmers, there was plenty of meat and to a growing family that was important. Not short of a dollar, good happy workmates, I suppose when I look back now the signs were there. It was too good to last. Everyone is born with his or her destiny. Some are lucky. They have all the happy times, while others are only allowed so much. While some people are very lucky others can try every day and never win anything.

However, when J came to Te Puia to inform me about The General I went to Ruatoria Police Station and was told that a helicopter was due down from Whakaahu any minute with a beheaded body and the police will be taking the same to Wellington for identification, etc.

I drove back to Te Puia Springs to tell Kath personally, crying all the way and drying my eyes before facing my wife, not wanting to hurt her more than she was already hurting. I suppose there are certain days in one's life we will never forget. That day will be etched in my memory forever.

The next morning I went to ask for time off while Kath as usual got the kids off to school. Then we were off to prepare the marae, etc for our son's tangi.

First we went straight to Amiria Ave, Ruatoria, not only to the very best Maori bread maker in the world but also a very special cousin, Mama Ngatai.

There were no words said as Kath and I walked in. Mama and her sister Teo were seated in her lounge. We all looked at each other and within seconds we were all crying our hearts out. In a way it was good to cry. It sort of cleared the miserable feelings I had been carrying around for weeks, for a while anyway. After this I kept Kath with Mama and Teo to do the shopping for the marae. I went to look for some help to kill some mutton at Waihuka, a family block which I was leasing at the time.

On our way there we stopped at my Auntie Sophie Haereroa's to ask for a bucket for our sheep's heads, livers, etc. As soon as Auntie saw me she started to cry and talking at the same time. According to her my son's death was due to a curse on Raniera Haereroa, my grandfather on my mother's side, but apart from that I never knew him. He also never brought up my mum so you can understand that I have very little time for this man. So to say that it was some curse connected to him caused my son to die the way he did was to say the least gut-wrenching. However, according to Auntie Sophie, all the first sons of the first of Raniera's progeny will die. My mother is Raniera's second child to his second wife. My mother's older sister and her daughter died within a week of each other. My mother's first son, Wi ote Rangi, died as a baby. Her brother Wi Pahau's son Tuta also died. Also, Mum's first to her second marriage, Eruera, my older brother, died as a young toddler. Raniera's eldest son, Teraumawhitu, died at about 25 years. His eldest daughter Kohimarama's son Dave is still lost at Horehore to this day. So whatever anyone believes, some of us have taken the precaution of having certain ministers remove the satanic curses from the face of the Earth, Amen. Although both my relations are long gone now I would like to mention their names, cousin Romeo Tuhura and Tewi ote Rangi Paki. My son's tangi lasted nine days. That's a long time making sure that everyone was fed. Kath and I cannot thank everyone enough: the Police, the speakers, everyone, the family, the workers at the back, everybody that gave koha, flowers, or helped in any way, for you all know who you are. Do you know that it is times like that when you know who your real friends are, may our father in heaven bless you all, especially all the Te Puia friends and neighbours.

*Just adding a little footnote to this excerpt. Paetene later elaborated on what he wrote about Kohimarama's son Dave still being lost up at Horehore. Paetene says that Dave, like Lance, was the victim of a homicide. Tohungas had told Paetene that Dave and another man had been up on Horehore Station. The other man had shot Dave and his horse and put Dave's body at the bottom of a post hole. The tohungas had told him where the post was but had advised him to leave the body where it lay. The man who had committed the crime had been made*

162

*aware that members of Dave's family knew what had happened. And the matter*
*had been left there.*

**Interview with Paetene Kupenga on Saturday, February 24, 2007, at his home in the Hiruharama Marae Papakainga (he had just turned seventy two weeks earlier):** Well it happened exactly like this. We stopped the car and I had three or four mates with me. We were just going along another half a mile down the road to a little farm I used to have then and kill some mutton. On arriving at Auntie Sophie's I realised that we didn't have a bucket to wash the heads and all that in. So I called into Auntie's. Otherwise I would never have heard this story. That's Auntie Sophie Haereroa. She married my mother's brother. But funnily enough, as soon as I walked in the road gate to her house, I was just coming through the gate and starting to ask for the bucket, and she come out of her door and she was already crying. No one told her Lance had died. No one told her anything. But she must have heard somehow and she was crying, crying and talking at the same time, talking about the curse on Raniera Haereroa.

Well, I was crying myself when she started to cry. But also listening to her, it took a while to sink in but it was devastating. You know, it's not the type of news you wanted to hear at that time.

But however being the woman she was I accepted her story. Well, I actually didn't accept it there and then. At that stage I just listened to her.

According to Auntie the curse came from land fights between my grandfather Raniera and a cousin of his. They were fighting over Puhunga Block. There's Puhunga there, from that bridge as you cross right back to the end of the river because on the other side is Matahiia Block, which, apparently, Jeremy Williams has just sold to an Englishwoman.

When they divided this land on Puhunga they cut all the manuka, the bush off it and farmed this side as Totaranui and then they done the same to the other side, which is Puhunga. They cleared it and farmed it also. They put the woolshed on this one, the Totaranui woolshed, and put a certain person as manager. All right? And when they cleared the other one and formed the Puhunga Blocks, they put a woolshed on it also. Now *this* manager wanted to be the manager of *that* also. That's when the fight arose. You understand? That's when him and Raniera had a fight. Raniera said, "Hang on. You got the other one. Leave this side to us." Cos Raniera owned most of the land anyway. But this fulla wanted the control of both. That's where the fight arose. And while they threw words at each other well, you know, dangerous. When Maori throw words at each other someone pays.

He knows he couldn't take Raniera out. But he can take the children out. Well, just as a guess, their powers must've been quite equal. He couldn't touch Raniera. But he could take his kids out. And that's how the curse came down.

If you want to go deeper into it you can check all the birth certificates and death notices.All the sons have been taken out. Eldest sons. Not second. Not third. Only the eldest sons. Well, it should have been the sons, but in some cases the daughters are older than the sons so it's their son that goes. It's always the senior son. If the first son is second, behind the daughter, it doesn't really take. It could take if the eldest daughter hasn't got a son.

About a year after we shifted to this house from Te Puia Springs in 1988 I brought Auntie here, right here. We discussed it all night.

Sophie had married Raniera's son. But he wasn't the son affected by the curse. See? There was one older than him who was taken out; Raniera's own son was taken out. Now that son who dies never had a son, but his older sister had a son, David Campbell, and he was taken out. See? Chris Campbell the Rasta came from the youngest brother, Willie. They're my cousins. Chris Campbell's grandmother and my mother are sisters. They're both daughters of that man we're talking about.

And another thing to disprove what Hone Kaa said in the trial of Joe Nepe. He said that in the original incident Kuku and Koro took Te Atau's life, that the younger brothers overthrew Te Atau, the chief, for playing around with their wives. So that's how he verifies this one. Now if the younger ones took out the chief, now it's the chief that's taking out the younger one. That's his version. Well I'd like to say he's all up the chute because Joseph Nepe is no senior to my son. If anything he's a junior junior in the genealogies. So it can't stack up, can it.

Now I'll tell you now, that man who set the ... onto my grandpa was Joseph's great grand uncle. You see now how the bearing comes. It's nothing to do with Te Atau whatsoever. Here it is here. And if Auntie didn't tell me and then come here later and explain it we'd be still in the dark about it.

*So you think that Joe and Lance were caught in the wairua of that curse that was placed on Raniera?*

Yes.

*They were taken over by the spirit of that curse?*

Oh yes. It's the wairua of that thing that overtook them ay. Cos they were friends, man.

*I remember Joe saying that he was hallucinating on Lance's face.*

Yeah.

*That he could see the devil and that he had to kill him.*

Well, like I said, about a week or so before Lance disappeared they were at home. Of course, they were mates. They'd sleep there, everything. Cos I mean, we're related.

The man who put the curse on Raniera is Joseph's great grandfather. Raniera is Lance's great grandfather. So they're the lines that this has come down through.

I didn't realise all this until we brought Auntie Sophie here all those years later.

I know Chris and John and these guys were trying to find out about the *thing*. They wanted to find out the prophesies of Pop Gage and maybe a few of them thought they were the chosen one. But I think most people have moved on from all that stuff now.

We've had people like Hohepa Delamere here. He died about a month ago. And he was well beyond any of that stuff. There are pure tohungas and there are make-up ones. Chris and them were trying to grasp the power of the *thing* really. They were trying to grasp the power of that kaupapa. But in my book there are only two powers: the Mighty Father and Satan. And Satan, if anything, his power is stronger. See, Chris and them, they were digging up graves. I know for a fact they used to go up on the graves and perform war dances to try and get the power and they were digging things out. Because we collected a lot of stuff and took it back to the cemeteries, took it back and buried them in the cemeteries. They had these relics wherever they went. A lot of it was just rubbish, I think. We managed to get some and we had to chopper them back up. There could be some still floating around, I don't know. But all the stuff we found, we took back... to Whakaahu.

See, there's a big graveyard on Whakaahu. In the old days it was a big pa, one of the strongholds of Te Aitanga a Mate; that's us. And Whakaahu was the sea stronghold. There was a bigger stronghold at the back of Hikurangi. See the Maori weren't as stubborn as most people think they were. At a certain time of the year when the pigeon was ready for harvesting, they lived back here. And ata certain time they knew the tides were good, they moved back out there near the sea.

Whakaahu's a gigantic graveyard. It's gigantic. That's how Nga Puhi from up in Northland thrashed us, over there. Thrashed us! Thrashed us properly. They reckon they threw five hundred in those holes where they found Lance. Aw yeah, well, they had the guns so they just slaughtered them. And I'll tell you it's eerie. Even in daylight, blue sky, beautiful, we choppered up, far out, it was blue, beautiful, not a murmur in the air... but when we got up there it was different. The chopper couldn't land.

*Do you think the Rastas spent too much time up there?*

Of course they did. It made them wairangi... mad. But, deeper than that, some of our leaders were giving these Rastas the wrong information. They were feeding them up with wrong information.

*About what?*

About everything. About the land. It was mostly about how the hell the white man got the land here, there. I don't begrudge their fight. What I do disagree with is the way they went about it. You can still fight them the proper way. Fight them in the courts, not all this put guns on people.

*What's your take on all this talk about the Williams having one hundred-year leases that had expired? Was there anything in that?*

I don't think so. See, I'm the one that's claiming for all these lands back right now. See how many books are there that I've been reading. But whatever happens this is the last opportunity that we'll ever have of trying to get some of this land back. Well, to be honest I can't see any Government or any Pakeha giving his land back but we know for a fact that we owned it at one time. I can show you all this. We owned it at one time. All of it. Jeremy Williams' old Matahiia Station is only a speck. It goes on and on and on. It's about a million acres. Matahiia's only a small block. This land was all owned by Te Aowera, Te Aitanga a Mate. I can show you the map.

(The tape's muffled for a few minutes, so I have no idea what we were talking about here.)

Look it doesn't matter how you write it. Your version will always be the Pakeha version, someone outside looking in. There's a difference, a lot of difference.

(The tape gets muffled again, but I'm pretty sure I'm mentioning that Colin Williams told me how Samuel Williams had taken over the lease of a huge block of land near Ruatoria from Sir George Whitmore. I'm asking Paetene how Whitmore got hold of it. Whitmore, with Ropata Wahawaha from Te Aowera and many of his warriors, had chased Te Kooti all over the place.)

I personally believe that Whitmore used these people. I think he just used his position and his power over his Maori soldiers, gained their confidence so he could get the land, which is what happened with just about all of them, before they knew what had hit them.

The Pakehas were taking land off people because they were involved with Te Kooti. It's just a pretty good excuse really. But why did they take land off soldiers that were helping them? See, they found ways around, whichever way that worked. There's many, many ways. They'd get them into debt. They'd get all Te Aowera here to go into Gisborne for the courts for certain blocks here and then when they get there, "Aw it's gonna be on February the 24$^{th}$." Right? Or whatever the date is today, the 27$^{th}$. And when they get there with their families, nowhere to board because they haven't got that much money. They just camp at the seaside there. And they tell them, "Aw, no, no, sorry, it's next month." Yeah. So what happens? Those poor families, that hapu, there's about a hundred of them staying there with their kids. So they gotta stay down there for that month. Then they say, "Sorry, it's another month." Well, by then they're heavy in debt to the shops. So it's all designed for them to get rid of their land. And it's exactly what's happening now.

See, I've been working on this for ten years. I put this claim in because of what happened to my parents and my mother especially. I saw her live with nothing all her life. I never saw her with a new dress. I told her, "Mum, sell your shares," in so-and-so block, which was being farmed by her nephew with a majority share there belonging to her sister.

She said, "No, I can't do that."

I said, "Sell it, Mum. We'll go and buy you a new dress. At least you'll have got yourself a new dress."

She said, "No, I can't do that. I've got to save the land for you people."

I said, "No, don't save nothing for us. It's not worth it. We'll only finish squabbling over your three or five acres. Sell it and buy yourself a dress."

That was my strong thing to my mother, all her life. And when I think of all these lands that were taken away and all the people that live richly in mansions and everything, it breaks me because I know how we lived and how my mother lived to bring us up. You can't get any poorer. Very few people in New Zealand lived a poorer life than we did. And when I know of all the lands that my grandfathers owned all being farmed by different Pakeha, you look for some sort of justice. That's why I really put the claims forward, not because I've got any hatred for anybody.

**Interview with Paetene Kupenga over the phone on Tuesday, March 13, 2007:** The Tohungas have cleaned up Whakaahu now. They can get rid of a curse on a certain place, ay. And that's what they done. But that's nothing to do with Lance. If you're going on that story, that Lance was killed because of...

*Te Atau and all that...*

... Because of taina-ship and all that, which I can prove to you is a lie, if you're saying that Lance was killed because he was junior on the genealogy to Joseph, well that's what the tohungas have done. They've cleaned that mountain so there's no more rubbish like that can happen up there again. So for the people who believe in that rubbish well they've got nothing to worry about. But that whole claim is just pie in the sky. I'd like to face John Kaa head-on one day on our maraes and get him to explain it to me because his rubbish won the case for Joe, this Lance being a taina to Joe. See, what happened up there two hundred years ago was the juniors getting rid of the senior. Now they're saying that the senior got rid of the junior. But Lance is not a junior.

*Is Lance a direct descendant of Te Atau?*

Yes, also, whichever way, whichever way. He's also a descendant of the junior ones, of Koro and Kuku. But as far as Lance being a Junior to Joe, he can't be. So you carry on with your story. If you believe that well that's fine.

*Well, it's not a matter of what I believe, Paetene. It's a matter of presenting what came out in court and then refuting it with your stuff.*

Aw no, you don't have to refute it. Carry on with that stuff there. They believe in it. It doesn't really matter. I told you the real story.

*That's right.*

It doesn't matter. It doesn't really matter if that's the one they want to believe.

*Well, the thing is I haven't added your stuff yet obviously because...*

Don't. Never mind. Let them carry on believing that, I would think, Angus.

*Well, Pàetene, the thing is what I want to do, the aim is to tell the story as close to the truth as possible.*

But no one's going to listen to that, ay. They believe in that Te Atau stuff and of Joe being the senior. But I told you, the whole thing don't stack. And the people that know, the people that do know the whakapapa, know it doesn't stack. If you want to just ring up Api Mahuika (the Ngati Porou runanga boss) and he'll tell you. But this is something we've always kept inside and we'll wait for the right opportunity to talk to this great John Kaa.

*Well, to me it's a matter of historical record that that is the defence that was used to get Joe off on insanity. So that's fact. Everyone knows that. What's new is what we've talked about.*

Yeah, but you see, I didn't want to get involved right from the word go. Tell me, who would want to be involved once their son's been beheaded?

*Of course. No one.*

You tell me. No one. No one would. But this is years later. Everything is cooled down and you can see black is black and white is white. I didn't know why it had happened to Lance until Auntie Sophie told me it was to do with an argument between my grandfather and Joseph's grandfather years ago and the facts are facts. And they've still got that land that they shouldn't have.

*Yeah, yeah.*

168

That to me was more realistic than the pie in the sky Te Atau two hundred years ago.

*So the tohungas went up to Whakaahu did they?*

Yes.

*And is the term that they make it noa? Is that the term?*

Yes. I was one of the ones that went up. So basically it shouldn't happen again, ever.

*And is it a process of karakia and sprinkling water and...*

Yes, yes.

*And basically just cleansing the area.*

Yes. And taking back the rubbish they had taken from the graveyards, the bits we could get.

*Aw yes.*

We had to put them back in the things up there.

*What do they call it?*

The urupai or the graveyard.

*So that day you were telling me you went up in the chopper, that was the day the service was held on the hillside. Would you call it blessing it?*

Yes, blessing it.

*And does that include the holes as well?*

Yes. Especially those holes.

*Well, look, I would like to use this stuff we've talked about because I think it's actually the most important part of that whole episode because it's the resolving of it and it's the making sense of it, I suppose.*

(Paetene and I have a long discussion about this, most of which is quite muffled on the tape.)

*Could you tell me how you managed to get the curse off – the one from Raniera down – just so that we can resolve it in the story?*

I don't want to mention people's names. They wouldn't want their names mentioned?

*Okay, that's cool. Can you do it without mentioning their names?*

Yes I can do. I came to Auckland. Then my sister and I went to Coromandel to see this...

*Tohunga?*

...To see this chief, yeah. Not only to lift our curse, but they got a curse on them also.

*Yeah, yeah.*

You see, it's quite deep you know, Angus. If you wanted to really get into the depth of it we'd have to spend a night talking about it. You see, because what happened to Lance is actually quite minor compared to other curses that are happening around here. Now for instance, I don't want to mention names, but three sons had died – smack! - in their teenage years – bang! – well, they blame the sun. They were just coming into this bridge and they blame the sun in their eyes. Anyway, the three sons died. Now another brother of theirs was burnt in the fire, the house burnt down. Now can you start to understand how deep these curses are?

They're our cousins. They've got their own curse that they're dealing with. And it's the same thing again. It's over land.

But that's only two. And I can carry on. A girl cousin got murdered, and so on and so forth.

But I think Lance's death brought all this to a head. And our other cousins and us decided to talk about it and do something about it.

See, some of these things, we become Pakeha-fied and call it a coincidence. But when you get three sons dying in one smack, it's starting to get serious now isn't it? Okay, it can't be coincidences any more. The other brother got burnt. These are the things, some of us will carry it on forever and some of us go and work in Australia, England maybe. But these things don't leave us... until we do something about it. Well, we've done it.

We went up to Auckland, as I said, grabbed someone to help us because my sister knew where to go and then we met up with this other family, which are our own cousins...

*The family who the curse originated from?*

Yeah. And then we went to Coromandel and sorted it all out there. And it must be powerful because...

*So far it's holding.*

Nothing has happened since as far as I understand. That would have been at least fifteen years ago. Lance died in '85 so it would have been in the early nineties.

*So when you go and do something like this what is the process? Do the families pray together or do they have to go to the place where it happened?*

All that. All that, if you can, of course, go to the place where it happened and the tohunga does the karakia over the place.

*And is that what happened with this one?*

Yes.

*So now the families are a lot...*

Oh a lot freer in heart, you know. They can have a good sleep and not worry too much. When these things happen over the years, those of us who knew, just look at each other, you see?

*Yeah.*

You know?

*Yes, yes.*

Not everyone in the family are aware of these things. A lot of them are highly educated. A lot of them are lawyers. A lot of them are well past this stage of curses. I mean, they'll look at that and think you're a fool. But when things happen...

*Yeah that's right...*

You know that something else is happening.

*Yeah, something a bit bigger than what we're used to, sort-a thing.*

Well, that's all I can say to you. I think you know the procedure, as most people do now. You see them do it when someone dies on the roads and so on, someone will go and put a blessing over where he died.

It's almost the same thing only it's a bit deeper because we've got to understand where the curses came from and try and get rid of that.

**Conversation with Joe Nepe in 2000:** *Have you made contact with the Kupengas?*

Yeah. No, we've made contact with that whanau. They're up here (in Auckland). Their family's up here at the moment. They come around here now and then.

*Aw, is that right? And it's all okay and that?*

Yeah. Na, it's sweet.

*What about old Paetene, is he still down there is he, the dad?*

Yeah, he's still in Rua, in Jeru (Hiruharama). Yeah. Na, him and I get on. We drink at the pub. We drink at the pub.

*I mean, have you made your peace with the Kupengas?*

Yeah. Mmm.

*Yeah, yeah, so you've explained to them where you're coming from and they're okay with that?*

They're okay with it.

*Yeah. Aw good.*

As long as you talk to them, ay.

*Well, you gotta talk, ay.*

You gotta talk.

*Yeah, well that's one thing that I was worried about, that you hadn't sort of had any contact with the Kupengas.*

Na, I've had a lot of contact with them actually, especially over the past three years. My mum's a teacher – she's passed away now – but when she was teaching the Kupengas were working with her. We used to have a lot of contact with them, their family up this way anyway, all his cousins and cuzzy-bros and sister-bros, all of them.

# PART 1 RASTA ROOTS

# CHAPTER 1

**THE EARLY DAYS**

**Isaac "Ike" Campbell, brother of Ruatoria Rastafarian leader Chris Campbell:** I knew that they were going to kill Chris, sooner or later. I always knew that. When things started to get rough, yeah, everyone knew Chris was gonna get killed.

My parents actually knew Chris was gonna die right from the time he was a baby. My old lady's a tohunga. It's a Maori thing. She's clairvoyant. They knew all right. That's how they could handle it. She already knew years ago. She came from a line of tohungas. She has dreams about all us kids.

Even Chris told me a couple of times, "They're gonna kill me." And they did.

**Constable Chris Bunyan:** I was in the same class as Chris Campbell in form one and two at Ilminster Intermediate in Kaiti here in Gisborne. I was also the policeman who comforted Chris as he lay in the driveway after Luke Donnelly shot him. As you know, he died later that night. So I had a long association with Chris.

In those early school days everybody just got on. We had a really good class and everyone was considered cobbers within the class. Although you may have had friends from your primary school days in the other classes, most of your friends were in your own class. Chris was just one of the boys. I knew he had a bit of a fiery temper. That was just his nature.

He wasn't a guy who caused problems in the playground. He was smaller than a lot of the other guys then. But he'd always wanna stand up for himself. He didn't take any nonsense.

He was quite an accomplished boxer and on more than one occasion he brought gloves along and wanted to fight guys. If there was ever a dispute about something, instead of having a bit of a wrestle and a tussle out on the playground, he brought the gloves along because he felt he had an advantage with the gloves on. It was always, "Come into the ring. We'll sort it out in the ring."

But he was quite chirpy, quite sharp-witted. And when we moved on to high school he was in my class in the third form at Gisborne Boys High and right through we crossed over in different classes.

**Gordon Sutton (childhood friend of Chris):** I remember one incident at Te Poho o Rawiri Marae in Cambridge Terrace, just down at the bottom of Kaiti Hill. All the kids had shanghais (slingshots) in those days, big shanghais that you could fire stones with. So we had a war between the Cambridge Terrace kids and these kids from out of the district who were visiting the marae.

It *was* a battle, mate. It was full on. You're talking about twenty to thirty young guys fighting us and there was only about ten of us. And things weren't going very well for us. They had driven us back to our houses. All we had was our hedges as the last bit of cover. We were buggered. We had to go and get Chris to come over and give us a hand and give us some control. And even though we were outnumbered, mate, he just went straight over the hedge and hit them up front, straight into them. He went up to their main man and bang, bang. There were shanghais firing ammo in all directions and he just went straight up to the main bunch of guys and just BOOM. He was only about twelve or thirteen but he was bigger than the other guys. And it was all over. *That* was all taken care of.

**Barney Campbell, Chris's brother and a former Ruatoria policeman:** Chris wasn't a troubled kid. I think he might-a been the old man's favourite, just quietly. That's just the way it was. I don't know if there was any special reason, really. He was quite an ordinary kid. You really had no idea that in years to come it would end up the way it did where he was concerned.

He was more or less just starting high school when I left. We both went to Gisborne Boys High. The whole family was living in town at that stage. The old man only went home after his brother died, back to their family land. Otherwise we'd left the coast at an early age. We were basically brought up in Gisborne.

We left Ruatoria, moved to Whangara, then to Gisborne, back to Whangara and back to Gisborne again.

Chris was into rugby, and boxing with Mal Watts. But I really had no idea that old Chris was heading down the opposite road to me.

**Gordon Sutton:** I met Chris when we were at Kaiti Primary School in Gisborne. His parents were living a couple of houses from us in Cambridge Terrace. His old man was a shearing contractor. And we were just little kids hanging out together.

Chris was one of those guys that always wanted to be the leader. He'd tell us where to go and what we'd be doing each day. You know, "What's goin' on here, ay. No, no. We'll change that around," – to suit him. We didn't say we wanted him to lead us, because we'd just as likely turn around and tell him to follow us, but at the end of the day he'd take charge. He was a bloody neat guy.

Like we'd go up the back of Kaiti Hill to check out all these horses. They'd be horses that belonged to other people. And there was Chris jumping on the horses and riding around and leading the way. We'd all just be sitting back and watching how he did it.

Then it was the school days and Chris was right into boxing. There was a bunch of them that used to train under Mal Watts. They used to win championships. And Chris was right up there. He was a good stylish boxer. He could-a went a long way.

I used to go along to the boxing. Mum wouldn't let me join because she thought it was too violent. But I used to go along and watch them train and spar at the gym. And I'd go along and watch them at the Poverty Bay championships and tournaments like that. And they were good. Chris had that Muhammad Ali sort of style. Ali was his boxing hero at the time. And that's the sort of guy Chris was. He was the sort of guy who you'd go into his room and there he is with the comb in front of the mirror, streaking his hair down, like this.

I'd say, "Aw, come on, Chris."

He was a real scrapper at school. If there was a fight Chris would be there. And he was a bit of a dominator here and there. He was pretty good with his dukes. He wasn't the type of guy who would walk up to someone and start a fight. But if it was happening he had to be there.

As far as sports outside of rugby, pretty average, I thought. He always thought he was better than he actually was. But when it came to boxing, he shone.

174

**Constable Chris Bunyan:** In the third form I noticed some of the characters Chris was mixing with were a bit of a worry.

Whenever there were unannounced staff meetings and there was spare time waiting outside classrooms, I always remember Chris and another guy knew how to get into that class. They could get through the locks. It was a bit of an exhibition by Chris to say, "Hey, look, we can do this." Now they weren't stealing anything at school that I'm aware of. But it was just, "Woah, these guys can get through that door." I hadn't noticed anything like that at intermediate.

And then basically, again, you go to a new school, you make new friendships and he sort of drifted away. And it wasn't until about the fifth form I noticed that Chris was getting into a bit of trouble along with a couple of the characters he was hanging with.

**Gordon Sutton (childhood friend of Chris Campbell):** Chris would always be arguing with the teacher at school and trying to put his point across. And he was right as far as he was concerned. And he wasn't going to take no for an answer. And then he'd start explaining his position on the subject to you, and I'd just be wondering where the hell he got all this knowledge. And then at the end of the day his position would start making sense. "Aw yeah. Okay, Chris."And then he would just pull out his comb and swish his hair back.

**Detective Sergeant Laurie Naden (retired):** I got on well with Chris. And I would have to say that if he'd kidnapped anyone else there was probably a strong possibility they would have died. I'd known Chris since he was in secondary school. I remember in about 1972 they were running dances at the Te Poho o Rawiri marae for secondary school kids. And there was quite a major stoush broke out there on this particular night. The district commander at the time said, "Well bugger it. We're not gonna let these kids stuff it up," cos it was actually giving the majority of kids somewhere to go.

So he called a meeting and they had the principals from Campion College and Gisborne Boys High and Lytton and Chris came in as a mediator. And that's where I met Chris. He was just a student, but competent, sensible type attitude. So I'd known Chris since that stage, since the early '70s.

He was very much a leader when he was at school. He was very, very eloquent, but not pushy. He didn't set himself up as the boss. But people did look to him for advice and assistance. And of course during the arsons I'd spent time with him at various stations.

So I think if he'd kidnapped anyone else it might have been a bit different.

**Sergeant John Robinson (retired):** I knew all the Campbells through Barney, who was a cop. Ike and Joe and Chris: they were all mates of mine. I got on well with them. Ike and Joe are good guys and so was Chris. He was a likeable rogue. But like so many others he became obsessed with the land.

He first came to notice in Gisborne in the early '70s when they had a riot at the Te Poho o Rawiri Marae.

The police and the local Maori had put on a blue light dance for all the kids. Of course, Chris Campbell and all his mates turned up and they wanted to bring alcohol and drugs in and they weren't allowed so they rioted. They started fighting with everyone there and throwing bottles and stuff. And he was the ringleader in that incident. He was only sixteen then.

Anyway he moved up the coast and the next time he came to notice was when a group of Ruatoria youths were at a party in Waipiro Bay. They had a loose affiliation to the Black Power gang back then without actually being Black Power. They ended up having a drunken fight among themselves and Rai Haua got stabbed. Rai's brother Cody Haua went to trial for the killing, but he was acquitted.

**Gordon Sutton:** Deep down Chris was a bloody lovable guy, a kind-hearted guy. We used to hang out together all the time. Him and me and Wade Lloyd and Heta Matete all hung out together for years.

Then all of a sudden his family moved. I was about fifteen when he took off up the coast. He was at Boys' High for a while and then he was gone.

They went back to the homestead up at Makarika, near Ruatoria. And I just lost contact with him basically.

**Detective Sergeant Laurie Naden (retired):** He was an interesting bugger, Chris. He passed School C at Gisborne Boys High. But he was never given School C because he hadn't done the required half days. And with that he just dumped the Pakeha system.

He moved up the coast, and started working on the family farm.

**John Gillies, author's brother:** I was covering a Labour Party regional conference at the marae at Waiomatatini near Ruatoria for the Gisborne Herald. It was the early '80s, before David Lange came to power. But Lange was there and was talking about how Labour would give Maori a forum for their treaty grievances so they could be tested by law.

I had a pad and a pen and was obviously a reporter. So Chris Campbell and a few of his mates came and started talking to me. This was before all the fires had started.

The two things that struck me about his physical appearance were that he had long dreadlocks and seemed to have hardly any teeth.

He gave me a lecture. Ronald Reagan, because each of his three names had six letters, had the mark of the beast. And the Bible said the great conflict was going to come in the east and there was no more eastern place than the East Coast of New Zealand.

His mates obviously looked to him as a spokesman and gave him their support.

I can't remember taking any notes and I never intended to write anything up on the conversation. But I think he talked to me because he guessed I was a reporter.

Part of me wrote him off as a bit of a rambler. But there was something quite different about him, too. The overall feeling I had when listening to him and being around him was one of intense uneasiness. He made me very uneasy.

**Ike Campbell, Chris's brother:** When we left Gisborne as boys to come back to Ruatoria, I don't know about Chris, but I'd only just learnt I was a Maori. You know how I learnt I was a Maori? One day, I heard the schoolteacher say, "You black bastard," and I looked around and I thought, "Shit, I *am* the only one he could be talking to." I would-a been about fifteen or a bit younger when I found out because we weren't taught about being Maori. The only Maori we knew was when our parents wanted to say something but didn't want us kids to understand. So they'd speak in that Maori, that old Maori. I don't know why we weren't taught. But I used to listen to them and I started to learn. But when I started to learn today's Maori I got confused and I couldn't understand it because today's Maori is very different from the old Maori.

## THE ROMAN CATHOLIC BEHIND THE RASTA MOVEMENT

*Ike Campbell isn't the only person who's ever been shocked to discover he's considered different and treated differently because of his race. The same thing happened to the great black activist and leader Marcus Garvey. According to his* reminiscences, *The Philosophy and Opinions of Marcus Garvey*, he discovered only in his fourteenth year that there was a difference between the races.

Marcus Garvey, the youngest of eleven children, was born into a poor family in St. Anne's Bay, Jamaica, in 1887.

While Rastafarianism started in Jamaica, Garvey was not a Rastafarian. He came before them. He founded the largest Pan African organisation in history, the Universal Negro Improvement Association, in Harlem, New York, in 1917. The first Rastas didn't appear in Jamaica until 1930 during the crowning of Ras Tafari as emperor of Ethiopia, after which Ras Tafari took the name Haile Selassie.

The Rastas believed the crowning of Haile Selassie had been prophesied on numerous occasions in the Bible. And they considered this proof that Ras Tafari was the Second Coming of Jesus Christ.

But it wasn't just from the Bible that the Rastas took their prophecies. Garvey himself had said: "Look to Africa, when a Black king shall be crowned, for the day of deliverance is near." Garvey was a strong influence on the Rastafarians, particularly his belief that people of African descent should return to Ethiopia. (Garvey believed the whole continent of Africa had been Ethiopia before whites cut it up into pieces to share among themselves).

But Garvey never accepted that Haile Selassie was the Second Coming of Christ. In fact, in E. D. Cronon's biography on Garvey, *Black Moses*, Garvey describes Haile Selassie as a great coward and as ruler of a land "where black men are chained and flogged". Yet, if there had been no Marcus Garvey, there may well have been no Rastafarians.

Another paradox: Rastafarians consider the Western culture of the white races to be corrupt and oppressive, they call it Babylon and consider it a conspiracy against black people led by the Pope; Marcus Garvey, who, more than anyone, is the historical inspiration of the Rastas, was a Roman Catholic.

Both Garvey and the Rastas continuously refer to scriptures to support their beliefs, but the Rasta emphasis is on Haile Selassie being the Second Coming of Christ, while Garvey's work remained within the traditional Christian context.

Garvey did emphasise a black God. And, according to Garvey, blacks were the chosen people, and Africa the chosen land. The Rastas adopted these beliefs. They believe that every Rastafarian is an Israelite, a descendant from the lost tribes of Israel. Reading the first chapter of the Song of Songs in the Bible's Old Testament, they conclude that Solomon was black and so must Jesse and David have been before him. "I am as dark – but lovely, O daughters of Jerusalem – as the tents of Kedar, as the curtains of Salma. Do not stare at me because I am swarthy, because the sun has burned me." Other texts are also cited to prove that the chosen people from the Bible were dark-skinned.

The flag of Garvey's UNIA was red, black and green. Red was the spilled blood of his people, black the colour of their skin, and green the colour of nature. The Rastafarian flag is the same, but with the black replaced by a band of gold, which Garvey received in a vision. The gold symbolises "rods of deliverance" (prayer sticks). These colours indicate the Rastas are true Ethiopians.

And like the Rastafarians, Garvey had a millennial vision. He foresaw an apocalyptic struggle: "I see the angel of God taking up the standard of the Red, the Black and the Green and saying, 'Men of Negro race, men of Ethiopia, follow me'."

Garvey said: "No one knows when the hour of Africa's redemption cometh. It is in the wind. It is coming. One day, like a storm, it will be here."

The Jamaican Rastas took Garvey's millennial concept a step further. They wanted nothing less than transformation of the world's social order, after which the Rastaman would live in peace in Africa. The transformation would come about through the judgment, the battle of Armageddon. The Rastas believe the time of judgment is at hand. It will be immediate and universal but it will happen only when God is ready. Every person will be judged and those who have not led a just life will be destroyed like Sodom and Gomorrah in the Bible. And, as Joseph Owens says in his book Dread: "The judgment will be a frightful holocaust... The Rastas often use sets of natural symbols to represent the judgment: blood and fire, lightning, earthquake, and thunder. Judgment is indeed understood to be a supremely natural event: it is the vengeance which the natural universe must take on those who have betrayed the laws of life. If the blood of innocents has flowed in the past, then natural judgment will require the blood of their oppressors."

In the early 1920s, Marcus Garvey bought steamboats and organised his Black Star Line to take blacks back to Africa. But in 1927 he was jailed and deported from the United States to Jamaica. He died in 1940 without his dreams being realised. But he was the first to establish a relationship between the West Indies, North and South America and Africa, and he challenged the black man to return to his homeland.

**Prof. G C Oosthuizen, University of Zululand, thesis on Rastafarianism, 1989:** Why did the Rastafarian movement originate in Jamaica? For an answer, we must look at the history of Jamaica, which was conquered by England in 1655 and was associated with the slave trade and other atrocities. Runaway slaves called "Maroons", considered the white man per se as an evil being, whom they hated more than the regime he supported. For more than eighty years after Britain took over Jamaica the Maroons warded off military efforts to re-enslave them. They believed the secret powers they had at their disposal, because of close contact with their ancestors, could not be overcome by the whites...

..."After the emancipation of the slaves in 1833 many joined the mission societies. However, when their material position did not improve, they founded or joined movements, which had Afro-religious elements in their approach. Mayalism, which included aspects of the black Jamaican religions in its belief system, experienced a revival. Its followers maintained that the world would come to an end and that Christ was coming, sent by Jah. Jah was their word for God – a word used later by the Rastafarians. The so-called "mial people" (from a syncretistic belief system called Obeah-myal) were the first to envisage a transformed social cosmos." (Cashmore E, 1979. Rastaman: The Rastafarian Movement in England.)

**Joseph Owens, from his book Dread (written about Rastafarianism in Jamaica):** The colonisation process was initiated by the missionaries, who would come preaching peace, but who would soon be followed by the predatory settlers, traders and conquistadors. The missionaries did a disservice to the native community not only in leaving them unsuspecting of the savagery of the white advance, but also in grafting on to them a religion where all virture is coloured white and all vice black. "They show you a white Christ, blond hair and blue eyes and all that stuff. The only thing I see black most times in those biblical picture is a black devil." (Jimmy)...


# CHAPTER 2

### THE LOST TRIBE


**Former Detective Sergeant Laurie Naden:** They were completely out of it. They had their own jargon. It was quite clever actually. A "steedless chariot" was a car of course. Anyone authority - it didn't matter whether he was the head of the Post Office or the social welfare - he was a baldhead. You didn't have to *have* a bald head to be one.

And they had terms for the police like whoever was running the police operation was a baldhead in the lead and things like that. So they became a strange little group of people.

**Beau Tuhura, one of the original Ruatoria Rastafarians:** We have to consider our dreams as a way of God revealing things. And I had a dream in which the constellations appeared like a gathering of the star signs for the twelve tribes of Israel. I could see the constellations for *all* the tribes, which is interesting, because, to date, the tribe of Dan is still missing. They're known as the lost tribe of Israel. But the placement of the constellation signified where the lost tribe was dwelling.

Of the star signs, The Scorpion best represents the house of Dan because it's got a tail on it. If you look out from here, it's sitting over the maunga, the mountain, right now.

Now some time later, in about 1979, I was at a kotahitanga hui, a tribal unity meeting, in Maungatapu, near Tauranga. Kotahitanga basically advocates that unless we unite then we can't accomplish our self-determination. Our efforts will be fragmented and nothing will be achieved.

Anyway I was standing outside one night at this hui and I saw the constellation of Dan up in the sky. And it was so clear that night that it was almost like the only constellation there. It was sitting right on top of the evening star.

I was with a kaumatua from another tribe. I showed him Dan sitting on top of the evening star. And he wept. He said he'd been waiting for this combination in the sky. It seemed like the fulfillment of a lifetime for him. He said that all his life he'd heard about this. He said he'd always looked for it but had never seen it. But he'd been told that there would come a time when someone would reveal it to him. And he felt that had now come to pass.

I noticed that the rest of the time he was there he was in prayer and weeping. Then that was the last I ever saw of him.

Now in Maoridom there's been a lot of prophecy that has been fulfilled in our time. But there's also been a lot that has been discarded in favour of the prophecies of Jesus Christ. And there were a lot of prophecies that were handed to *different* tribes, concerning the time, as it got closer, to those days when the Son of Man would arise from the East.

We learnt about these prophecies that have been handed on to *other* tribes through our involvement in the kotahitanga movement of tribal unity. As the tribes came together so did the old prophecies that had passed between tribes.

And this kaumatua told me one of them. It was a prophecy that he was to pass on to the person who revealed to him that combination in the stars.

The prophecy came in the form of a vision. It was of a dog-haired or dreadlocked man walking down the main road of a town with the hills on either side on fire.

I didn't know what it meant. I couldn't foresee that churches were going to be burning and houses were going to be burning. It wasn't the method that I'd looked at to address land issues.

**Tape recorded note to myself after Cody Haua took me to visit John Heeney:** The Rastas do believe that the Rastaman is the lost tribe of Israel, the tribe of Dan. According to John Heeney, the lost tribe of Dan were known as having two blessings. They were a sea-faring tribe of great warriors and they were skilful carvers, the same as the Maori.

*I couldn't find these blessings in the Bible. So I went on the internet and Googled "tribe of Dan blessings in the Bible skilful carvers". I came across "The Tribe of Dan, excerpted from The Secret History of the World, by Laura Knight-Jadczyk". And here is perhaps some good news for the Rastas. She confirms the blessing about the tribe of Dan being skilful carvers. She says they were also sea-faring people (like the Maori) and also that Samson was from the tribe of Dan (I mention this because I remember Chris Campbell saying during his trial for kidnapping a police officer that he felt like Samson). Anyway, she also argues that the tribe of Dan became the tribe of Judah. Knight-Jadczyk says, "If the tribe of Judah is really the tribe of Dan, then that means that the House of David is the tribe of Dan. And following the clues, we discover that this lineage belonged to Ishmael and Esau, not to Isaac and Jacob." Interesting place, the internet. Another reason I mention all this is because Jesus and Haile Sellasie are both said to be direct descendants of King David.*

**Megan Goldin, Reuters, August 21, 2000:** 2,700 years after the 10 tribes of Israel were taken into exile and vanished, the fate of the lost tribes remains one of history's most intriguing mysteries.

In 722 BC Assyrian warriors captured the northern Kingdom of Israel which was home to 10 of the 12 tribes of Israel and took the inhabitants into captivity.

The Bible's Book of Kings records they were exiled "in Halah and in Habor by the river Gozan and in the cities of the Medes." The other two tribes, Judah and Benjamin, which lived in the southern Israelite Kingdom of Judah, were forced into exile by the Romans centuries later in AD 70. Unlike their northern brothers who were assimilated, these tribes maintained their identity and are the ancestors of modern Jews.

Rabbi Eliyahu Avichail has been hunting for the lost tribes for decades. He has undertaken dangerous journeys to Myanmar (formerly Burma) and other war-torn parts of Asia to pursue the descendants of a people who disappeared almost 3,000 years ago. "I am looking for Jewish customs and Jewish signs among people who are not Jewish. That's what it says in the Bible," Avichail said.

The Pathans of Afghanistan and Pakistan head the list of the peoples Avichail believes are lost tribes.

Avichail says the Pathans' ancient name is "Bnei Yisrael" or the sons of Israel and many of the clans are named after the 10 lost Israelite tribes like Ruben, Asher, Naftali and Ephraim.

But even more convincing are Pathan customs which mirror ancient Jewish rituals still practiced today.

Like Jews, Avichail says, the Pathans marry under a wedding canopy, light candles on the eve of the Sabbath and wear prayer shawls similar to those used by religious Jews. He says they even circumcise their eight-day-old sons as Jews do.

Avichail believes that after the Assyrian conquests, the tribes scattered along the Silk Road to Kashmir, China, Burma and Thailand. He suspects they may have gone as far as Japan.

"We had in the Bible a very clear tradition that the 10 tribes were exiled to the east of Israel and the prophet Isaiah in the Bible told us they will come back from this direction," Avichail said.

Not content to just study Isaiah's prophesies, Avichail is trying to fulfil them by bringing people he believes to be from the lost tribes back to Judaism and the Holy Land.

One of Avichail's biggest success stories is the Shinlung people from the Myanmar-Indian border who believe they are the Israelite tribe of Menashe. He has already helped around 500 of them move to Israel and convert to Judaism.

According to Shinlung legends they are one of the 10 tribes of Israel that was exiled in China and later expelled to where they live today. They practice sacrifices similar to those in the Bible and celebrate holidays reminiscent of ancient Jewish harvest festivals.

So strongly do they believe they are Jews that some members of "the tribe of Menashe", as they call themselves, have begun to practise Orthodox Judaism and teach their children Hebrew.

Esther Thangjom moved to Israel and converted to Judaism to fulfil her belief the tribes must return to the Holy Land.

Thangjom, who proudly wears a Star of David around her neck, has no doubt that she is descended from the tribe of Menashe.

"As a child every time something was mentioned about Israel my heart would move," she said.


## THE BAD SEEDS


**Laurie Naden:** Chris underwent a real dramatic change in his personality. That happened after he dropped out of the education system and went to Ruatoria. That really blew him out of the water. And I think he said, "Fuck ya. I don't want any more to do with you. I'm out of here."

But then I didn't see Chris for a long time. And when I did next run across him he was into dope in a huge way. And it was hot and cold. If he was straight: good as gold. If he wasn't, he was always a bit cautious. But, yeah, it was when he got into dope that I noticed the big change in him. Well, he may have been into dope when I first met him. I don't know. But there was a huge difference when I met him again later when he was up the coast.


**Conversation with Joe Nepe in November 2000:** *There was a lot of dope around in the old days. But you guys never made a lot of money out of it, ay?*
Just smoking it.
*Was there a bit sold here and there?*
Nothing big.
*Was there a tie-up with you guys and the Black Power back then?*
Black Power and Mongrel Mob and Headhunters.
*Aw is that right? With the Rastas?*
Mmm.
*In what way?*
They used to come and buy herb off us.
*Aw yeah okay.*

Bulk that is.

*Yeah. And then they'd just take it back to Auckland or Wellington or wherever.*

That's right.

*So was there much money around in those days?*

Na, not really.

*What, were they ripping you off?*

Na, they gave us a good bargain. They'd buy a pound for three grand.

*Aw yeah.*

But in those days that was big money. A pound now, you can get a pound for seven grand now. So you can see how big it's gone up, ay?

*Yeah, shit yeah. And that would be really good quality?*

Yeah. That would be our top stuff.

*But three grand, what was the money being spent on? Legal fees and stuff?*

Cars.

*Aw, cars?*

Cars, saddles, horses, horse back riding materials, bridles, food to keep us going.

*So you were never going to get rich off it?*

Na. No way. No way you get rich off that stuff.

**Sergeant Alex Hope, police report, "History of Recent Problems in Ruatoria" (Alex has since retired from the police force and is now a lawyer working in Hamilton):** The present problems in Ruatoria began in the 1970s with the emergence of the Black Power gang in the area. A Black Power convention was held at the Hiruharama Marae in the late 1970s. It was organised by some local people who supported the Black Power.

Members of the Hikurangi South Maori and Hiruharama Marae committees opposed the convention. One person and his supporters locked the marae gates. But this person's mother and aunts opposed him. A large police operation was mounted to prevent trouble. The meeting caused major ructions within the community.

The Black Power movement in Ruatoria collapsed after a number of incidents, which resulted in the jailing of Chris Campbell and Michael Heeney, who were part of the leadership of the group.

The appearance of Rastafarianism occurred at approximately the same time that Campbell was released from jail.

**Detective Sergeant Laurie Naden (retired):** Chris was a very, very intelligent, very eloquent sort of a person. Probably if he was still alive and if he hadn't stuffed his brain with dope he could-a become quite a top-class leader in Maoridom.

At some stage Chris started gathering other people around him and the Black Power group evolved from there.

They held this national meeting, which was a flop. A woman, Sue Nikora, who became a little notorious as life went on up there, was one of the main people who tried to get it going.

And really after that fell over Black Power up there basically became the Rastas. Actually, it's a bit of an insult to the Rastafarian faith, but that's what they wanted to be called.

**Former Rasta Beau Tuhura:** Tigi Ness is the father of the hip hop singer Che Fu. Tigi was one of the first guys in New Zealand to be into Rastafarianism. Chris met Tigi in jail and Tigi got Chris into it. I knew Tigi when we were up in Auckland. I was about twenty, so this would have been in about 1972.

I was living in Auckland, listening to Bob Marley's music and hearing the message and curious about who Rastafari was. So I began reading books on Rastafarianism and his Imperial Majesty Haile Selassie. And from there my awareness of who he was and the whole movement in Jamaica grew. We started getting into bands like Third World who were both political and religious. As a Maori I found their beliefs very similar to what I was about and my own identity.

So I came back here and we just took the Rastafarian faith on board in our greetings and then in our fellowship. And then, as our group, we more or less separated ourselves.

We were the only Rastafarian group in the country back then. All the Maori youth were into Nga Tama Toa, which was the only political pressure group, and I was involved in that too. And the Islanders were into the Polynesian Panthers.

Black Power was a movement that was strong on the East Coast. I didn't get much into gangs in Auckland. I was more into the political angle than the gang mentality.

But when I brought the music back, of course, it just spread like wild fire. Everyone, like myself, was touched by the music and the messages and the rhythms and everything. It was new and it was different from all the other music we'd ever heard and Bob Marley was so much more powerful than all the other reggae singers. He was really more spiritual in his lyrics, too.

Even dope wasn't around here then in the early seventies. There might have been one or two who smoked, but not many. Even in Auckland while I was there,

there wasn't much of a dope culture. I remember, Larry Morris, the singer, got busted for having a joint on his person and he did *time* for it. And later Bunny Walters got busted and it got huge headlines in a place like Auckland. That was when Thai Buddha was the go. Nowadays you got skunk and all these different overseas brands.

**Detective Sergeant Hemi Hikawai, interviewed in 2000:** Do you understand how this whole thing eventuated on the coast with the Rastafarian?

The coast is basically regarded as being Black Power territory. But you must first and foremost remember that twenty-five years ago, here in Gisborne, Maori were not into dope. Maori in those days, twenty-five years ago, were piss-heads. They were juice-freaks, mate. They weren't heads. You know what I mean? And if you look at the policing that went on there, it seemed to be brawls and all that: the DB, the Sandown, the Albion, the Masonic. It was all big brawls because Maoris then used to drink and fight. And they were working, all working, and there was a lot of bloody money about and jobs were plentiful and so that was the lifestyle.

The drugs at that time or the cannabis use at that time was restricted mainly to non-Maori. The bohemians and the surfies were more into it.

And if you can imagine, the coast was Black Power. Then what happened was you had Maori that had left the coast and had gone away to the cities who were coming home and bringing those city habits back with them. You had it slowly starting in Gisborne and slowly infiltrating its way up the coast.

Then what happened was with that cannabis culture came the Bob Marley music. And Bob Marley is Rastafarian, right? And if you listen to that Rastafarian music it speaks of struggle, it speaks of slavery, it speaks of Ethiopia, Haile Selassie, and all that.

Now then, there was a fight. A man by the name of Beau-Beau Tuhura was the controlling person there. And Beau-Beau and Campbell fought. And Campbell won. So Campbell then became the dominant man there.

And if you can appreciate that the Rastafarian movement is meant to be a religious movement. Right? Now you have these self-styled Rastafarians who were formerly Black Power setting themselves up with their own cult on the coast. So they had to find a religion. And the closest thing that they could find that was not anything to do with the white man and that associated itself with Maori struggle was the Ringatu religion. So they identified with the prophet, Te Kooti (who started Ringatu). So much so that at one stage Chris Campbell used to quite openly believe and boast that he was Te Kooti reincarnated.

One of the other Rasta leaders, John Heeney, then took up the same stance and said that he was Ngarimu, his uncle, the VC winner, reincarnated.

So together they convinced themselves that they were indestructible because of whom they modelled themselves on.

**Beau Tuhura:** The Rastafarian movement really started in Ruatoria when I came back from Auckland in 1977 with about three Bob Marley tapes, some seed and some herb and started to grow. The group of young fullas around at the time started listening to the music. Chris had moved back up here by that time. He would have been in his mid twenties. Bob Marley was played on the airwaves a bit by then, and there were a few guys who'd heard his songs but couldn't get hold of the music.

I remember having arguments with people about who wrote I Shot The Sheriff: Bob Marley or Eric Clapton? Some would even say Bob Dylan.

So the music was very new and partaking of the herb was a very new experience for a lot of people around here. And the herb just took off. In a couple of years all the young kids up and down the coast were into it. Before you knew it dealers and tinny houses started springing up here and there. The fullas, of course, started growing their own, at first without success. You know, they couldn't wait for it to mature. But eventually they got the growing techniques down to a fine art and they were producing good mature seedless heads. And today, hell, the strain is better, the smoke is better, the cultivation of it is of a very high quality and it's too big for the police to stop now.

It's probably one of the only industries that bring any money into the coast. It pays bills. It puts fullas into wheels or whatever they want that they couldn't afford on the dole. It enables them to enjoy the comforts of home: television, sounds, those sort of things you take for granted as a basic part of the household.

**Raewyn Rickard, Beau's sister:** The first contact I had with the Rastas was through my brother, Beau Tuhura. He was very religious. And he turned up with his hair-do, the dreadlocks and the music and the ganja. So he turned into a bit of a rebel. That was years ago. I was little.

And then when I come through from college it had built up. That was about 1977. By then he just rode around on horses and he had the hair-do and they were involved in land rights issues. It was Beau and Chris and they had a few others with them by then.

# CHAPTER 3

## MANSLAUGHTER TRIAL

*In February 1982 Cody Haua (who will later become known as one of the hard core Ruatoria Rastas) appears in the High Court in Gisborne. He's charged with the manslaughter of his brother, Tukihimia (Rai) Haua. Cody pleads not guilty.*

*Crown prosecutor R. B. Squire tells the jury that the case against the twenty-three-year-old special scheme worker is both simple and tragic.*

*He says that on November 5, 1981, Cody Haua, his brother and some friends travelled to two or three hotels on the East Coast, ending up at the Manutahi Hotel in Ruatoria about 7pm.*

*Most of the group stayed at the hotel until closing time and went from there to the Haua home, where they started a party in the kitchen.*

*Squire says that a fight started between Cody and Rai and that Cody took hold of a knife. As other people in the room tried to break up the fight, Cody stabbed his brother in the left-middle chest area. Rai was taken to hospital but was dead on arrival. He died from hemorrhaging associated with the stab wound.*

*Defence lawyer Michael Bungay concedes it was "the hand of the accused that held the knife which inflicted the injury which resulted in death".*

*The author's brother, John, is covering the case for The Gisborne Herald. During a break in the trial, he overhears Michael Bungay talking to a few people in the court. "You've got a big haiwy-arsed Mawi coming at you with a woasting fork. What are you going to do?"*

*The answer to be inferred is obvious.*

*Bungay doesn't present any defence evidence to the jury. He stresses that the onus of proof is on the prosecution. The Crown has to prove beyond reasonable doubt that the stab wound, which led to death, was intentional. He says it's not enough for the Crown to prove that a fight took place between Cody and Rai Haua. An unlawful act, which resulted in death, has to be identified. If that's* accomplished, then the Crown has to show that self-defence or an accidental stabbing can also be ruled out.

Squire points out that in Cody Haua's statement to the police, Rai was seen with blood on his head and cheek. This, he says, suggests a second wound inflicted by the knife, which, in turn, suggests the wounds weren't inflicted accidentally.

Bungay says the kitchen, where the people were gathered when the incident occurred, was only about five metres by four metres.

"In that kitchen were a double bed, a mattress on the floor, cupboards, a table and seven people. All these people had been drinking for the best part of a day. You would not expect a clear picture to come out of all this. That is not the defence's fault. It is the Crown's job to prove the case."

Bungay says that Rai Haua was known to be quick-tempered and aggressive if he'd been drinking. He says that Rai became angry with another person at the party, and that Cody told him to "forget about it".

"But the defendant's brother got a knife and put it in a door in such a way as to prevent the door being opened. The accused took the knife out of the door – that made his brother angry. We know that he got up and in one motion struck the accused in the face. Then we have the matter of the fork."

Evidence has earlier been given that Rai had moved towards Cody, brandishing a roasting fork. Bungay notes that Rai was the bigger and stronger man. "He has a weapon and he is coming towards you. How would a person react? Your back is really up against the wall. It is sudden, it is surprising and it is violent. None of it is coming from the accused. It is all coming from his brother. What would you do if you saw a larger, stronger, violent man who has already hit you, coming towards you?"

Squire questions whether a fork was involved in the incident at all. He says it's interesting that in his first interview with police, Cody didn't tell them about Rai brandishing the roasting fork. In fact, the fork wasn't mentioned until Cody made a written statement. Only one witness had seen the fork. Another said a "flash" he saw could have come from it, but "two witnesses did not see the fork". "They were there and saw the start of the fight and saw no fork. Even if the defendant's brother did have the fork, was it reasonable for him (the accused) to stab him? If the defendant was genuinely threatened with that fork, I suggest there would have been some injury."

After deliberating for three and a half hours, the jury finds Cody Haua not guilty of the manslaughter of his brother, Rai Haua.

# BABYLON, ZION AND OTHER LAND ISSUES

**Denis O'Reilly, CEO Group Employment Liaison Service, report on Ruatoria to Secretary of Labour:** I can tell you that the Ruatoria Rastas differ from most Rastafarians in a number of ways, not the least of which is their millennial vision of the "Coming of the Most High" occurring on Mt Hikurangi or thereabouts. The Saviour coming from the East has its emphasis on East rather than Saviour. This ideological feature is held nowhere else in the world. These people are definitely "Rasta Ki Ngati Porou" and in fact are more Ngati Porou than Rasta.

While some familiarity with an understanding of Rastafarianism is necessary to even begin communication with the group (members) one can easily become sidetracked.

**Joseph Owens, Dread:** Babylon is, in sum, the whole complex of institutions which conspire to keep the black man enslaved in the western world and which attempt to subjugate coloured peoples throughout the world. Against this power the Rastafarians fight continually and trust in the help of the Almighty to fell this ancient enemy once and for all.

**Detective Sergeant Hemi Hikawai (retired):** They regarded Ruatoria as being Babylon and because you had Mt Hikurangi, which was the first bit of dirt to get the sun, they believed that that's where Christ was going to come. So they then had to rid Ruatoria of everything that was evil. And churches were regarded as being evil, so they started burning those down. The white man was seen as bald-heads, so they had to get rid of him.

You see, there was no land confiscation on the coast at all. There was no land confiscated. The non-Maori that are there were there legally. They'd purchased the land. They had a right to be there.

The next significant thing that occurred was that you had some unscrupulous, racist Maori who saw those boys as a means to an end. So then they started influencing them to get rid of the Pakeha. Elder Maori were influencing the boys, elder racist Maori, people with chips on their shoulders, two people in particular. One of them is a Keelan. Sue Nikora is her married name but her maiden name is Sue Keelan. The other one was her brother. I can't remember his name. He might be dead now.

**Sue Nikora (an early influence for the Ruatoria Rastafarians, and a mine of information on East Coast land rights issues and traditional healing):** I never for one moment told them anything about the land issues. But they have grown up in that atmosphere of unrest because of the alienations of the lands.

We always had the understanding that the land went into perpetual leasehold, full stop. It was said that if Sir Apirana Ngata can't do it, who can? You see? So it was a waiting game for the expiration of those leases.

I don't think the Rastas were aware of the legality or the illegality of the leases. All they knew was these Pakeha people were on these lands. I never for one moment told them about any of our researches into land claims. Our researches have been confidential researches, confidential to our land claims committee and to Crown Forest Rental Trust. And our research was just starting out then. But it was happening when our parents were alive, but in the Maori perspective. They had hui after hui after hui after hui. Then it came in the form of the movement for the unification of the Maori people. And all the Maori issues would come out.

We never really told them as much, you know, "We own that land. You go away and shoot whoever, burn whoever." No. No.

A lot of those boys couldn't speak Maori and I never taught them about the old customs. In fact, they were the type of kids who were unteachable as far as formal teaching was concerned. They were a lot of boys who were dropouts. They were boys who agitated against the system. They were boys who had been in jail and had learned about the world in jail. I never tutored them in any way whatsoever. We were there. Right? We were there if they wanted. Once or twice they would ask a question. And rightly so we should answer them because we would be the best ones to answer. But we never really sat them down formally to tell them this and tell them that.

**Barney Campbell, Ruatoria policeman (retired):** In the early 80s I was stationed in Wellington. Then the old man got crook. It was Maori sickness. It's hard to explain to a Pakeha. He just seemed to be sick for no reason at all, you know? And I know he went to see a chap around here, a Maori guy, and he seemed to tell the old man what his troubles were. I think you'll find a lot of Maoris still go to see *somebody* if they're ill, even if they're still going to the Pakeha doctor. The old man was crook anyway. And when I found out how crook he had been, I decided I was going to go home to help him. So I resigned from the job whilst still in Wellington. After I resigned, I think it was my last day in the job down there, I changed my mind or certain people in the heirarchy caused me to change my mind about leaving the job. I was told that I could come home to Gisborne as soon as there was a vacancy here - you see? - nearer the old man. So that worked out fine. I ended up over here for a year. And then I was told I'd get the next vacancy at Ruatoria. And I still wanted to go there. I didn't see any problem really. I was going home. And that's how I ended up there.

**Sue Nikora :** It's a sickness of the mind known as mate Maori, unique to Maori alone, and it can be treated by Maori only.

It can manifest itself either through a transgression of tapu, or through what they call a kanga – the Pakeha would call it a swear word or curse. And sometimes it isn't directly aimed at the victim, but because he's vulnerable at that time he gets the flak for it, especially if the guy doesn't belong to the whenua, to the land. That's what happens. And it can also be caused through thought provocation called makutu. People would say, "What the hell's he doing here, ay. I'll put some sort of curse or makutu onto him." The victim could be oblivious to what's going on. And it could affect him. The mind is affected and he's oblivious to what's going on around him.

That type of illness is not recorded in Pakeha medicine because they don't know the cure and they don't suffer from the illness. But a lot of our mental health problems start off as mate Maori and end up as schizophrenia and all those sort of sicknesses. But they could be saved by Maori prayers, or incantations or mind reading, or through blessed water or whatever.

**Sergeant Alex Hope's brackground report on Ruatoria (for police):** At the beginning of 1984, there were a number of adherents to Rastafarianism...
...Some of these persons were ex-Black Power (Chris Campbell, Michael Heeney, Dick Maxwell and Cody Haua). Initially they preached peace and quoted regularly from the Bible. They strived to learn and speak Maori and to learn their Maori history, genealogy and customs, which to a large extent were lost to them. The group consisted of about a dozen persons. They were led by a group of three persons: Chris Campbell, Bobo Tuhura and Rawiri Marunui...
...The three leaders approached a local kaumatua (Tom Te Maro) in order to learn Maoritanga, whakapapa (genealogy) and Ringatu (a Christian sect established by the rebel Te Kooti).They became involved with the Treaty of Waitangi and Kotahitanga issues and some took part in the Hikoi Ki Waitangi (protest March to Waitangi).

**Beau Tuhura, early Rasta leader:** See, the philosophy of Rastafari actually supported our own views of Tino Rangatiratanga, or Maori sovereignty. At the time we were involved in Kotahitanga as a movement for tribal unity and self-determination. Incorporating Rasta into that was quite easy. We could draw from Bob Marley's lyrics. His slogans like, Hold On To Your Culture and Get Up Stand Up were quite powerful to us. It was adding to our own taha Maori and our own Tino Rangatiratanga. Lyrics like, "Why can't we be free to roam this open country?" We felt that we had the right to do as we liked basically.

In the Treaty of Waitangi, we didn't concede our Tino Rangatiratanga to the Queen. What we did concede to her was for her to govern the country. That was our understanding. We were fine with that as long as it didn't affect the lifestyle we wanted to live on our own land.

**Barney Campbell:** My first year or so stationed up in Ruatoria, there was no inkling of the things that were going to start happening up around there. I saw a bit of Chris in that first year. The Rastas might have been a group by that stage but I wasn't aware of it, really. It was just normal run-of-the-mill police business as usual sort of thing, you know. You just went out and did the job and that was that. And they weren't any more prominent in the community than any other group of people.

I was up there about four years. It was good until the shit hit the fan and the Rastas started fence-cutting because that was the start-off, ay, when they went up Taitai, Stuart Williams's place, and cut all the fences around there. I think they went to Matahiia, all around there, and cut all the fences one weekend.

It turned out about twenty or so of them rode up there overnight and just went on their merry way cutting fences. And then I know we had a bit of a meeting. It was just myself, Waho Tibble – the other Maori policeman up there at the time, Tom Te Maro, because they seemed to have a bit to do with him through the Kotahitanga movement. It was a political party. I became aware that they were seeing a bit of Tom or he was seeing a bit of them. Tom's an uncle of mine and he was a bit of a mentor to them. But as far as I was aware it was all to do with the Kotahitanga movement. And that was just a passing thought. I never thought that perhaps old Tom was teaching them a few things, being an elder. It didn't occur to me that it might lead to other things. And I can't say that's what caused it, you know. But they might have been on to the Maori thing, I suppose: the land and all those things.

**Beau Tuhura:** When we started to get on the bus to attend Kotahitanga (tribal unity) rallies with people from the Tuhoe tribe and attending the Ringatu church services and looking at our own back yards we felt that we needed to push issues of our own that were happening here. For instance, we felt we wanted to stop forestry being planted on Maunga (Mount) Taitai. I think that was the first political move we did was by cutting the fences there. Stuart Williams had just negotiated the sale of that place to the Government who in turn sold it or leased it to the forestry.

# CHAPTER 4

## THE RASTAS TARGET THE WILLIAMS FAMILY

**As explained by Rastafarian Cody Haua and Sonny Brown, the father of Rasta Hamana Brown:** The Rastas had been told by some of their elders thatthe Williams family had acquired certain blocks of land off local Maori on either ninety or one hundred-year leases. The Rastas believed that the lease had expired on Stuart Williams' land on Mount Taitai. But instead of returning the land to the Maori, Williams sold it to the Government, who onsold it for forestry. The Rastas were outraged. So they went on their first fence-cutting spree, all over the mountain.

**Sergeant Alex Hope's report on Ruatoria for the police:** During 1984 members of the group were regularly appearing in court facing possession of cannabis/cultivating cannabis charges. The Rasta image began to tarnish as abusive scenes took place at court when Rastafarians refused to acknowledge the court. The group had also begun to read The Bible with a local slant to their interpretations of it. They foretold the second coming of Christ on Mt Hikurangi (the highest mountain in the East Cape area, a symbol of Ngati Porou, and reputed to be the final resting place of Maui's canoe Nukutaimemeha). Hikurangi was Mt Zion and they were to clear "Babylon" (the devil, Pakeha, anyone who disagreed with them) from the land between Hikurangi and Whareponga. According to some, Chris Campbell saw himself as a messiah.

They became involved in land issues and took particular exception to the proposed sale of Taitai Station to the New Zealand Forest Service. Taitai Station included Taitai Mountain, which was apparently an old fighting pa. The land was owned by one of the Williams family, who are the East Coast's equivalent of the landed gentry. They are descended from an early missionary who acquired large amounts of land reputedly by dubious means on some occasions. It was alleged that Taitai was obtained by dubious means. Not only was the Williams's ownership of it disputed but also the proposed sale of it to the NZFS.

**Jeremy Williams, East Coast farmer:** The first time the Rastafarians impacted on my life was in 1984 when Stuart Williams sold his property, which was the other half of the original Matahiia Station to the Crown for forestry. Not long after the sale went through a dozen or more guys rode cross-country and cut every fence and hacked through flood-gates. They did a circuit right around and came back down and rode out. They did it in broad daylight.

I'd actually been to a Lion's Club working bee. I saw them all riding out of Whakapaurangi Road with their Rasta flag. I didn't know what they were doing. I didn't even really know who they were at that stage.

They'd cut the boundary between other Maori farmers and Taitai Station. And it was just after that I heard for the first time this idea that a hundred-year lease had fallen due, etc, etc. We used to hear this notion that an area from the ranges to the sea was all leased land. If you take Ngati Porou, they, as I understand it, sided with the British in many instances way back. And as such the British didn't confiscate land off them like they did in Taranaki and Waikato. And therefore the huge land claims are not prevalent in this area compared to the land claims in other areas. But I'm no authority on it.

In terms of our own property we have almost no leases. And any leases that we do have, have a finite period. Basically, our property's free-hold. There's a small piece of Maori leased land at the back of Taitai and a little bit of Maori lease just down by the river. And I have a maize lease with Ike Campbell (Chris's brother) which is for a finite period. So as far as I'm concerned we're a free-hold title. Ninety nine percent of the land is paid for.

**Joe Nepe, one of the original Ruatoria Rastas:** There was no talk of fires at that stage. That didn't come 'til later. Some people talk about fire being a symbol of purification. But I think we used that method because it was effective.

My grandparents brought me up. And I got involved in the Rastas because I was just around in the place at the time. I was in a certain place, mixing with everybody else. And then me and Chris met. And then me and Beau met. And then John Heeney met us. And then we just all came together as one. The originals were: me, Chris, Beau, John, Hata Thompson, Diesel Dick Maxwell, Cody and a few others. We talk about "the twelve" and twelve's a good number but I think there were more. We just used whoever was around at the time to make up the twelve. There was a basic twelve in the movement, like there was always twelve members there all the time. We were all related and all from the same area. I think that's what made us so strong, ay.

The first episode that took place was the fence-cutting at Taitai Maunga. Stuart Williams was running the place at the time. It was all over our land grievance we had with the Pakeha.

Actually that Taitai Maunga's a good story, how we developed that one. We were all at Totaranui at Beau's place that morning all horsed up and we planned it. We'd ride out one night and we'd hit the mountain. They rode out one night when I was still at work at the marae and the next night I rode out, me and my brother, and caught up with them. And we cut all the fences right around the whole mountain. But we had to go back and fix them up, believe me or not. And we had to pay a hundred and twenty-five dollars each. That was a bummer. I didn't go that day to fix the fences. The police didn't come and pick me up. Old Barney, Chris Campbell's brother, was the policeman running things back then. Chris and Beau weren't happy at all about having to go back and fix the fences. I think it spurred them on a bit more.

**Jeremy Williams, Pakeha farmer:** The story went that they believed that Jah was going to appear on a white stallion on the side of Mount Hikurangi. The story also went that they used to ride from the valleys around Ruatoria to Hikurangi and that if they went through Sir Peter Tapsell's property and up through the back of Waiangakia, or they went through Matahiia and right across the back of Parsons they'd see Jah on his stallion. But I haven't seen anyone walking on water yet and they didn't see anyone riding a white horse at midnight. The other notion was that Jah put the Rasta on this earth to roam free and he was put on earth before fences were built. Therefore any fence in the road is to be cut.

## "THE TWELVE"

**Early Rasta leader Beau Tuhura:** People talk about "the twelve". The twelve are the original members of the Rastas we used to put together our House of Israel.

Now in Maori culture you have the marae with the poupou (centre posts) holding it up and the slabs of carved totara representing tipuna (ancestors) around the sides and the end. And in the marae each poupou symbolises an important ancestor or chief.

Well ours was a symbolic house. We had twelve poupou holding up our house. Each post was a member of our Rastafarian group. And each member of the group was linked to one of the twelve tribes of Israel. The tribes came from the sons of Jacob, who changed his name to Israel (in the Book of Genesis, Old Testament).

I was of the house of Joseph. One of my blessings was that I would be the one separate from my brethren. So throughout the years, I was separate from a lot of the things that went on. Although we are one, I was not really a part of the group. Joseph also has the blessing of women and children.

**Detective Sergeant Gary Condon (retired):** I do know that Beau Tuhura's name came up initially and he was right into it. I think he was there in the initial part of it. But I think as time went by he slowly but surely weaned his way out of it. I think Beau's biggest problem was he had too many women around town and he had too many children. He had about ten or twelve children.

**The Bible, Book of Genesis, Chapter 49, Jacob's testament:**

Jacob called his sons and said: "Gather around that I may tell you what is to happen to you in days to come. "Assemble and listen, sons of Jacob, listen to Israel, your father…"

22   "Joseph is a wild colt,
       a wild colt by a spring,
       a wild ass on a hillside.
       Harrying and attacking,
       the archers opposed him;
       But each one's bow remained stiff,
       as their arms were unsteady,
       By the power of the Mighty One of Jacob,
       because of the Shepherd, the Rock of Israel,
       The God of your father, who helps you,
       God almighty, who blesses you,
         With the blessings of the heavens above,
         The blessings of the abyss that crouches below,
         The blessings of breasts and womb,

26 The blessings of fresh grain and blossoms,
    The blessings of the everlasting mountains,
    The delights of the eternal hills.
    May they rest on the head of Joseph,
    On the brow of the prince among his brothers.

**Raewyn Rickard, Beau's sister:** I remember when Beau went to jail in the mid-eighties. Mum refused to pay his child maintenance. They used to put you in jail if you didn't pay your maintenance. Luckily, he wasn't in there long, about two and a half months. But rather than pay it, Mum thought she'd let him go to jail and scare the hell out of him. She was worried for him the way everything was brewing up around here.

They grabbed him when he was in bed at our grandmother's house. He didn't even have time to get changed. When he turned up in town at the courthouse he had his Roman sandals on and our nanny's curtain wrapped around him. Mum was spewing. She brought him a change of clothes.

**Beau Tuhura:** Chris was seen as the prophet or the seer because that's the blessing of the house of Gad. He also had the blessing of being attacked, but of being a smart tactician.

### Book of Genesis, Chapter 49:
19 "Gad shall be raided by raiders,
    but he shall raid at their heels."

**Early Rasta leader Beau Tuhura:** Now the blessings of the twelve sons of Jacob that were handed down to the different members of the Ruatoria Rastas were also seen as the twelve sun signs in astrology. So we studied our births and when we saw our House of Israel it was actually representative of those births. Each person had his own birth sign and along with it came the blessings of that birth sign.

Twelve is a number that keeps popping up.

There's a twelve-year cycle in Chinese astrology, which we also studied. There were twelve apostles following Jesus. We were the twelve apostles who followed Haile Selassie, the second coming of Christ. He was the atua (god) or cornerstone of our house.

So by studying all these things we gained an overall picture of how we fitted in together, what our strengths and weaknesses were and what we had to offer each other.

**Angus:** And were there twelve people, like each one for a different month?

**Joe Nepe:** Well, that's what we worked it out to be, ay. The twelve tribes of Israel and each person had to represent their month. My month was Benjamin so that was March. My birthday is March 28.

**Genesis, Chapter 49, Jacob's testament:**
20   "Benjamin is a ravenous wolf;
Mornings he devours the prey,
And evenings he distributes the spoils."

## WHEN GOOD KIDS GO BAD

**Sergeant Alex Hope's Report on Ruatoria:** On 1.8.84 approximately 10 kilometres of fenceline on Taitai were cut in numerous places. This incident established notoriety for the Rastafarians who were immediately identified as the culprits. A Dept of Maori Affairs community officer together with a forestry worker who was a local kaumatua (elder) sought to deal with the matter "in-house". The incident quickly became national news. A meeting was held involving the people of Hiruharama (a small community near Taitai), kaumatua (elders), parents, Rastafarians and interested persons...

...The aim of the meeting was to resolve the problems by getting the whanau (family) together – offenders and their families – and obtaining restitution.

At the meeting, the Rastafarians admitted cutting the fence and agreed to pay restitution. Chris Campbell apparently refused to pay. However, restitution was paid by his family. Some persons (particularly members of a land rights group) supported and encouraged the Rastafarians in their actions. One person told them to go to jail rather than give up and pay restitution.

The stated reasons for the Taitai incident were (from the Rastafarian viewpoint).

Taitai belonged to them (their ancestors).

The Williams had no business selling to the Forestry.

Pine tree must not be sold to the Forestry.

Taitai must be returned to the rightful owners.

They wanted all Pakeha out of Ngati Porou.

They wanted all Ngati Porou land returned to the rightful owners.

They wanted to live freely in the way their ancestors did in the past.

**Colin Williams (landowner and farmer):** Now I remember one meeting that we all went to at the hall at Hiruharama (Jerusalem) just after it started. There was a whole team of Rastas there. All the parents and different people in the community were there to try and get these boys back on the straight and narrow path. And it was heartbreaking. The parents were down on their knees at that meeting praying that these boys would listen and come back into the community. They were living terrible lives.

**Tom Heeney, the former deputy chief of the Ruatoria Voluntary Fire Service and the father of Rastafarian John Heeney:** John was a great kid. You couldn't have asked for a better kid. You didn't have to tell him anything, whereas with the rest of the kids we had to tell them to mow the lawns and you even had to threaten them sometimes: "If it's not mowed by tonight you'll get a belt when I get home." But he'd just get up, go out, do it. There was never any problem. Kept himself clean, tidy. His bike was marvellous. His bike was the only bike that was shiny.

He went to Hata Paora, the Maori college in Feilding. He was a good second five for their rugby team and a good athlete. He was also a very bright kid and wanted to be a pilot. That's partly why he had to come back. They didn't have physics at Hata Paora so he had to come back to Ngata College here in Ruatoria. Then he went into the Air Force. But he pulled out in the end. A lot of the officers he reckoned were pretty bloody thick. He wasn't too impressed by some of them. But he got into the drugs there, too.

After that he joined the P&T. He was working on the lines for the Post Office and did a course in Wellington.

**Bob Kaa:** I remember the first public meeting that was held in this area, as a consequence of what was happening. The word had got around this group called the Rastafarians was gonna take the town over. Anyhow I got a ring from the chairman of the Hiruharama Marae asking me to co-chair a public meeting with him. And I said, "No problem," because I was the chairman of the Te Aowera Marae and Sarah Sykes was our secretary.

And the mother and the aunties of the Heeneys were at the meeting. And we had the Rastafarians there. John Heeney was there and Beau-Beau (Tuhura) was there and one or two other of my nephews were there. So we gave them time and we said, "What do you guys want?"

And they said in the most descriptive language, "We don't want a fuckin' thing from any of you bastards. We're gonna *take* what we want."

And poor Peggy – that's Tom's wife, John Heeney's mother – she was standing up and throwing her arms out, and saying, "What do you want son?" And he turned around, spat on his mother and told her to fuck up. Yeah. I was there. And I couldn't believe it. And she just fell on her knees and just bawled her eyes out. That's Tom's wife and *his* mother. I'll *never* forget that.

But however, obviously Peggy still loves her son, even today. You'll never take that away from *anyone*... despite the fact she was spat on. As far as she's concerned, that's her son.

**Bailey Mackey, TV producer from Ruatoria and friend of the author:** I remember flicking through the channels and coming across an interview - I think it was on National Radio one Saturday morning - with an old Catholic brother. He'd taught at Hata Paora College. And he was telling the interviewer that in all his years of teaching there was one student who stood out more than any other. He said this kid was the most naturally intelligent he'd ever come across and had the most potential to become whatever he wanted. Eventually I realised he was talking about John Heeney. I couldn't believe it. It sounded like he reckoned John Heeney was a genius.

**Colin Williams, Pakeha farmer:** I grew up with the parents of a lot of those boys and played rugby with the fathers. They were terrific people. They really were. They were tremendously community orientated. And I can't think of any of them that didn't really pull out the plugs to give their kids every chance in life and a really good education. They worked their butts off to get those boys away to college. Nearly all of them went out of the district and were educated outside. And, you know, they just turned round and did that to their parents. It was very, very sad to see parents who'd done so much to give their kids a good start in life treated like that.


## "THE GOOD NEWS"


**Beau Tuhura:** There were so many things revealed to us through the Kotahitanga and the Ringatu: like there would be this group of young people coming with a new message of hope or *the good news*, and that that group would be an insignificant group of people that you wouldn't give tuppence for. Everything that was revealed indicated that *we* were the group of people and that it was the right time. And yet it also became a *dread* time for a lot of people because they thought, "What could this group of people do? And how could they be the chosen few?" They were disbelieving. "It can't be them. It can't be that that prophecy would be fulfilled today with this lot." But it did, according to the korero (talk) that I heard. It referred to the dread, to the appearance, to locks and the hair. It was said there'd be something about their appearance that would indicate they would be tapu (sacred, set apart).

And now when I think about it and after reading the scripture concerning the vow of the Nazirite of separation to the Lord in Numbers 6, which says you must not take a razor to the head or partake of the vine, I can see all these things were in the korero that the old people were talking about. We didn't drink back then. We only smoked the herb.

**The Bible, Numbers 6:** The Lord said to Moses, "Speak to the Israelites and say to them: 'If a man or woman wants to make a special vow, a vow of separation to the Lord as a Nazirite, he must abstain from wine and other fermented drink and must not drink vinegar made from wine or from other fermented drink. He must not drink grape juice or eat grapes or raisins. As long as he is a Nazirite, he must not eat anything that comes from the grapevine, not even the seeds or skins.

"During the entire period of his vow of separation no razor may be used on his head. He must be holy until his period of separation to the Lord is over; he must let the hair of his head grow long. Throughout the period of his separation to the Lord he must not go near a dead body. Even if his own father or mother or brother or sister dies, he must not make himself ceremoniously unclean on account of them, because the symbol of his separation from God is on his head. Throughout the period of his separation he is consecrated to the Lord.'"

**Sergeant Alex Hope's backgrounder on Ruatoria:** In retrospect, the following factors in relation to the Taitai incident were noted:

Those involved were led by Chris Campbell, John Heeney, Rawiri Marunui and Beau Tuhura.

With the exception of the Maxwell brothers, Dick and Doe, all those involved were from Hiruharama, just south of Ruatoria.

All those involved were under some degree of influence from Sue Nikora, Sam Keelan and Sue and Sam's brother in law Sonny Brown (East Coast Genealogical Society).

All were unemployed.

All were heavy users of cannabis.

With the exception of the Ngarimu family (John and Tina Heeney) the leadership within each of the Rastafarian's whanau was weak.

*The likes of Alex Hope and Hemi Hikawai claim the Rastas were under the influence of Sue Nikora. So what sort of thing was she telling them?*

**Sue Nikora (interviewed in the early 2000s):** The Williams family was the third cousins to Queen Victoria of England. And they were sent out to the colonies with a Bible in one hand and a gun in the other. Meanwhile, think about what's been happening lately in Zimbabwe, Fiji, the Solomon Islands and even Te Kooti's Hau Hau rebellion in Poverty Bay in the last century. Anyway, the Williams were sent out to deal with the natives and convert them to Christianity to make them more sophisticated so they wouldn't remain primitive forever and a day.

So they came out here and they preached The Bible. They were the ones who were responsible for the Declaration of Independence in 1835. They were responsible for the signing of the Treaty of Waitangi. And they were responsible for looking after the people of the Tairawhiti area. The Tairawhiti area stretched from Te Aute in Hawke's Bay right up to Te Hiro in the north, at Cape Runaway.

But the Maori here wouldn't listen to what was being said. And at the same time, they were responding to the infiltration of the Hau Hau movement, the Pai Marire movement from Taranaki around to the Waikato area because their lands were being confiscated. It had nothing to do with anything else except the land confiscation and the land alienation from Maori so that the settlers could come and settle in our country. That was the simplicity of it.

That was the reason the Williams family came. They came explicitly for that. Then their uncle or grand uncle, a man called James Busby, because the Maori wasn't listening to what they were saying, he went to England and he said to Queen Victoria, "You know those Maori people won't listen." He had come from Kerikeri up north. They'd been trying to take land from the Nga Puhi people as well. Then they came down here. And he said, "They won't listen."

So she had a gospel, the word in Maori is Rohopai, the good word. Her good word was, "You know, James Busby, you go back. If they don't want to listen to The Bible, shoot them."

We have evidence of that document.

He was designated the trustee for the whole territorial boundary, which was three million acres. That all went under his jurisdiction as the trustee of the Maori people in the Tairawhiti area. So what they did was they brought all their Williams family and settled them throughout the territorial boundary. And the

Williams family administrated Maori lands so that they could have perpetual leases. Perpetual leases were ninety-nine-year leases with no rights of renewal. That's exactly what has been happening in Fiji right now. And the ninety-nine-year leases were instrumented in New Zealand from 1895 to 1994. So the perpetual leases were completed in our area in 1994. So that's when they expired. And what's happened is the Williams family are still sitting on those lands. The question is why don't they just give it back. But they've been on it for so long – for four or five generations – that they seem to think that they own it.

So what we're doing now is we're claiming our lands back through the Waitangi Tribunal. But we don't have to claim it back. They should just say, Right, here you are, Maori. Have your land back.

But they want us to prove it beyond reasonable doubt.

We expect to get our lands back at the end of this year and next year. Our claims are going through now. We want every inch of that land back, plus compensation over a hundred and fifty six years because we haven't received a single wazoo for the leases that were in operation.

They said in the instruments that they were paying thruppence per acre. But they never ever paid it. My parents, my grandfather, my great great grandfather never got that thruppence. And they stayed at thruppence per acre all those years. There was no market value corrections put on them.

And this is the scenario that these children have been born into. Our parents, and grandparents have always agitated for return of our lands. And these kids have been born into that environment. And of course some of them went away to school. Some of them were dropouts. But there are ones who went away to school and learnt the intricacies of property ownership. They were the ones who came back and said, "Those Williamses are aliens. We'll burn their barn down. We'll tell them to get off. And if they're not gonna get off we're gonna steal their horses as some compensation for what has happened." Some of the ninety- nine-year lease deals were fair enough but some of them were straight up, "You either listen to what we're doing or we'll shoot you." James Busby used the constabulary to bring law and order. He used whatever he could use. They brought their guns over and used their guns to force us to submit. It was all intentional.

There was a block of land in Ngatapa, another one back here in Tauwhareparae, Matawhero, Waerenga-a-hika. We were rather lucky that we were a bit isolated. The Crown had got to some of our people and we formed the nucleus of the constabulary. That is why we are really known as the kupapa, or the loyalists. We were loyalists to the crown of England, under the leadership of

Major Ropata Wahawaha, under Major Tuta Nihoniho, under Porourangi. The main leaders of that constabulary came from the Ruatoria area.

They were the kupapa that met at a place called Popoti, which our hapu own. And they called some of our people in and they were the ones that came forward to Gisborne to hunt out Te Kooti Arikirangi.

But Te Kooti belonged to our hapu as well. The Crown made a brother fight against a brother. And all the time the reason was because of the taking of the land. That was the simplicity of it.

Because of the fact they had already been recruited into the constabulary. And the constabulary was paying the five leaders of the constabulary fifteen hundred pounds each per annum to lead our people. And they rallied up the hapu to form an army. It divided our people no end and it divides us to this day.

And the ramifications of what really went on with Te Kooti ended up with these boys and their Rastafarian movement. It didn't start with them, it started with the Black Power gang, and then the Mongrel Mob. But it was the Rastafarians who took the flak in the end.

I'm as bold to say that a lot of those Black Power members went and formulated the Rastafarian movement. I think Chris himself was a Mongrel Mob in the beginning and then went straight into the Rastafarian movement.

**Barney Campbell, former Ruatoria policeman:** So we had this meeting about the fence-cutting on Taitai Mountain. And it was agreed that they would go back up there and fix them all up. I don't know who decided that it would be done that way to be quite honest. I don't know why we didn't just charge the lot of them with willful damage. I know we went back up there to fix them up because we went with them. We took them up there. I remember Chris was there, but I can't remember if John Heeney was.

I know I remember thinking, "This might be the start of something." I wasn't quite sure what though. There was just something about it really.

*After the Taitai incident, the community becomes more involved with the Rastafarians. A meeting is held at the Mangahanea Marae, where it's agreed to set aside a block of land next to the Hiruharama Marae as a garden for the Rastafarians. The group suddenly becomes involved in gardening on a fairly large scale.*

*Another feature of the Mangahanea Marae meeting is a leadership struggle between Chris Campbell, Rawiri Marunui and Beau Tuhura. Campbell triumphs and, though not acknowledged as such, becomes the leader from this time onwards.*

*March 1, 1985: Gisborne CIB and Ruatoria police team up for Operation Gorilla. A number of Rasta houses in the Whareponga area are searched simultaneously after the police receive some chilling tip-offs. They've been told the Rastas are:*
  *Building an arsenal of firearms.*
  *Receiving training in guerilla warfare.*
  *Growing cannabis on a large scale.*
  *Four people are arrested on cannabis and dishonesty charges. None of them are hard-core Rastas.*


## SORTING IT OUT ON THE RUGBY FIELD


*As winter approaches, the Rastas decide to start their own rugby team. They call the team Nga Tama Toa, which is the name the Rastas also use for their group. It means The Warriors. The team plays in the Rasta colours of green, red and yellow.*

**Former Rasta Beau Tuhura:** They tried everything to stop us from entering the competition. But they couldn't stop us.

The game we had against our old club team, Hikurangi, was more of a bloodbath than a game of rugby. I was more or less the player-coach and I switched between halfback and first five. The less time I had on the better. I just wanted to give all the young players a go. That's why we pulled away from Hikurangi and formed our own team in the first place. There were a hell of a lot of young fullas who couldn't make the A team. And it wasn't until we formed Nga Tama Toa that Hikurangi said they wanted us to become the Hikurangi B team.

We said, "Na, we just want to get right away from you fullas," because they had their clubrooms but we wanted to go back to the Hiruharama Marae and make the marae our clubrooms. And we actually started that thing of hosting away teams and feeding them.

Hikurangi was our old club and they were all whanau. It was family against family, brother against brother.

The main thing that sticks in my mind about that game is the blood. They wanted to teach us a lesson for abandoning the club. And we were out to prove we were just as good as they were and that some of our players should have been in contention for that No. 1 team, because a lot of our fullas were coming through, while a lot of their players were at the end of their careers but they were hanging on.

The confrontation on the field was pretty ruthless. The poor old ref, there was no way he could control it because the battle lines were drawn as soon as the teams walked on. And that's what it was. It was just a physical battle. Tackles were big. And if anybody went on the ground, he soon became part of the ground. I've never seen so much blood. There were missing teeth, broken noses, black eyes, the whole works, a lot of bruises, broken ribs. I don't think there's ever been a game played like it since. It made Geyer versus Wally Lewis in that State of Origin match look like child's play.

But I think it turned out to be a bloodbath *and* a hiding for us at the end of the day.

I didn't attend the do afterwards. And I don't think the dread did either because the rules at the clubrooms were no swannies, no gumboots, no drugs, and no dreadlocks. So no Nga Tama Toa. The boys didn't bother turning up.

We only lasted one year. We were doing all right in the competition. We were holding our own. The only thing that stopped us from carrying on was that half the team ended up in jail.

**November, 2000, interview with Joe Nepe:** *What position were you?*

Front row prop. Chris Campbell was the hooker and Willie Tangira was the other prop.

*Cos old Beau told me about the game you guys had with Hikurangi. He reckoned it was a blood bath.*

Ha ha ha ha ha. Aw fuck, all our rivals, all our oncles. Fighting our oncles. *Ha ha ha.*

Fuckin' bloodbath all right. I remember that.

*Did you guys win?*

Na. We lost that game. Chris had a scrap with Victor Takarangi. Victor was a *big* man in those days. He went on to become one of the kingpins in the vigilantes. He was more hardcore than the likes of Bob Kaa. They had one lot of vigilantes with the police – Bob Kaa's lot - and another lot that took the law into their own hands, and that was Victor and them. They were bashing up Rastas. At that time we were all in jail, see.

*Yeah. So there wasn't much you could do to get them back.*

The only thing we could do was **burn** them.

*What position was Victor playing?*

Ah, first five.

*Not an amazingly big guy then?*

He was a big guy *then*.

*What was he doing at first five? He just fancied himself as a bit of a ball-player?*

Ha ha ha ha ha ha ha. I think he just wanted a bit of action that day. He got it, too.

*Ha ha ha. So what happened?*

Chris got the better of him.

*So it was an all-out brawl in the middle of the field? Ha ha.*

Yeah. In the middle of the field.

*Just the two of them?*

Farck.

*Doomp, doomp, doomp.*

Doomp, doomp, doomp, doomp. You cunt!

*Ha ha ha ha!*

Boom, boom, cunt, doomp, doomp, doomp, doomp.

*How did it start off?*

I dunno. One tackled the other head high or something like that. The next minute, "You fuckin' cunt!"

*Any broken bones or anything?*

Na, just a punch-up. Sonny Bartlett also had a fight.

*Sonny Bartlett?*

He was one of the twelve. He stays in Gisborne now.

*And he was one of the original ones?*

Yeah.

*Cos he never turned up in any of the newspaper clippings or anything did he?*

He was a good boy.

*Aw is that right? He was into it for the philosophy alone.*

He was a good boy. He kept to himself.

*Did he stay out of it a bit?*

Actually he was in there for a while, cutting fences and all that.

*But when it got a bit more...*

When it got a bit heavy, he just eased on out.

*So he had a dust-up that day too?*

Yeah.

*What position was he?*

Number 8. He was a big fulla.

*So what was it like at half-time? Didju guys have the edge?*

No we didn't. The edge was 3-nil at the edge, at halftime.

*Is that right? They were winning 3-nil?*

They were winning 3-nil. We gave away a penalty and they got it. They only beat us by a try.

*What was the final score? Do you remember?*

Na, 12-10 or something like that. It was a close low-scoring game. But they won.

*What about John Heeney? He would-a been a winger was he?*

He was our first five. He was a good player too.

*Yeah, well I'd say he'd be pretty quick, ay. What about Chris? They say he was more of a journeyman than a...*

Hee hee hee. Ha ha ha.

*Everyone says he was a good boxer. But everyone laughs if you ask them about his rugby. He was a pretty average rugby player was he?*

Na, he was a good rugby player, Chris.

*Aw, was he?*

Yeah.

*Just solid?*

Solid. Played rugby in his younger days.


## RAEWYN'S AWAKENING


*Raewyn Rickard is the sister of former Rasta Beau Tuhura and the wife of Rasta Anthony Tuhou. Raewyn is the Ngati Porou victim support co-ordinator, which uses whanau-based solutions for helping at-risk youths. I chatted with her at her work in Ruatoria. Here are some snatches of what she told me.*

My husband, Tony Tuhou, was one of the last to join the Rastas. But he was there during the mid-80s when all the hu-ha was going on.

I mainly lived in Gisborne when all the trouble was happening but my brother used to come through. I never went on any of the land marches or anything. I was considered a baldhead by the Rastas and by my brother. I was going to school and getting an education. And I went on to work at Maori Affairs.

Beau used to come over home and pull out The Bible. We'd discuss it because I'd gone to a Mormon College. So we had two different philosophies.

I used to find it hard when I looked at Haile Salassie's life and how his people lived so poor. I just couldn't click to it. So Beau and my mother and me had some interesting talks.

Chris and the other guys brought up some major issues that we had as a people such as: how do we open up our maraes. There was a way of life that our people had and yet now it's governed by laws where you have marae committees saying, "You cannot live there." No one was allowed to build homes around the maraes. We had laws here that we could only build homes down by where the dump was. That was the housing zone of Ruatoria. And it only got changed when they built the papakaianga out at Hiruharama.

We had years there when no one could build on their land because of the by-laws.

It was land alienation.

What was really hard for me was here I was at Maori Affairs. I was the leasehold clerk. I worked for the Maori Trustee in Gisborne. I caused a lot of land alienations and I did a lot of stuff not knowing what I was doing, being as young as I was. So I perpetrated these laws and enforced them. And then I had my brother and cousin on the other side, from the other whanau, who were trying to stand on the other side of ourselves. They were saying, "We're the chiefs around here and this is what we stand on, our whakapapa (lineage) to these maraes. This is our land and we should have rangatiratanga (sovereignty) over it." But they didn't.

One of the first things I noticed in my job as leasehold clerk was that Maori land was worth less than European titled or general land. It's still the same today.

If you were paying a lease on Maori land you wouldn't have to pay as much as you would if it was European land. And you'd pay much less in rates. The rates were really cheap. You had all the terms and conditions of a lease, but less of the expense.

At the time when I worked there we still had land that was going for a shilling a year, on ninety-nine-year perpetual leases. Some of these blocks of land that were going for a shilling a year were a hundred acres, some were even over two hundred acres with a right of renewal.

What they did is you paid your rental to the Maori Trustee's office and it was distributed through the Maori Land Court to the beneficiaries, the landowners. And you can imagine: you've got ten cents and you've got a couple of hundred landowners. It takes years before they get five bucks back on their land.

The other thing that happened was there was also a law that when the revenue from your shares was reduced past a certain point, you just fell off the register. Your land just disappeared off your beneficiary card. Your money would then automatically go to the Maori Trustee. It would just be held there with the other unclaimed dividends. And it earns no interest.

No one ever moaned because the Maori Trustee had this title. But really he was Mister Government. The Crown was taking back the miniscule amount of money you made off your land. That's land alienation. There's heaps of land that's just disappeared and it's just ended up with the Maori Trustee.

A family might have only a little piece of land left whereas they knew that in previous shares they might have owned lots of land. They'd look and know they used to own from that hill over there to that other hill across there. They'd only ever been paid a pittance for the lease. And now the land had been taken away and they got nothing. Because the land was leased to people, you weren't even allowed to walk on it or do anything on it.

Eventually they decided to address it and change those laws, which stopped those perpetual leaseholds. Now they lease the land for a percentage of the land value. But the land value is still worth less than it's really worth.

Now when you get a Government valuation of the land, you draw all the things off like improvements that might have happened to the land. So say someone has been leasing your land and their lease expires. You need to pay them back for all the improvements. And you can't afford to buy your own land back.

I remember I used to be very bureaucratic when I worked as a leasehold clerk. I didn't understand a lot of the things then that my brother was breaking his heart over. To me they weren't important. But when I look back on everything today, I feel so guilty.

I didn't even wake up to what was happening with the leases. I used to order for Government valuations. And I just accepted everything we did. We had a book of laws. This is all the Maori Land Acts and then at the back there was: This is how you do such and such and these are the forms you use. And I just followed the instructions.

But I had my eyes opened when I came back from Gisborne to live at home in Ruatoria. I'm the chairperson of our family land now. We nearly lost the lot through debts. We had an uncle that gradually declined into Alzheimer's.

Nobody realised what he was going through. It was one of those ugly GST debts with penalty tax. Other than that they didn't pay a mortgage where the family had taken out a loan to buy back land that we had lost.

We used to have two hundred sheep and a lot of cows. But they're all gone. They were rustled. And our fences were cut, but not by the Rastas, by other people. The Rastas took a whole heap of flak for what a lot of naughty people were up to at the time. They just became the general scapegoat for everything that went wrong. It was just blamed on the Rastas.

# PART 3 COP KIDNAPPED

# CHAPTER 1

## THE POLICE STATION/COURTHOUSE BURNS

*Thursday, November 7, 1985: Te Puia woman Francine Gilvray, her mother Polly and cousin Shane are woken in the early hours of the night by crackling and popping sounds. Luckily, they've been sleeping in the new family home because only a metre away, Francine's old three-bedroom family home is well ablaze.*

*Francine calls the fire brigade. The timing of the fire's uncanny (an uncle and aunt were going to move the house to a new site in Tokomaru Bay this week). The fire's also suspicious (there's been no power to the old house for nearly a year). So what started it?*

*Neighbour Don Tamihere arrives at the scene with his hose. As flames quickly engulf the old house he tries to make sure they don't jump the narrow gap over to the new one. The old home's been in the family twenty years. But there's no hope of saving the uninsured contents: clothing, furniture, a new* mower, jewellery that had belonged to Polly's grandmother. The Te Puia firemen arrive and take over the battle to stop the blaze.

The Tokomaru Bay firemen provide backup. But the Ruatoria brigade's late with the water tanker. It's sputtered to a stop on the highway. Thieves have siphoned the petrol. The firemen are able to pirate the two-stroke mix from their portable pump and are back on the road in half an hour. But that's a long time for an emergency service to be delayed. When they arrive they're able to help dampen the remains of the old house (the new one has been saved). But the robberies are a concern. Petrol thefts from the tanker now amount to about two hundred litres over several burglaries, while five bunker coats, complete overalls and sets of boots have also been stolen.

**Friday, November 15:** A hedge fire is lit on Whareponga Road. There are no houses around. The fire brigade arrives at 10.50pm. Paper and matches are found at the scene.

**Tuesday, November 19:** Just after 10.30pm a person is heard running away from the Ruatoria courthouse. Several people hear noises. A rubbish tin is knocked over. Flames are already creeping through the building. At 10.58 a fireman living near the courthouse sees the fire and raises the alarm. But it already has a good hold. The orange glow is visible all over the district. The cracking windows and exploding roof tiles bring residents from their beds.

The courthouse-cum-police station is just across the road from the fire station, about fifty metres away. But the blaze is beyond control when the firefighters arrive. The flames are leaping through the roof. The township's been robbed of one of its more attractive buildings.

Thirteen Ruatoria volunteer firemen, backed up by eight forestry fire crew and a Tikitiki team of ten, battle to protect the flanking buildings - a new unoccupied police station and the public health nurse's home. Fortunately, there's little breeze. And they manage to contain the fire to the courthouse, apart from some blistering to the nurse's house. Police and fire teams from Gisborne also rush to the scene. Most of the firemen are there until 3am and a crew stands by until daylight.

**Wednesday, November 20:** By mid-morning between twenty and thirty police and fire officers are investigating the latest blaze. The new Ruatoria police station is suddenly the base for the police operation, several weeks in advance of the official opening. It was designed to blend with the courthouse next door, but will stand alone now.

*It's a rough introduction to the coast for chief inspector Whiro Ratahi. He arrived in Gisborne only yesterday to take up his new post as deputy district commander and has immediately been called in to head the inquiry. The investigation's a big change from his previous position as head of the diplomatic protection unit.*

*In tandem with the fire inquiry police investigate a garage burglary on the same night, hoping to find a link. Not long before the fire the Barry Avenue premises of T and S Motors Ltd were entered. Tools, tyres, a battery and other items are missing. The anger felt by some Ruatoria residents in reaction to the fire is also a concern for police.*

**Lyn Hillock, Gisborne assistant fire commander (retired):** We get really serious when they burn down the courthouse and the police station. Ian Clark's fire safety and I'm the third officer for the coast. We spend five days sifting through the whole remains of the courthouse. The only thing we miss after four days is a little square of glass, which was in the front door. And they've broken this little square of glass and reached in and unlocked the door. We realise they've used some accelerant that was in a little room just off the front door to start the fire. We trace the path of the accelerant right through the courthouse.

*Thursday, November 21: Chief Inspector Whiro Ratahi and his team conclude the fire was arson. He says the fire started in the police office in the courthouse. Articles were stacked against a heater, causing the fire, which then spread through the building.*

*Tuesday, December 4: Fire fighters attend a house fire call at Tikitiki. The call is traced and police question Rastafarian John Heeney.*

*Saturday, December 8: A near-new woolshed worth over $100,000 and a hayshed containing about two thousand bales are destroyed by fire in Ruatoria.*

*Ruatoria's recent record for fires is now the worst in the North Island and investigations have already confirmed suspicions the latest two fires were deliberately lit.*

*The fires are on two different stations. The woolshed's on Koura, while the hayshed's on Waiomatatini. Both went unnoticed until staff arrived to find smouldering wreckage.*

*Electrical fault has been ruled out as a cause for the woolshed fire because the power wasn't connected. And as far as the hayshed goes, fire officers say spontaneous combustion's not an option.*

*Koura hasn't yet shorn the bulk of this season's wool. But some bales went in the blaze on Sunday night with the loss put in six figures.*

*The common theory is that the arson of the Koura woolshed is a Rasta retaliation to Operation Whareponga, after which Chris Campbell was convicted for trespassing on Koura, and other Rastas were charged with theft and receiving. As mentioned earlier, Koura Station belongs to the Ngarimu family. John Heeney's mother Peggy and her sister Kate Walker, who lives on Koura, are both Ngarimus.*

**Jeremy Williams, Pakeha farmer:** They burnt the Koura woolshed down twice. The old Koura woolshed was pretty run-down and old but they were still using it. They built a brand new one and that was burnt down, too.

*Wednesday, December 12, 1985: The house in which Rasta Gallace Hongara lives is destroyed by fire. The house is in Whakapaurangi Road, the same road as Te Aowera Marae. Extra police are sent to Ruatoria to investigate. Len Kirikino owns the house. Alan Murray Kirikino and Lee Wayne Kirikino are both Rastas. In his backgrounder on the Ruatoria troubles, Sergeant Alex Hope notes: "This happens at a time when Gallace is trying to extricate himself from the Rastas."*

*The suggestion, it seems, is that the Rastas lit the fire as a message to Hongara.*

*But in a story on the Close Up current affairs programme, reporter Genevieve Westcott takes a different angle. She says: "Residents here decided to fight fire with fire. And this Rasta stronghold just outside of town was burned to the ground. For the people of this community it was utu, revenge."*

*Westcott reports from the scene of another incident: "This house was to be the second target of the anti-Rasta backlash. Women and children were inside when several men attacked with batons and stones."*

*Thursday, December 26: The fire alarm goes up from a shearing shed on Gate Station, inland from Ruatoria, at 8.30pm. Property owners are able to confine the fire to a hay bale and it's extinguished before fire fighters turn up. Police are treating the fire as a possible arson. But Ruatoria's Sergeant Norm Gray says there's nothing to link it to the recent spree of suspicious fires.*

**Excerpts from a story in the Gisborne Herald on Friday, December 27:**
As one man guarding family property put it, "You sit there in the dark thinking,

'What am I doing, here in this day and age? We're going back a hundred years.'"...

...Ruatoria people have heard talk about a "plan" to raze Ruatoria and rebuild it, talk of a hit list and threats to many individuals in the town...

...The town is on edge but so far there has been success in containing talk of retribution from within community ranks. But if the crime continues, the police cannot guarantee the lid will stay on.

*Also today, it's announced that Lands and Survey, owners of the old theatre building in Ruatoria, will be asked to demolish it soon because it's a fire hazard.*

*Recently, it had been used as a store but it's now derelict. The building's open to the street because its windows are smashed and the fire service regard it as an extreme hazard.*

*The county council will tell Lands and Survey to "pull it down before someone puts a match to it".*

**The Gisborne Herald, Saturday, January 18, 1986:** Ruatoria is an unusual sight by night. When Herald staff passed through at 2am on a recent weekday the town was lit up like a Christmas tree. Security lights burned at woolsheds, maraes, houses, barns and right through the business and residential area of the township.

The eyes of the neighbourhood support patrol miss nothing. There is a feeling of being watched from the moment you are within a few kilometres from the town.

## THE GOSPEL ACCORDING TO BOB

**Bob Kaa:** My view is the reason these problems started is it was all over land. You're probably aware that a Maori is very jealous of his land. It doesn't matter if it's covered in gorse, blackberry or what. Land to us is, well, you can't buy it. And people will fight to the death for land. And this particular episode was all over land.

And the perpetrator behind it is a family called the Keelan family, headed by Sue Nikora, who lives in a nice home in Gisborne, in a nice comfortable street, with nice surroundings, plenty of water, plenty of power. She lived there before all this happened. And I don't blame her. She actually went through the system to find out what happened to her parents' shares in this particular land, which is out towards Whareponga, where this guy was ... only to discover that her family were no longer shareholders. Well, even a bloody goat can't stand on it but that's beside the point. We perceive land in a totally different way. So she went through the system to find out what happened to those family shares. But the system didn't work for her. So she thought, Well stuff it. There's only one way to do this: intimidation. We'll try and scare *some* bastard.

And at that time a lot of the boys were talking about Rastafarianism and a lot of these kids were her nieces and nephews just as they were mine. And she thought, "Shit, this is the vehicle I'll use." But the problem was she couldn't control them. She hyped them up. She said, Get those bloody Pakehas. This is our land. Burn those trees.

At a time when the New Zealand Forest Service was starting to plant trees she was saying, Burn those bloody trees and cut those bloody fences. Those so-and-sos. Do this fulla with our land. And she really hyped them up and instilled into that organisation that that was the kind of thing to do to get our land back. And they did what she suggested. But then Sue just faded back into the background and the boys took over.

**Former Detective Sergeant Hemi Hikawai:** Sue Nikora and her brother used their influence over these boys and they fed them full of bloody propaganda. They made the bullets and those boys fired them. But then what happened was as these fires mounted up the cause was lost and it just became something to do. "There's a fuckin' house; let's burn it down."

A lot of the families in Ruatoria were criticised. They were accused of knowing who was burning these places down and not helping the police. Well, I don't blame any of those people up there for that. It was out of control. Even the parents of the families were scared. Those boys were terrorists. And they had the whole community hostage.

**Sue Nikora (who was, it's said, herself prepared during childhood to become the next great leader from Ngati Porou and who made headlines in the mid-2000s for trying, with the help of a hulking supporter, to collect "rent" from Pakeha business owners in Gisborne):** I never ever for once riled anybody up because if I saw them doing anything wrong I would tell them, "That is not the right thing to do." They were coming to me. "Is this the right thing? Is that the right thing?" If it wasn't I'd say, "No." I never ever tried to get them to do things against the law.

**Sergeant Alex Hope, former head of police in Ruatoria (now a lawyer):**
The Rastas did have some concerns that had a historical basis. There *were*
disputes about land in the past and there *were* underlying truths and unsettled
grievances about how people had acquired certain bits of land, including the
Williamses... and *even* in relation to Lance Kupenga being killed by Joe Nepe.

When Nepe killed Kupenga, he talked about utu and things from the past.
And one of the old kuia in town said to me afterwards, "Well, yes there was
something between the families in past generations. It could have been utu."

Maori in particular, but probably not just Maori, believe that your sins are
visited back on you and your family.

And in the early stages with the Rastas when they were just getting set up, I
remember they were living on Te Aowera Marae. And I recall that Sue Nikora
and her brother Sam Keelan, Hamiaora Keelan, had involvement with that. And
on the other side of the community – this was before the disbandment of the
Department of Maori Affairs – you had Kate Walker and Marie Collier. They
were the two Maori Affairs community officers. And they were also working
*hard* around those Rasta issues. And they came into conflict: Kate and Marie
against Sam and Sue. That over-simplifies it.

But early on in my career in Ruatoria, Sam Keelan died, Marie's husband
died and JohnWalker, Kate's husband died. And more than one person said to
me they all lost a husband or a male member of the family because of what they
were involved in with the Rastas and what they were doing.


## THE SIGNIFICANCE OF THE 12<sup>TH</sup>


*Wednesday, February 12, 1986: Another suspicious fire... A Ruatoria*
*resident notices flames shooting from an unoccupied police house in Mangakino*
*Street at about 10.30pm. The fire service is called and within an hour the blaze is*
*out. But the twenty-year-old, three-bedroom house is extensively damaged.*

*Constable Waho Tibble had lived in the house until December, but it had sat*
*empty since then. Tibble's replacement arrives tomorrow. The arsonist has*
*pulled off a pointed and well-timed welcome.*

*Just like when the courthouse was burnt down, the target is again a symbol of*
*the law. Ruatoria is now a community of two extreme stances: those who consider*
*the establishment an ignorant enemy, and those who consider an affront to the*
*law to be a personal affront.*

*A pattern has emerged of incidents occurring on or near the 12^{th} day of each month, and everyone in Ruatoria knows the significance of that day.*

**Beau Tuhura, one of the early leaders of the Rastafarians:** We took on the Ringatu beliefs as set down by the prophet Te Kooti, who also had a prominent position in our house of Israel. We attended Ringatu services, which were held on the 12^{th} of each month. So you go into the marae at mid-day on the 12^{th} and they shut the doors. You stay overnight and fast for twenty-four hours and pray and take part in the service. And then they open the doors again at noon the next day.

*Thursday, February 13, 1986: A police team of fourteen from Gisborne and stations along the Coast is investigating last night's blaze, assisted by the fire service and an electrician. Police have no doubt that it was arson. The officer in charge of the inquiry, Detective Sergeant Gary Condon, says it appears an accelerant was used. Police presence in the town has increased since it has become obvious a pattern of deliberate fires has developed.*

# CHAPTER 2

### A SECRET MEETING AND AN OFFER

**Bob Kaa:** I'm not sure if any of the locals have taken Sue Nikora to account for what she did back then to hype the boys up. I can recall the day she came here. My wife will testify to what I'm saying. Sue and her two brothers wanted to buy my garage out. They wanted to get rid of me, probably because I was opposing them. I was on television. I was in the media. As fas as I was concerned it wasn't so much *them* that I was opposing. I was opposing what was happening. As far as I was concerned they were just a pack of unemployed bloody wankers. I wasn't prepared to have any unemployed prick come up to me and say I want the shirt off your back. I'm not going to take it.

And so what she was saying was, we want you out of the equation. She offered us sixty-eight thousand to walk out of the garage.

I said, "You add a one in front of it and I might think about it "

She said, "No, I've got the cash."

"Show me."

"Doesn't matter where it is. And I need an answer by this afternoon."

Needless to say I told her to go and get stuffed.

This was at the height of the troubles. She was still involved that late in the piece.

There's a place called Tauwharanui on your way back to Gisborne. You would have passed the Hiruharama Marae on your right coming into Ruatoria about 10 Ks back. There's a long straight before that about two or three Ks. Opposite that is a stream. And there used to be a woolshed there. That area's called Tauwharanui. And there used to be this old dilapidated woolshed there. You may not believe it but what they did – and I'm talking about the Keelan family and the boys – they actually built another home inside it. And I'll tell you what: it was beautiful.

They invited me there to one of their meetings, to discuss the issues, and I couldn't believe it. When you looked on the outside, you wouldn't have known there was a home in there. But they had everything inside. They just didn't want everyone to know they had this nice place.

I went to the Keelans' place. Sue and her brother Sam were there and so was Beau Tuhura, who was one of the Rastas. They wanted me to make a public apology via the newspaper about the things I'd said about the organisation. I told them, no way was I gonna do that. I had nothing to apologise for.

They put on some food. Someone was doing some cooking.

They also said I had to go to court with them and support them because by this stage one or two of them had been apprehended by the police and were about to be prosecuted. I'd act as a witness for them. And this took about an hour of to-ing and fro-ing. Anyhow I stood up and I said, "Well, I'm sorry."

They said, "Well we've got some food on the stove. We were gonna give you some. But seeing as you didn't compromise, you can go and get fucked."

*Friday, February 14, 1986: Another fire: this time the Ruatoria Aero Club is gutted during the night. The original club was torched just four years ago. Insurance money and a fund-raising effort from the local Lions Club paid for the latest building, a lined garage that hadn't been completed.*

**Bob Kaa:** After I met Sue Nikora and her brother Sam and Beau Tuhura at Tauwharanui there, I came home and I said to my wife, "Bugger it. I'm going to go and see Chris's father." I knew Chris very well. I knew his parents very well.

I said, "I'll have a talk with his old man and see if I can talk some sense into his father in particular." His mother is a very humble, placid woman. So I went out there and drove through the creek. And somehow Chris's mum must've known I was coming because his dad was waiting for me. He saw me, he pulled his gun out and he said to me, "Bob... fuck off."

I said, "Hey, hang on, Bill." I asked him where his wife was.

He didn't want to be friendly. He just said, "Na."

"Why can't we talk?"

"I'm not talking to you." He cocked the bloody trigger on me.

I thought, "Fuck this," and left.

At that time I was publicly opposing what Chris and the boys were doing. And the grapevine works wonders along the coast. And I guess it got back to Bill's place that I was opposed to Chris. And he would have thought, "That bastard Bob Kaa," because Chris was his son. It wouldn't matter whether Chris was the devil himself; he was still his bloody son.

I wanted to talk with Bill and maybe we could've arrived at some sort of solution. Bill was a farmer in his own right, working on a family farm. He was one of my best bloody customers, Bill. But he really turned sour.

Anyhow a few days later, for some unknown reason, Chris Campbell came to see me. I was doing some work for the Iwi Authority at the time. He came and sat in this vehicle I was working on. And he said to me, "Bob, I amthe Christ."

And I said, "Yeah, well, fair enough. I could say the same too."

"Yeah, but the difference is, I can do things that you can't."

"Such as? Burning the fuckin' township?"

"No, no, no. I didn't do that."

"Well, what are the kinds of things you can do?"

"I can perform miracles."

I said, "Aw, you're all, you're all shet."

And he said to me, "The day's gonna come, Bob, and you mark my words, things will happen and I'll be there."

"What the hell are you talking about?"

And he said, "Things will happen." And he got out of the vehicle. I don't know what he was talking about but not long after that he disappeared over the hill there and kidnapped Laurie Naden.

*Saturday, February 15, 1986: Police are treating the airstrip fire as suspicious. The cause isn't known but police say fences in the area had been cut.*

## "THE VIGILANTES"

*That night the anger explodes. And Gisborne couple, Paddy and Forli Brown, are caught in the middle of it.*

*After visiting Paddy's father, Sonny, on the outskirts of Ruatoria, they head off at about 11pm to pick up a tyre at an address in Whakapaurangi Road, Hiruharama. Paddy's brother Hamana, a member of the Rastafarians, is with them.*

*When Hamana gets out of the car to open a farm gate, a group, who've been hiding, suddenly jump out and attack the car with fence batons and other weapons. The windscreen, rear window and all but one side window are smashed. Forli and Paddy are struck around their heads and bodies.*

*Hamana manages to get back into the car and they drive off. They report the incident to Ruatoria police and also give them a piece of baton used in the attack. They tell police that they recognise one of their attackers as a member of the neighbourhood watch group known locally as the vigilantes.*

*The couple then drives to Gisborne. They're treated in the accident and emergency ward at Gisborne Hospital. It's discovered that Forli Brown has suffered neck and shoulder injuries, including a broken collarbone. Her husband has a wound stitched behind his ear. The doctors tell him that if he'd been taller, he would've been seriously injured.*

**Sunday, February 16:** *Paddy and Forli Brown now face a $1500 repair bill for their car. They're angry and they want the vigilantes to pay.*

*On Sunday they return to Ruatoria, and attend an informal meeting with Maori elders and members of the surveillance group, who deny any responsibility or knowledge of the attack at Hiruharama.*

*Co-chairman of Concerned Citizens of Ruatoria, Bob Kaa: "It was definitely not members of our team. We keep a complete log of all activities and know where everyone is. I regret what has happened but it happened beyond our control."*

*Kaa admits that tempers are frayed within the surveillance group and that it's hard now to restrain people wanting to take the law into their own hands. But he says if any of his group were involved then he'll do his best to see that they're brought to justice.*

*Kaa says he's aware his group is known as the vigilantes. "It's unfortunate that we've been labeled with this name. It has an unlawful connotation. But we are just concerned citizens working within the law, protecting community property. "*

*Then Kaa announces his (temporary) resignation as co-chairman of the group, citing business reasons. He says it definitely has nothing to do with the trouble on Saturday night.*


**Notes tape-recorded following a conversation with Sonny Brown in November 2000 at his home on the corner of Whakapaurangi Road, Hiruharama (Sonny's a widower; he'd been married to Sue Nikora's sister and is also the father of an old workmate and friend of the author, Kathy Akuhata-Brown):** Sonny Brown said it wasn't just the Rastas cutting fences. The *vigilantes* also cut some. They cut fences on the Keelans' property, which also belonged to him through marriage. Sonny said that someone came and told him that they'd seen the vigilantes cutting his fences down the road. So he went down to see who it was. He was on his way down when a cop came along. He told the cop what he was going to do and the cop told him not to bother. Sonny said, "You and me, we'll both go down."

And the cop said, "No, no, no, just leave them to it."

Then, for Sonny, the penny dropped that the cops were involved. Sonny believes the cops and the vigilantes were working together.

**Hughie Hughes, Pakeha electrician, whose business is in the main street of Ruatoria (interviewed in late 2000):** It just got to the stage of fire after fire after fire. It became the thing of the day to burn something or pull down fences. There was this sort of idea that, "The whole land belonged to us. We're all one family. There shouldn't be any fences stopping anybody. And everybody's cattle is our cattle."

People were even cutting their own father's fences. There's one paddock just south of here, at Hiruharama, where it's only in the last two years that it's been re-fenced. That land has laid to waste ever since 1986 or '87. The father died and the fence has just laid there. That's at the Keelans' property, at Sue Nikora's brother's property.

And I know the Kirikinos had their fences cut, and young Alan Kirikino was a Rasta.

**Sue Nikora, early influence on the Rastas:** People say I told the boys to go out and cut fences but the main fences that were cut were ours. They belonged to our family. Why would I be saying to those boys to go out and cut fences? You tell me.

I reported it to the police that our fences were cut. They took no notice. All our fences were cut down. We were the ones that had our fences cut during the unrest.

But I knew it wasn't the Rastafarians because those boys were our own kids. It had to be someone else who cut the fences. We were running a farm then. We had sheep and cattle and a shearing shed and quite a lucrative business. Someone else must have done it because I'm sure it wasn't the Rastas. I don't believe for one moment that they would go along and cut their own fences. They were our children.

**Sergeant Alex Hope (now a lawyer), interviewed on October 5, 2002:** After I left the coast I ran into one of the Neighbourhood Watch guys at a party over here in Hamilton. He was intoxicated. And he told me that there was about half a K of fence along the main road in Ruatoria and that he and another guy had put a chain around the fence and hooked their 4-wheel drive up and just driven up the road. They ripped hundreds of metres of fence off the property.

**Raewyn Rickard, Rasta Beau Tuhura's sister:** Death threats started coming to Beau and his kids. We don't know who they came from. Mum received these letters saying that they were going to kill Beau and his line and their mokopuna. The letters weren't signed. But there were a few families getting them.

I know my mother was worried because I had to come up and she said, "Go and spend time with your brother."

I was heavily pregnant at the time. I went over to see him with my big stomach. And he'd emptied out Nanny's house and he was just waiting. He was waiting for whoever wanted to kill him. All he had was the couch and the fire, the butcher's knife, the axe and his Bible.

It's not like Beau couldn't sleep. He's not afraid of anyone. And if anyone did turn up it wasn't gonna be a lay down and die job.

The thing was, Lance had died and there was a real backlash towards the Rastas. It was stressful for Beau, not knowing who was threatening to kill him and wondering when they might strike. But no one ever came around.

*Violent incidents between members of "the vigilantes" and the Rastas are becoming more common. Early in the morning of Wednesday, May 21, 1986, a man answers the door of his house in Whakaangiangi, near Te Araroa, and ends up being held at gunpoint with his feet and hands bound. He's kept like this from 2am to about 5am. When he's finally untied by his assailant, a fight develops. The victim of the home invasion suffers a suspected fractured skull but manages to overpower his captor and hold him until police arrive.*

*(The attacker is later described as a twenty-year-old from Te Araroa.)*

**Detective Sergeant Laurie Naden (retired), interviewed in early 2000:**
We had some funny situations with the vigilantes. A joker from the Neighbourhood Watch Group gave Dick Maxwell's brother a bloody good hiding, this Doe Maxwell, who's now brain damaged because Dick smacked him over the head with a rock a few years ago. Dick just about killed him. Doe had to go to Waikato Hospital.

Anyway, Doey got a bit of a smacking one night. So he nominated a couple of bloody suspects. So we went round, did our inquiries, you know, straight down the middle.

And I remember one of the boys coming back to me. Aw, you told me to go and see so-and-so.

"Yeah."

"Well it probably was him."

And I said, "Yeah. What'd he say?"

He said, "No it wasn't me and Doe can't identify me cos I had my motorbike helmet on at the time."

That's what you were dealing with, ay. He'd beaten the shit out of Doe. I think he might've broken his arm.

**Notes tape recorded following a conversation with Cody Haua and Sonny Brown:** Apparently when Dickie Maxwell beat up his brother, he beat him with a mere, not a rock. They were drinking at one of the marae and Dickie and another guy were urinating out the front.

His brother Doe said, "Hey! What are you doing? Cut it out and go to the back of the marae if you want to have a piss."

They reckon Dickie had this mere and just smacked him with it two or three times and then dragged him off away from the marae and beat the shit out of him.

Doe's a cripple and he'll be one for the rest of his life. He's slowly coming right with the brain damage, but he's still not quite there.

But, according to Cody Haua, it wasn't all one-way traffic. Cody reckons Doe once stabbed Dickie eight or nine times with a broken bottle. He says Dickie was stabbed many, many times in his life.

**Senior Sergeant Alan Davidson (retired):** Now people used to get confused. Dick Maxwell and Richard Maxwell were two different people. But they were actually brothers. Dick was known as Diesel and Richard was known as Doe.

**Sue Nikora:** Dick Maxwell was given the name Diesel because he went and got some diesel and, thinking it was petrol, siphoned it out and put it into his car. That's why they call him Diesel Dick.

He was quite a character. He was always very respectful. But I think a lot of people saw him as a negative sort of person. But, you know, he was funny.

**Tom Heeney, Rasta John Heeney's father:** Diesel Dick lived just on the corner as you go into Ruatoria. His father was a fencer for this farmer.

Well the Neighbourhood Support Group was doing one of their patrols up and down the streets. And they put the spotlight on old Diesel. So he picked up this molotov cocktail and he was gonna let them have it in the car. Trouble was his arm came back and he just splashed the petrol right over himself. He ended up putting himself on fire.

So the neighbourhood support guys had to jump out of the car and put him out. Then they had to take him down to the hospital and get him doctored up.

I don't think he was too badly burnt. His arm, I think, caught most of it. Diesel was just being the tough guy and it didn't quite work out. Life never quite worked out for Diesel.

*Saturday, May 17, 1986: One of the staunchest members of the Neighbourhood Watch Group appears in court in Gisborne. It's forty one-year-old self-employed builder Victor Takarangi. He's charged with assaulting Dickie Maxwell's brother, Richard "Doe" Maxwell, and assaulting him with intent to injure. The alleged assault took place in Ruatoria on January 11.*

*This is Doe Maxwell's version of events. He's sleeping in his car at Hyland Place, Ruatoria. He wakes up early in the morning, looks out the window and sees a group of people nearby. Takarangi's among them, carrying a stick about a metre long.*

*Takarangi walks up to the driver's seat side of the car and speaks angrily to him. He opens the car door and swings his stick inside, striking Doe Maxwell twice on the thigh.*

*Maxwell gets out of the car and tries to talk to Takarangi. But Takarangi keeps swinging the stick. Maxwell backs away, backs away. Then makes a* desperate grab. *Takarangi strikes him twice on the shoulder. Maxwell is struck on the arm while shielding a blow, and again on the shoulder and now the legs. The incident ends when Takarangi breaks the stick over Doe Maxwell's head. Maxwell rings the police and goes to hospital with a cut on his arm. The arm is put into a cast.*

*Questioned by Takarangi's lawyer, Tony Adeane, Maxwell says he walked to the car to see his nephew, who'd been driving it. But he refuses to elaborate on what he and his nephew were doing because it might incriminate him.*

*Adeane says he can't proceed further because Maxwell refuses to answer any more questions, and that Maxwell's evidence should be discounted.*

*A second witness, Terry Carl Gibb, also gives evidence. Like Takarangi, Gibb's a member of the Neighbourhood Watch Group. This is his version of events. Maxwell wakes him in the early hours by banging on the door of his Hyland Place home. Maxwell wants him to step outside but he refuses. Maxwell leaves and returns about fifteen minutes later frightening Gibb and his family. At daylight, Gibb goes to see Takarangi. They decide to visit Gibb's brother-in-law in Hyland Place. Gibb and Takarangi are standing outside the brother-in-law's gate when they see a car parked nearby... Gibb refuses to give further evidence, saying it would put his family in jeopardy.*

*It seems both sides in this case have too much to hide.*

*Prosecutor Chris Douglas says he can't continue with any questions and won't call more evidence.*

*Adeane asks the two justices of the peace hearing the case to discharge Takarangi because of insufficient evidence on both charges. This is granted and Takarangi walks.*

**Lyn Hillock, former Gisborne deputy fire chief:** One night I'm coming out of the pub, down the front steps. Dickie Maxwell's on his horse and he's riding the horse into me and pushing me into the wall of the hotel. I've got my Holden, my fire brigade car parked outside there. And I always carry a cigarette. And I've got my smoke hidden in my hand where Dickie can't see it because when you're up the coast you're always watching your back. So I shove this glowing cigarette into the side of the horse. The horse leaps across the footpath. A hoof lands on a car. It eventually sets itself right and charges onto the street and Dickie Maxwell's down the road, gone in seconds. Little things like that are just wonderful.

**Former Detective Sergeant Laurie Naden:** We had this team arrive from the Bay of Plenty and they were going to solve these arsons. This joker Chris

Keightley was adamant he was going to get a cough out of a Rasta. Well, there was this little chap up in Ruatoria, Hamana Brown - thick as two short planks but quite a likeable little rogue. I said, "Well go and talk to him. Go and talk to Hamana."

So about four hours later Chris came out and said, "You know, I've just convinced him that there was a yesterday."

And I said, "How did that come about?"

He said, "I asked him what he did yesterday. And he said, 'There's only today.'"

And this is how they used to go on. They used to talk about the I and I. You'd say, "What did you do yesterday?" And they'd say, "I and I stayed here."

Chris said, "I don't know how you jokers have put up with this." But, as I say, after four hours he finally convinced him, probably with a slap in the ear. "Hey, where were you before you got up this morning?" type thing.

You could never ever mention The Bible to them, because they would just rattle off and prattle, prattle, prattle for hours and hours and hours. And it was nothing like I ever read in The Bible. They made things up to suit themselves.

So to come home it was quite nice to sit down and have a *normal* conversation.

# CHAPTER 3

### THE RASTAS KIDNAP A COP

*Monday, February 17, 1986: Graeme Mathieson spends most of the day searching for his three horses. They've disappeared from his employer's property in Makarika, near Ruatoria, and the eighteen-year-old shepherd's furious. Two rifles were stolen from a Makarika house yesterday and Mathieson, a member of the Neighbourhood Watch Group, is certain the Rastafarians are responsible for both offences. He goes up in a helicopter and spends ninety minutes looking for his horses from the air to no avail.*

*Early in the afternoon, Mathieson's fellow watch group member Albie Walker sees three horsemen –Rastafarians Chris Campbell, Hata Thompson and Cody Haua - riding across Koura Station, where Walker's employed.*

*It seems binoculars, two-way radios and notebooks are now regular equipment for local shepherds. Walker is in radio contact with the Neighbourhood Watch Group headquarters in Ruatoria. He contacts Mathieson, who's sure the Rastas are riding his horses, and other members of the group. They get together and head out towards the hut, used by the Rastas, on the hill at Whakaahu. From their vantagepoint, they see Campbell near the hut carrying a rifle. They radio that information back to watch group headquarters and it's passed on to police. Mathieson, Walker and the others remain on observation in the area until relieved by two policemen.*

*Police decide that members of the Gisborne Armed Offenders Squad, led by Detective Sergeant Laurie Naden, will surround the hut at dawn.*

**Tuesday, February 18, 1986, The Gisborne Herald:** A policeman was held hostage but later released as Armed Offenders Squad members closed in on armed Rastafarians in bush country near Ruatoria this morning.

Police believe they have the group of three men contained in bush near a hut at Whareponga, a few kilometres out of Ruatoria.

District commander Superintendent Paul Wiseman said that earlier this morning Detective Sergeant Laurie Naden was taken hostage by three men but at 9.10am he was released unharmed and was picked up by police helicopter.

Officer in charge at the scene Chief Inspector Whiro Ratahi confirmed that the three men were Rastafarians but said at the moment there was no further contact between them and police.

Police are still in position at Ruatoria and are being reinforced by armed offender units. Napier district Armed Offenders Squads have been mobilised and were to be flown to the area this morning.

**Detective Sergeant Gary Condon (Condon transferred to Gisborne in 1984 from Masterton, where he was in charge of the CIB. He also played flanker for the Hawke's Bay rugby team during the Ranfurly Shield era):** Laurie Naden got kidnapped as a result of the fires. We'd been up there a lot investigating the arsons. What happened in the lead-up was Hemi Hikawai and I had gone up there to investigate. Somebody had burnt down the aerodrome, which really was just a small shed, and the police house in Mangahaere Street.

While Hemi went on investigating those fires, we heard that three weapons and three horses had been stolen from a property near where Jeremy Williams lives in Matahiia. We knew it would be the Rastas. Also, that same night, about a million and a half dollars worth of forestry was burnt down in a block just north of Ruatoria, heading towards Te Araroa. We were pretty sure the Rastas did that, too. Later, Albie Walker, who farmed that area, saw three guys on horseback through his binoculars. We guessed that it would be Cody Haua, Hata Thompson and Chris Campbell. And they vanished into the forest.

So we had the arsons and we had the three horses and the three weapons stolen. And we knew that two of those three men were wanted on warrant anyway. So to cut a long story short we managed to trace them to the hut at Whakaahu. We saw the horses. We knew they were armed. So I called the armed offenders. And the rest is history.

**Hata Thompson, interviewed in Gisborne in July, 2001:** All I remember is we were asleep in the hut up on Whakaahu there. They chased us the day before from the ranch that's over at Makarika. I pinched some horses from there. *I* pinched those cos I had no horses. And I needed something to ride. And those horses happened to be right there. They chased us all the way up to the hut on Whakaahu.

We'd been on the run for the whole day. And we'd just woken up after sleeping in the hut. Suddenly, we hear this loud speaker: "Chris Campbell, Cody Haua, Hata Thompson, this is the police; we've got you surrounded. Come out with your hands up." And we're lying there really stoned. The next minute we thought we were having a bit of déjà vu, just lying there. Then the bro sits up and goes, "Fuck, I'm sure that's the cops outside?" And it was dark as It was just coming up to daybreak when it started. I said, "We better lie flat on the floor."

"Why?" asks Chris.

"Because I think if we don't, we're gonna get taken out to be quite honest."

"Aw, okay."

So we were lying there for a while.

Then Chris says, "I'm not staying here, bro. I'm not gonna get taken by them. No way. I'm outa here." And he ran out and ran straight into Laurie.

**Bob Kaa, Neighbourhood Support Group:** Well, it serves Laurie Naden right, the stupid bastard. We offered, the local people, offered to go with him up the hill to try and find Chris. I mean, the locals know this country better than anyone.

We said, "We'll give you two guides. They'll take you up there and they'll put you on to these guys just like that."

He said no, and what happened? He got kidnapped. Of course, Chris knew that country much better than they did. They had helicopters zig-zagging all over the place looking for him. We could have saved the taxpayer a lot of money.

The hype here was that bloody high, we wanted to get that prick out of there so we could all settle down to a normal bloody life. That's all it was. That's why we wanted to help. But they weren't interested in that.

**Laurie Naden:** What happened was there were warrants out for Chris's arrest. They were on a property, which belongs to the Walkers up there. And there was a hut right up the top of this place. They'd just cut fences and cruise on to people's properties. You owned nothing. It was theirs. And they were in this hut. And Chris had been causing a few problems. He'd allegedly done some burglaries. We put a team in to see if they could find him and they found him and two others, Hata Thompson and Cody Haua, in this hut.

So the armed offenders, which I was part of at that time, we went in the next morning because we knew they had firearms. They'd been seen with firearms. We did the standard cordon and contain voice appeal. And he broke every rule in the bloody world.

Instead of sitting in the house, saying, "Get stuffed, I'm not coming out," he come charging out the door. He *ran* out the door with a firearm. And he confronted a dog handler, who was just alongside me. But he was real crafty. He never actually presented the firearms at any stage, which, in those days, you really needed to be in fear of death before you could shoot'm. So the dog was going mad and the dog handler was having problems. So I yelled at Chris to distract him basically. He dropped out of sight and I started moving around. The next minute I got a thing in the back of my ear. "Stay where you are." And it was Chris. He realised it was me. And I'm thinking, "Oh, shit."

The initial thing wasn't too bad but he was scared he was going to get shot, which he bloody would-a been. He was probably more scared than me at that stage. He didn't know who was around, he didn't know how many were around so, basically, he got me to call up on the radio and tell them what had happened. And we have procedures when that happens and everything changes. He was quite happy once I'd told them. I had a pistol, which he took, and he fired a couple of shots over my head.

It was quite strange cos my youngest daughter, it was her birthday about a week later and I thought, "Thank Christ I've already bought her a trike," because I didn't know which way it was going to go. I was actually on holiday when that happened. Like a fool I'd gone up the police club for a beer and we got called out. Even if I'd been at home they would have found me and I'd've gone out anyway.

It was a bit strange for a while. And then he settled down. He wanted to know what I was doing there. And why hadn't I come and knocked on the door like I used to do. He was frothing at the mouth. It was quite strange. I just talked my way through it, saying, "Well you know Chris, we knew you had firearms and we didn't know whether you'd been smoking and we don't know how you're going to react when you're smoking."

And, of course, I was getting it back. "I've never harmed you Laurie. We're mates."

I was probably talking at about two hundred miles an hour and thinking about six hundred miles an hour. But he calmed down.

He had the upper hand. I was buggered. He had his gun and my gun, and the radio. So we walked back up to this clearing to where the hut was and I'm not too sure what was going on with the other two. They really didn't want to get involved at that stage. I think they'd realised, "Oh shit."

Anyhow, Chris took over the situation. We wore a beret in the Armed Offenders Squad and he took that. And he took my gun belt and my radio and stuff like that. We went back to the hut, sat down. The other two come back with four horses. Chris went and lit up a bloody big joint and offered me a smoke. I told him to stick it up his arse.

Tim Reedy, who was one of the armed offenders and a relation somehow to Chris, he called out to him in Maori. And, of course, that pissed Chris off because although Chris was so much Maori he couldn't speak the language. So then Tim switched to English. And they had a conversation. Chris was calling back to Tim, trying to get him to come out to where we were. "Come out, bro. We can sort it out." Of course our rules were, "No, no, you stay where you are."

After a while we got on these horses and away we went. The AOS had no option but to stand by and watch them ride off with me. They had the reins and I just had to hold onto the front of the saddle. We went down to a sacred pool, which gives me a little bit of a shiver because Chris was telling me about this huge massacre that had taken place there and... A lot of it was folklore. You know, a lot of it was bullshit. It was stuff that *they* had decided. It had just slipped into one of his visions.

We all had to get down and have a bloody wash at this pool. In his mind, because of this battle, there were spirits there and we had to wash the spirits off. I did whatever they asked me to do. If they wanted me to say a prayer, I said a bloody prayer. It was actually a very nice area, very isolated, a lovely creek running into the pool.

**Barney Campbell, Ruatoria policeman and Chris Campbell's brother:**
We were told to stay up on the hill and keep an eye on the hut where Chris and the others were staying until the administration could set up the operation.

It was up at Whareponga on Whakaahu Station. They attached some spiritual significance to that place.

There was a lot of talk on the loud haler. The thing that annoyed me was we were supposed to be in charge up there. The police were supposed to be in charge. They woke them up from their sleep. And it turned into a bloody fiasco. The AOS were there to do the job they needed to: call them out and do whatever it is they do if things don't go according to plan.

I wasn't down there. But I was on the AOS in Wellington. The rule is you call the man to surrender and if you feel you're in danger well then you let one go (a shot).

I asked Chris what happened. And he said he realised they were surrounded. And he thought he might make a break for the bush. And he took off with the gun and fell over and the gun discharged. I remember him saying, in that time, he thought, "Shit, I'm going to get it." He expected to be shot there and then. But it didn't happen and he dived into the trees. And he knew they were there somewhere around him. And then he said, when he gathered his wits andadjusted to the situation and looked around he saw Laurie. And he had Laurie before Laurie could do anything. I think he just snuck up on Laurie. What did Laurie say? Mmm. Well, I don't want to speak for Laurie, and if Laurie said that he wasn't in any danger I'd believe him.

While that's all happening I'm up the top and I heard the shot go off. And I'm thinking, "Well, somebody's probably been shot." But then you could still hear the loud haler. And I think you could hear Chris yelling back and different ones running around like I think Cody and Hata were out of the hut by then. I don't know when I realised they'd captured Laurie.

But I know during that sort of loud haling period or that stand-off sort of thing I thought, "I should go down there and I might be able to sort this out." But we couldn't get hold of anybody on our radio. It did occur to me to call and I think I did but I couldn't get anybody. And I didn't want to go down there and balls up the whole operation. But if I'd gotten the word to go down there I would've been keen because I thought I might've been able to help. Well I would-a gone down there, see, cos at no stage did I think they would-a shot me, really. There were times when I was wary of them.

Yeah, and it was a relief when Laurie turned up and he was released.

**Laurie Naden:** Chris only ever had one bitch with me. We had 357 magnums at the time. And there's no safety catch on them. You just pulled the trigger and they went bang. And Chris, somehow he got it in his mind that I'd told him there was a safety catch on it. And in some totally irrelevant piece of cross-examination in the court case this came up. He was defending himself. And I said, "Well there's no safety catch on the thing." And he really did the haka. "You told me there was a safety catch." And that was the only bloody disagreement he and I had, even after he kidnapped me.

**John Heeney, interviewed in early 2000:** Chris told me what happened. Laurie Naden got his own gun stuck in his ear. He got his own 357 Smith and Wesson magnum with no safety catch stuck in his ear. "What the fuck's this, Laurie?!"

*What was the story with the safety catch? Laurie told me he only ever had one row with Chris Campbell. He said it was to do with the safety catch but he didn't really elaborate.*

Of the 357 Smith and Wesson. When they surrounded him it all backfired, ay. They expected the boys to stick their tails between their legs and come out like this: "I surrender. I bow down." No way. No way. And even today we haven't bowed down. This isn't finished yet. Because, you know, the blood of our brothers, justice hasn't come for it yet. They got murdered. Chris Campbell and Dick Maxwell were murdered in cold-blood and the system cleared the murderers.

And the Bible says, "It is an abomination when the innocent man is found guilty and condemned to death and the guilty man is found innocent. It is an abomination."

*Where's that? Is that in Revelations, too?*

I think it's in Proverbs. They went up there and surrounded the hut. And it backfired on them. Chris told me about when they were in the hut. The cops surrounded them and said, "Come out with your hands up," and all that sort of thing. The bro grabbed the gun and stuck one up the barrel. The other two in there had a quick, you know, "What's going on?" And Chris ran out and when he ran out the hut he tripped over and the gun went off. And he told me there was another policeman there with a dog. The dog handler was there and he had a gun too. He couldn't aim his gun and control his dog at the same time so he opted to bail down the bank.

Then Sam (Hata) Thompson came out with a 22, pointed it at the dog handler. The dog handler pointed his gun at Sam. And Sam's gun had no bolt, couldn't shoot. See? So Sam would've been in the shit if they'd started exchanging lead.

But that gave Chris enough time to get off the ground and run and jump over the bank. And when he jumped over the bank Laurie Naden was right there. And he landed right behind Laurie, stuck the barrel of his rifle in Laurie's ear and said, "Take that fuckin' thing off Laurie." Laurie took it off and gave it to him. "What the fuck's this?!" A cannon, ay... a 357 Smith and Wesson. Not a police issue. That's not a standard police issue. No. That's Laurie's toy gun from Australia. At that time the police issues were those 38 Specials. Now they got those Glocks, ay. And I suppose Laurie didn't tell you his bullets were all dumdum. Dumdum bullets: the ends flattened off. The brothers had two bullets and they knew. We still got those two bullets. Dick had them. We took them from Dick because Chris wanted to show his mokopunas, "This is what the police came hunting the brothers with." Dumdum bullets are against the Geneva Convention. You're not even allowed to use those in war. And what's a policeman from Tokumaru Bay doing running around in our hills with a 357 Smith and Wesson? That's a cannon.

And Chris was tutuing around with it. He's going, "Where's the safety catch?"

He reckoned Laurie was saying, "Don't play with it! Don't play..." And BOOM! Off it went, the second shot to go off accidentally. Chris could have died with those guns going off. But if the brothers died up there, then a lot of *them* would-a died down here because we knew where they were all staying. We were just waiting for that one false move and then the whole town would've just come with their little 22 single-shot shotguns and would-a had a go at them because no one comes into our town and think they can murder Maoris and get away with it. And, you know, and then we go to their big city and then we smoke a couple of joints and they throw us into jail for a couple-a months. And they come here and kill the bros. And just because public say, "Aw no, they No. 1 public enemies, ay. We don't want them."

"Why?"

"Because, you know, they smoke pot, they got hair that looks like rope." And yet at the time we were wholehearted with The Bible.

**Hata Thompson:** When we were riding along, I remember Chris saying to Laurie, "What's all this bullshit you guys are bringing up here. Look what's happening. There's no need to come up firing guns. Why didn't you just send Barney up? Send my brother up. He would-a brought me back down, Laurie." We all had respect for Barnes.

# WHY HATA WAS THE REAL DANGER MAN

**Gisborne Superintendent Paul Wiseman (quoted on Tuesday, February 18, 1986):** We are concerned about the mental state of one of the persons.

**Hata Thompson:** Laurie could-a been in danger from us at the time. I remember when Laurie and Hemi and about another four of them gave me a good hiding. And I still remembered that. I'll never forget it. It was one time in Ruatoria. I was taken from Te Aowera Marae. I ended up spending a night down in the cells. Robbie (John) Robinson was the night jailor that night. I remember because when I came in I was all skinned up. And he asked me, "What happened there? You look like you've been in the pub having a bit of a spar."

I said, "Yeah, I have been in a bit of a fight, John, actually." Me and him were laughing about it.

"Who'd you have a fight with?"

"Aw, with Laurie."

"Who won? I suppose you won."

"Yeah, but then I got a good hiding from the rest of them."

And he goes, "Aw, okay. D'you wanna make a charge against them?"

I said, "No, it's all right. No skin off my nose."

Those guys did a lot of fullas up there. There was a lot of other fullas got done.

**Detective Sergeant Gary Condon:** I think Laurie was most concerned about Hata Thompson because Hata's a bit mad. He's a bit of a meathead. He always went off about things. He was a loose unit. I interviewed Hata after we'd got them all. He just sat there. He wouldn't talk.

*I haven't got Laurie's version of the fight he had with Hata. So I should mention that Hata tends to exaggerate his own advantage and cast himself as the hero when telling stories about scraps he's had. And the reader should bear that in mind. Of course, who won is hardly relevant anyway.*

**Hata Thompson:** Going back to that scrap I had with Laurie, it all started when I was caught on Te Aowera Marae with an ounce on me. So they found that and that was okay. I thought they were going to take me down to the police station to be charged. They said, "We're gonna charge you then we're gonna send you down to Gisborne."

That didn't bother me. I thought, "In the morning I'll just go straight across to social welfare and get me a ticket home."

And we were driving down the street and Hemi and Laurie were coming out of the pub and just walking up the road. They were pretty full. And the cops with me pulled up by the side of the road. And Hemi looked in the car and said, "Aw, too much. We've got you, ay."

Then Hemi pointed at Laurie and said, "Whadya think *he* looks like?"

I thought, "I'll tell him what he looks like."

I said, "He looks like a egg."

"Aw, okay, tell Laurie that. Hey, Laurie, Laurie, come over here, mate."

Hemi told him what I'd said. And Laurie's going, "Aw, okay, you called me a egg, ay. Let's have a fight."

I said, "Okay, well take the handcuffs off then, if it's gonna be me and you."

And he looked at me and I was only a young fulla. I was only about sixteen... seventeen. Then I said, "Look, I don't really wanna have a fight, Laurie."

But they took the handcuffs off and dragged me out of the car. And Hemi Hikawai goes, "Come over here and you guys can have a fight."

I thought, "Aw, okay." I don't mind having a scuffle. I've got a few scars to prove my worth.

So Laurie and me were sizing each other up. Then he had a bit of a go. And I said, "Right, you really want one?"

"Yeah, yeah."

"Okay." BOOM! Out! Just gave him one punch. Knockout!

He gets up and he's stumbling around in front of this person's garden for a while. And the cops didn't like it. So they held me down and they all had a bit of a go and they put a few into me, a few boots.

Then they let me go again and I got straight up and knocked him straight out again. Boom!

And they didn't like it. So they held me down again. And they gave me another kicking. And I got back up and Laurie's mouth was bleeding and he's going, "I'm gonna give it to you young fulla."

And I'm going, "Mate... I just bowled you over twice, Laurie. And you didn't even see them coming. You're fuckin' pissed, man. Go home." I was just a young bugger cos I was only sixteen. But I'd just dropped him twice.

"Aw well," he said, "come on then. We'll do it *again*."

And again they held me and gave me another good hiding, you know, they gave me a few boots.

Then I was up. "Right, where's Laurie?" WOOF! Out again. And I got on top of him and I started beating him up in this garden. We were having a scuffle right there in this driveway of the house next door to the pub. And then the whole lot of them stretched me out and started sticking the boot and everything into me. I ended up on the road outside. I'm just sixteen or seventeen and here's six grown men beating me up. And these were demons, you know, some of these guys were detectives. And then they took me down to the station, charged me, stuck me in the paddy-wagon and sent me all the way to Gisborne. Then when I got there I had to be charged again. That's when I saw old Robbie (Sergeant John Robinson). And he saw the scrapes on my arms from being dragged around. He goes, "Aw, what've *you* been up to?"

I told him and he asked me if I wanted to lay charges.

"No."

"Why not?" And he had a bit of a smile on his face.

"Aw, you know why, Robbie."

"Why?"

"I'm not a fink... I'm not a fink, mate. And I got my own back anyway. I got Laurie a couple-a good ones. So I'm happy."

I had a few fights down there after that. I ended up having a few scuffles down in the police cells. I had a beauty one night: me and about fuckin' eight cops having a scrap down the back. They were big guys, too. I thought that was quite even actually. I kept knockin' them out. Next thing: four cops are tackling me and I'm in the handcuffs. They left me alone after that. This was before we kidnapped Laurie.

**John Heeney (one of the Rasta leaders):** Laurie Naden's a whanaunga, a relative, from Tokumaru Bay. He's related to all of us. All the Maori along the coast are related.

Donna (John's wife): What's the Maori connection?

John: I dunno. But if anyone wants to examine it: the Nadens from Tokumaru Bay - there's the connection.

*That's probably why he didn't get blown away by Chris, you know, when he was kidnapped.*

John: No. He got *saved* up there by Chris.

**Hata Thompson:** When we had Laurie that time I wanted to give him a hiding. But I tortured him with a bit of the old verbal. You know, "Remember that time when we had that fight, Laurie, and all those cops beat me up?"

"Aw, *that.*"

"Yeah, *that*. When all those guys ganged up and gave me a hiding. Remember that?" I said, "You remember it. I won't give you a hiding right now. I just want you to remember it, Laurie. You see, I'm in conrol now, Laurie. Not you. This might be a short space of time. And I know I'm gonna be hunted after this, Laurie. But I'm in control now."

**Laurie Naden:** As far as the other two were concerned I'd never got on well with Hata Thompson. He was an arsehole. And we didn't like each other. But I think he realised, "Shit, we've done it now."

But with Cody Huau, I'd always got on reasonably well with Cody. And he was saying, "Bro, bro, bro, we don't want any part of this."

And Chris was saying, "You shut your mouth," cos he had the two guns.

So they were rather compliant as well. I wasn't happy but I wasn't too concerned at that particular point.

We left the sacred pool where we said the prayers and by that time you could hear the choppers up in the air. I think Dennis Hartley was up and there was one from town. And we came out of that area and up on to a ridge. It was quite clear and there was a chopper and Bruce Meredith was actually in it. He used to be one of the sergeants here. And they weren't far away. They only looked about twenty yards away. But Campbell pointed his rifle up at them. And I said, "Don't do that, Chris."And he said, "Mind your own business."

But fortunately they saw him and the chopper just turned away.

So we turned around. He said, "We're going down to Whareponga." And he gave me this story about another murder down there or another bloody battle or something. And with that we turned around and Chris had disappeared. And to this day I will say he abandoned the other two. I believe he had a, "Jesus, I'm out-a here." So Thompson and Haua and I, we're going through the bush. And eventually Cody says, "Where's Chris?"

I said, "He's fucked off and left ya."

"Na, bro, he won't have done that."

I said, "Well where is he?"

So they sort of accepted, "Well, he has gone." And Haua said to me, "Boy, get off your horse and get out-a here because if he gets you down there, he'll kill ya."

So that's what I did. I got off the horse and ran in the exact opposite direction to everyone else. And I got up on a high point. A chopper came and picked me up and we went back.

By that stage things were starting to go, like the anti-terrorist squad had arrived. All the armed offenders had arrived. And it became quite a major operation.

Thompson and Haua were subdued and uncomfortable, I'd say. In a normal situation, they'd be the smart arses at the edge of a crowd throwing bottles. I actually said in trial that I had no problems with them at all during the kidnapping. And I didn't. They just seemed to be overawed with what had happened, cos I was basically saying to them, "As long as I'm with you, you jokers have got problems because the cops aren't going to stop until they get me back. I think they realised, "Well, piss off, get out of here."

**Hata Thompson:** He wanted to come, old Laurie. First of all he didn't want to come with us. But after Chris took off, he wanted to come with us: me and Cody. And it wasn't 'til *after* I realised *why* he wanted to come with us. It was because he was frightened. He thought the bro (Chris) was waiting in the trees to give him the chop. And I said, "No, no. If I know the bro, he'll be long gone by now."

We headed for a place we said we'd meet Chris at. But our man never showed up. So we made a decision there and then: "Get rid of Laurie. We can't have him running around in the bush, carrying him around with us."

So I took him past this old homestead place in near Tuparoa and Whakaahu. We just rode along this stream. And we just left Laurie right there. I told him to walk back up the track to these yards about four hundred yards away up the hill and to just stand out in the open. We knew they'd find him, because once we got to these yards I just happened to look around and I could see them on this other ridge. They were behind us. But they couldn't get us because we were too far away from them.

I said to Laurie, "What are you gonna do?"

"Come with you."

"Na, you can't come with me." And he was just about begging. But I had to get out of there and tell him to let go or else I'd have to give'm a hiding. So he went up the track and that's when they picked him up in the helicopter. My heart was in my mouth the whole time.

**Detective Sergeant Gary Condon:** We went up in a chopper to look for Laurie. We went past the disused sheep yards, over the hut and then coming down a gully towards Whareponga we could see guys on horseback. And we could see Laurie's glistening head in the sun. I'm sure he'll be pleased to hear that. But we actually could see Laurie's head coming down. And as the chopper

241

pilot moved in a bit closer Campbell got down off his horse and pointed his gun at us so we backed off. Then probably two hours later Laurie came running out into a clearing, naked to the waist. His shirt was tied around his stomach.

And we thought, "Shit, shall we or shan't we?"

**Sergeant Bruce Meredith (retired):** All of a sudden we saw Laurie Naden appear in quite a big clearing below us. And he was on his own and running like hell. So I said to the pilot, "Right, let's get down." And we did. We made a very steep descent, hovered on the ground, picked up Laurie Naden and just took off. And that was it. We just got out of there.

**Laurie Naden:** I know a section of the military – and you'll never get this confirmed – had contingency plans to deal with them in a similar vein to Northern Ireland. These guys were driving people off the coast. You couldn't get insurance past Tolaga Bay unless you were prepared to pay huge premiums.

## ON THE RUN

**Hata Thompson:** While we were on the run, I couldn't even talk for four days. People would talk to me and I just wasn't interested. My mind was thinking at a hundred miles per hour. My mind was full of ideas. It was super- sharp... *super-sharp*. I know the feeling of a hunted animal now. I've felt it once and I'll never forget that feeling. It's an unreal feeling, being hunted. You're not a human any more. You've got men hunting you like they'd hunt down a bad dog. And we knew they wanted to *beat* us like dogs, too. That's exactly what they wanted to do to us for taking Laurie. But not only did they want to beat us, they also wanted to *shoot* us. My mates told me the police were staying at the marae. The Armed Offenders Squad had *machine* guns. They were all dressed up like *Rambo*... hanging out of *heli*-copters.

That day we took Laurie, me and old Cody sat up above these yards all day, from morning until dark. It was hard case. They were Neil Furnell's yards. He was a real estate guy who used to sell houses in town. He owned a farm there. And we were hiding in some trees just inside his property. The police were using his place to take off in their helicopters. We were sitting up above them in the trees just watching them come and go.

And Neil came out to the boundary with his dog this day. And he rode out on this ridge. We'd cut a little hole in his fence, just big enough to get our horses onto his property. And he was riding up and down the fence line and he got quite close to us. But he didn't see where we'd cut the fence. We were lucky he didn't continue round the ridge cos he would've spotted our tracks and he would've thought, "Foo, these guys have just been here. They must be just around here somewhere." And we were. We were right there. It was hard case. We were having a smoke. I had some herb and I said, "Aw, bro, we might as well roll this up. It might be the last smoke of our lives." So we're smoking away. Andthe first thing we notice is that the horse's ears prick up. Then, fuck, we notice Neil's dog. It's smelt this rotten sheep in a ditch and it's gone running over. Then it turns and spots us. The wind's blowing and it must have smelt where the horses have pissed. So the dog runs right up to where we've parked with our horses. It won't go away. And it starts to growl at us. "Grrrrr... grrrrr." Then I heard someone coming. I took a look and it was Neil Furnell riding past on his horse. He was calling out to his dog and whistling to it. He was only about thirty metres away. The dog was growling and looking at us, then turning back to where Neil was whistling and calling. We were gesturing that it should go away and return to Neil. But it was looking at us suspiciously, torn between whether to obey Neil immediately and be a good dog or dob us in and perhaps be considered an even better dog. Well that's how it seemed. Eventually, it turned and ran back to Neil. I waited until it was out of sight and finally exhaled a cloud of sweet pungent smoke... as quietly as possible.

I said to Cody, "I thought we were gonna get snaptured there for a second."

Just after that, an Iroquois helicopter flew over me. I thought it had caught me at one time cos I had to go away to use the old toilet. And I had to go well away from where we were hiding. I think the helicopter actually spotted me, but it wasn't too sure. I had to hide behind this tree and concentrate on becoming part of the tree. It stuck around for about five minutes, hovering over me. I had to go from tree to tree, hiding until I made it back to Cody.We had no gun, nothing. We had nothing really. We just hid in the bush when it was light and moved out into the open when it was dark. We could see the lights of torches as people moved into the bush to search for us at night. So we just stayed out in the open. Whenever we saw a light coming our way we'd just duck off, get cut of itsline.

***Wednesday, February 19, 1986:*** *Armed policemen from throughout the North Island are back in the bush country behind Ruatoria today as the manhunt for the three Rastafarians continues.*

*Armed Offenders Squads and specialist teams from Wellington and Auckland flew to Ruatoria by Air Force Iriquois helicopters late yesterday. Police aren't saying how many men are involved, but there are dozens, including Assistant Police Commissioner Stuart McEwen, who has an operational expertise in armed manhunts. Civilian patrols are also helping out.*

*The search area is now between Tuparoa in the north and Waipiro Bay in the south – a coastal belt of hill country about ten kilometres long.*

*Gisborne District Commander Superintendent Paul Wiseman: "We wish to try to have a peaceful settlement and avoid a confrontation situation unless some person's life becomes endangered. We hope that time will bring them to their senses. They have moved away from a confrontation situation. They have had ample time to think of what has happened and what is likely to happen."*

**Detective Sergeant Gary Condon:** When Laurie got kidnapped I went up on the Saturday and I never got home 'til a month later. I'd just ring my wife and she'd put a suitcase together for me and send it up. My wife got used to it after a while. The wives put up with a lot.

*Thursday, February 20: The manhunt enters its third day and police release the names, descriptions and photographs of the three fugitives.*

*Christopher Campbell is a twenty-nine-year-old, 173 centimetre tall Maori. He has tattoos on his hands, specifically "J to L" on his left hand. He was last seen wearing a grey nylon windbreaker with a white zip and white zipped angle pockets, and dark tracksuit pants, possibly red.*

*Cody Haua is a twenty-seven-year-old, 172cm Maori with cross and swastika tattoos on the left thumb. He was last seen wearing a black woollen coat down to his waist, dark trousers and running shoes. He was carrying a grey canvas bag over his shoulder. And he has dreadlocks and a wispy beard.*

*Hata Thompson is a twenty-year-old, 172cm Maori. He has tattoos of a ship and a boat on his left hand and dots and spots under his left eye. He was last seen wearing a black jersey, dark trousers and red track shoes. He has dreadlocks and his face has recently grown thinner.*

*Police are assuming the men are still in the same twenty square kilometre cordoned area. The policemen are staying at the Ruatoria Hotel, the Hicks Bay Motel and the Ngati Porou Marae in Ruatoria. The Rastas aren't happy about the police staying on the marae. They don't like the idea of a local marae looking after the people who are hunting down whanau.*

*There have been other incidents of fence-cutting since the operation began. The three fugitives aren't believed to be responsible. But it's possible other members of the Rastafarian sect are.*

***Friday, February 21:*** *The hunt is stepped up following a sighting in Tokomaru Bay at 7.15pm. A Ruatoria resident sees a person fitting the description of one of the offenders in a Rusty coloured Torana or Hillman.*

*The resident reports the sighting forty minutes later, after returning home to Ruatoria. The police estimate the car, heading south, would be just north of Gisborne. They set up a roadblock at Pouaua Bridge and all cars coming south are checked. A person is arrested for the possession of drugs, but they're not one of the offenders.*

*Meanwhile, the police make early morning and late afternoon sweeps in a specially-equipped helicopter. It's been brought in from Auckland and has FLIR (forward-looking infra red) scanning equipment capable of detecting the presence of humans or horses in the bush.*

*Supt Paul Wiseman: "The helicopter has located rabbits and sheep. If they were there it would find them. But the cordoned area is wide and they could easily have got through it. It is a huge area of bush. This check is also being made well outside our cordoned area. We have been checking out what we consider target areas and all those target areas have been checked out with negative results. Also, we have looked at the possibility of other people assisting them. I suggest that anybody who contemplates this gives consideration to possible criminal acts on their part. We have named the people so everybody in Ruatoria is well aware of whom we are talking about."*

## THE KIDNAPPERS ARE CAUGHT

***Saturday, February 22, 1986:*** *Early this afternoon Chris Campbell walks on to the family farm at Makarika, near Ruatoria, and gives himself up to his brother, police constable Pani (Barney) Campbell. He is charged with unlawfully detaining Laurie Naden.*

**Barney Campbell:** Whiro Ratahi was the inspector. And I said to him, "Aw well, this might be a good time for me to not come to work for a couple of days."

Chris was still on the loose and with the anti-terrorists up there, I thought there was a good chance that somebody was going to get shot. I didn't want to be there. And I thought, "Well if it's going to happen I want to be mentally prepared and to give the old man and them a bit of support and an idea of what might happen." As it turned out the old man had a fair idea it could turn out that way.

Anyway, I went home. I knocked off work. And to get away from my house, where I was living, I used to go out to the old man's every now and then, cos you gotta go along a little road down the river to where he is. And I didn't think the TV people would take the time to follow me there. Mind you there were helicopters flying all over the place. I basically stayed out there to keep out of the road until one day my cousin told me Chris had come home during the night.

I had to look after my own back, you see. And they said, "Go talk to him." And I said, "No, no, I'm going to see the boss first. We'll take it from there."

John Bethwaite from Napier was now over-seeing the whole operation because Whiro Ratahi had to concentrate on the Queen's visit to Gisborne. John could-a done it the other way. He could-a said, "You stay here and we'll go up the hill and get him." But he said, "Do you think you can get him in?"

And I said, "Aw, well, I'll do the best I can." So we got him in.

When the trouble starts the cousins from the north generally come down. The whole family had been up the hill to see Chris. They'd just come back. He was less than ten minutes away. I knew he wasn't far away. It's really not heavy bush country. You can stand anywhere on our old place there and you can see everything around you. But if you're in the bush, it's only manuka bush, you can see who's coming and who's going. So I dare say that if Chris saw an army of policemen coming across the paddock he would-a just gone back deeper into the bush. He knew the lay of the land. I went out with Mum, the old man, and I don't know who else. But he saw us coming and he just came out of the manuka and we went up to the house to try and sort everything out.

I was telling Chris, "You'll be going in. You have to come in and it would be preferable if you walked in," that sort of thing. I wasn't threatening or anything. I was just laying it on the line. "There's really no way out. The sooner you get it over and done with the better."

But I sort of half-way got the impression he might resist. And I just wasn't too sure, if it came down to a good old scrap, he might grab a spade and bang me with it and there were little kids around, you see? That was my main concern. I didn't worry about having a scrap. And I was a bit wary of my other brother, Joe, cos I couldn't see him. Joe was also in the Rastas. And he was mouthing off, too. Not so much rarking Chris up, he was just saying that he didn't think I should be doing what I was doing. Joe's the youngest.

In the end I just said to the brother in law, "I'm gonna grab him and I might wanna hand."

And he said, "Yeah, I'm with ya."

So we just walked around to the front of the house where Chris was talking and I just put my hand on his shoulder and said, "Well, we're away. You're comin' in." He didn't resist. He wasn't violent or anything, really. But let's just say he took a long time putting one foot in front of the other one. You know?

I said, "No. You gotta come in. I can't go back to the police station and say I let you go." Then I just yelled out to one of the cousins to ring the station and tell them I was bringing Chris in. I had to scream at her to do it. She didn't say she didn't want to do it, but she sort of looked at me and I said, "Ring the fuckin' police station now!"

They sent the helicopter out and Malcolm Meihana was in it with them. He made them land on the flat about half a mile away, where they had a good view but they weren't too close. I remember him telling me later, "I didn't think they needed to land at your old man's house with all their armoury." Malcolm had been a policeman up there too before my time. So he was very polite.

Then a car came up with a couple of the locals, Dave Neilson from Gisborne and one of the others. Anyway, they came up and we just put Chris in the car and away to Gisborne. And that was him out of the road.

**Hata Thompson:** Cody and I took off to Rotorua after letting Laurie Naden go. We were in Rotorua by the following night. We were heading to the Dire Straits, Brothers in Arms concert up in Auckland. We were thinking of going to the concert and then handing ourselves in straight afterwards. But we ended up doing a circuit up around the North Island. We drove straight through two police roadblocks on the coast. They had a look at me and we just cruised through. At one stage we pulled up next to Sergeant John Robinson at the lights. I waved out to him. But I don't think he was looking at us because he's normally got a photographic memory for faces. We all looked a bit the same with our dreads and our beards anyway. So we carried on. Cody's sister helped us out for a couple of days. But she freaked out after we saw John Robinson at the lights. After that she told us we were on our own.

Me and Cody, we left my grandmother's house just outside of Gisborne and walked for a couple of hours. We stayed the night under a bridge, with a raincoat for a blanket. The next morning we sat up in a tree and watched the cops driving past. Eventually, we split up. I was caught when I was hitchhiking up the coast from Gisborne to Ruatoria. I was walking along the road, right in the middle of nowhere. A police truck came along and they were gonna go right past me. The cops looked at me and I waved out, and they waved back. Then suddenly: Errrrrrrrrrrrrr (their tyres squealed to a halt). The cops told me I was the last one; they'd already caught the other two. As it turned out they only had Chris. Cody was still out there. They caught me on the main East Coast highway near Tolaga Bay on Sunday at 11.35am.

**Former Sergeant John Robinson (retired policeman):** When Laurie Naden got captured it made the Gisborne Armed Offenders Squad the laughing stock of the rest of the New Zealand AOS squads. It should never have happened. There weren't enough men for a start. We just had the Gisborne squad and we needed more. The planning obviously wasn't up to scratch. But our guys weren't very popular with the rest of the Armed Offenders Squads after that.

*Monday, February 24, 1986: Campbell and Thompson appear in Gisborne District Court charged with unlawfully detaining Laurie Naden.*
*The large scale police operation centred on the Ruatoria district has now been scaled down. Wellington and Auckland staff, including Assistant Commissioner Stuart McEwen, have now returned home. But a fresh team from Gisborne has been sent to Ruatoria to maintain police numbers. That night Cody Haua surrenders.*

**Barney Campbell:** The phone rang about 11pm and it was Cody's family, saying he was at home and he'd had a good chat with his mother and he was ready to come in. And we just went out to get him.

And then the next day we had to get some stuff they had out in the bush: tear gas and a radio and some other stuff. He wasn't going to tell us where it was because he didn't want to involve anyone else. So we went and told the boss. "We'll get the stuff back. He'll tell us where it is as long as we don't involve anyone else."

So we had to sneak him out in the daylight. That's another thing. John Bethwaite, who was in charge, had told Genevieve Westcott, the reporter from Close Up, to get as far away from the police station as possible. But they put a camera outside. There was a vacant paddock next door to the station back then. They mounted their camera there and aimed it straight at the police station. And they had a cameraman on it all the time. So we had to sneak Cody out during the daytime. And he took us up the road to get the stuff back. It was all hidden under culverts and what-have-you. Then we had to take him back in again. And then we had to take him out again to take him to Gisborne. But by the time we were ready to take him to Gisborne we weren't bothered whether they filmed it or not.

The car was right outside the door and all we had to do was get in and drive off. And Westcott was standing in front of the car going like this, mctioning for us to stop. Well, she got out of the road. Otherwise I would-a gone straight over the top of her. Mind you, I suppose she was only doing her job.

The next morning Mallie Meihana and I were in the police station but we only had Swann Dris on, see? It was raining outside. We were leaning against the public counter and Westcott came in and we all said, "Good morning."

And Malcolm said, "Aw, lovely day today."

And she says to him, "Are you Barney Campbell?"

And he said, "Aw, no, no."

And I said, "What you want him for?"

And she said, "Aw, I'd like to talk to him."

And I said, "Well I'm not sure if he wants to talk to you."

And she said, "Well I'd rather get *his* story from *him*."

And I said, "Well I'll tell *him* when I see *him*." You know?

And she went out. One of the cops said to her later, "He's the one you were talking to." Apparently, she did her nana, ay. But by then she wasn't gonna get anywhere near me. So we had our lighter moments.

*Tuesday, February 25, 1986: Cody Haua appears in the Gisborne District Court charged with unlawfully detaining Laurie Naden.*

# CHAPTER 4

**BARNEY QUITS THE POLICE**

*It was about this time that Barney Campbell decided to quit the police force. The final straw was when he was questioned about the arson of the police station.*

**Barney Campbell:** I was actually on leave when the police station went up on November 19, 1985. But I'd gone back in on the day to tidy up my correspondence.

Then a couple of months down the track the police started questioning me about whether I lit it. The first I knew about it was when John Robinson, the cop from Gisborne, told me. He was relieving for us at that time. John called me up on the radio and said, "Barry Hunter, the Detective Inspector from Napier, is in town. He wants to talk to you." That's the first I knew about it, that they'd come to see me.

It was a real surprise. I sort of expected to be spoken to a lot earlier like even the next day because I knew I was the last one in the police station that night. I thought as a matter of procedure they would talk to the guy who was last in there. But it was some time before they talked to me. And I thought, "Crikey, have they run out of good ideas or something."

They caused me to think that I was a suspect for the fire, for burning the police station down. They questioned me for an hour or so and asked me eighty-five questions. I had that figure in my head for a long time. I counted them. I remember saying to Hunter, "I didn't burn the police station down. I'm telling you that right now."

I know my old boss Norm Gray was heavied by the cops who went to interview him. He told me. I think he might've been in Otahuhu by then.

The good thing was I told Hunter what I thought of the way I was treated. But no, Norm didn't do that. He just didn't have it in him to do that sort of thing. And I was glad. I was happy when they caught the real arsonist.

After that I quit the police force. I couldn't believe they'd suspect me of burning down the police station after everything I'd been through in Ruatoria. And I didn't like the way I was treated. I might've left because of my family involvement. I might've. But I didn't. Then with that one I thought, "If they're looking at you sideways, mate, you're better off out of it."

**Sergeant John Robinson (retired):** When the courthouse and police station building got burnt, three days after the fire Barney Campbell told the CIB guys that he'd heard that John Heeney and David Mataira had done it. He'd heard through the grapevine that Heeney and Mataira had started the fire.

But the CIB guys never ever wrote that tip-off down. They didn't do anything about it.

Anyway the forensics showed that in the fire these tyres had been stacked up and burnt.

Now Barney Campbell, Norm Gray and Waho Tibble were the three cops in Ruatoria when the court house-cum-police station got burnt. So they asked them, "Were any tyres in the station?"

And they said, "Yes. There were some tyres there. They were exhibits from a case we were working on."

And then they asked a cleaning lady: "Did *you* see any tyres there?"

"No. There were no tyres there."

'Hello, who's telling lies? The police are. The police are telling lies.'

Weeks later, a detective comes up from Hawkes Bay. By this time, Norm Gray had gone to Otahuhu in Auckland, Waho had gone back to Feilding and Barney was the only one left.

And this guy came up and he interviewed Barney Campbell as a suspect, and he interviewed Norm and Waho as well on the grounds that a cleaner had said she saw no tyres.

And yet three cops said there were tyres there and they believed her instead of the cops. They checked us all out at different times. Secretly they inquired first to see if the cops had done it themselves. 'We can't get anyone else, we'll see if it's one of our own.' So we were scrutinised quite closely. After a while, you had to write down all the time where you were and what you were doing so that if they asked you at any time, you'd be able to show them.

Anyway Barney was devastated that he was a suspect. Shit, you couldn't have got a straighter guy than Barney. And he said to this guy, "I told them who did the fire three days after it happened."

So the detective looked through the whole file. And he said, "There's no record of you telling them that."

So they got a team together and they went out and they interviewed those two guys, Heeney and Mataira. And they arrested them.

And I remember I was still relieving up there when they brought Heeney and Mataira in and charged them.

I went around to see Barney and said, "They've just charged those guys with the arson of the courthouse and the police station."

And he said, "Oh, at long last."

But by then he'd already decided to leave the force. And I couldn't talk him out of it.

I sent a message to Waho and to Norm Gray to tell them that they'd made two arrests and they both sent messages back thanking me.

*Thursday, March 6: Chris Campbell is charged with having cannabis in the Gisborne police cells.*

*Friday, March 21: The new police station is opened in Ruatoria. The Minister of Police Ann Hercus makes a speech, praising the Concerned Citizens of Ruatoria, also known as the Neighbourhood Watch Group and the vigilantes.*


## RASTAS IN COURT FOR KIDNAPPING


*Monday, April 7, 1986: The depositions hearing against the three Rastas charged with unlawfully detaining Laurie Naden begins in Gisborne.*

*Chris Campbell faces additional charges of threatening to kill, making use of a firearm to prevent arrest, armed robbery and burglary.*

*Raymond Maraki (Hata, Sam) Thompson faces two additional charges of burglary, making use of a firearm to prevent arrest, unlawfully taking a car and possession of cannabis.*

*Cody Haua faces two additional charges of receiving, and one of burglary.*

*In his evidence Naden relives the day he was taken hostage:*

*The Armed Offenders Squad take up positions fifty metres away from the hut. Voice appeals begin at 6.39am. Naden sees Campbell outside the hut with a 3030 rifle across his chest. He tells Campbell to drop the gun. Campbell falls to the ground and the rifle goes off. Haua and Thompson appear. He loses sight of Campbell. A short time later he feels something at his neck. Someone yells, "Drop that gun or I will blow your fucking head off!" He turns. Campbell's holding the rifle to his neck.*

*"What the fuck are you doing here, Laurie, hunting me like an animal? We used to shake hands and now you are hunting me!"*

*Campbell takes Naden's pistol. He says he'll count to ten. If the other members of the Armed Offenders Squad haven't gone, he'll shoot Naden.*

*"Don't be a fool," Naden tells him. "That won't help you."*

*"I knew it would come to this," Campbell replies. "This is a civil war and I will die and take as many people with me as I can."*

*Naden sees Haua and Thompson. Thompson's carrying a .22 rifle. Naden uses his radio to tell other members of the Armed Offenders Squad to move back.*

*Campbell talks about being hunted, but says he feels safer now that he has a hostage. He takes Laurie's gun belt and beret and puts them on. He puts Laurie's pistol in the holster. "I've always wanted one of these," he says. "Now I'm a real armed offender."*

*He asks Naden if he knows why police didn't shoot him, then answers his own question: "Because I am Jah and you can't kill The Almighty These others are also protected by me."*

**Dread, by Joseph Owens:** Even more common than the name "God" is the name "Jah". One can only conjecture how this word has come to be the predominant divine title among the brethren. One sometimes hears the Hebrew word "Hallelu-jah" pronounced with a hard 'J' sound and a strong stress on the last syllable. The Jehovah's Witness' Bible, sometimes found among the Rastas, translates Hallelujah in Revelation 19 as "Praise Jah". It seems quite possible that this is the source of the name.

*Campbell unloads Naden's pistol and looks at the bullets. He becomes very angry. He accuses Naden of using dum dum bullets.*
*Campbell tells Naden how he got his rifle. He says he took it from a house near Ruatoria. He says its owner had threatened to shoot Campbell and his wife, and the police had done nothing about it. Naden asks if he can smoke a cigarette. Campbell says yes. Campbell takes out some cannabis for himself and rolls a joint. "I am a Maori warrior," he says, "and we now have a war. Cody, point the pistol at Laurie." But Haua's not keen. He says he doesn't want to be involved in any killings. Campbell says he'll shoot the Queen because she has no right to rule New Zealand. He describes her as the harlot of Babylon. (It's not an original tag. Rastafarians all over the world refer to the Queen that way.)*
*Campbell asks for his brother Barney, some food and some cannabis to be brought to him by helicopter. Naden says this will be done. But it isn't.*
*Naden continues the story to where he's picked up by police in a helicopter. After the evidence-in-chief is accepted, Chris Campbell cross-examines Laurie Naden. He asks why the armed offenders were sent to execute an arrest warrant. Naden says this was a command decision and that he had no part in it.*

**Dread, by Joseph Owens:** The present queen, Elizabeth II, is considered to be Elizabeth I reincarnate, and both are new embodiments of the ancient whore of Babylon. After reading Psalm 137:8, "O daughter of Babylon, who art to be destroyed; happy shall he be that rewardeth thee as thou deserved." one Rasta stated: "Who is this whore do you think? It's the queen! It must be a queen because she is the daughter of Babylon. It must be Elizabeth."

*Wednesday, April 9:* Chris Campbell is back in court. He pleads guilty to a charge of having cannabis in the Gisborne police cells on March 6.

*Police officer Chester Haa tells the court that a strong smell was noticed coming from Campbell's cell. A search revealed that Campbell had a plastic bag containing cannabis inside his trouser leg.*

*When Judge Hole asks if he has anything to say before receiving his sentence, Campbell in turn asks that he be given a Bible. "Why do you need a Bible?"*

*"So I can offer an explanation." Campbell then quotes a passage from The Bible, which he says invokes people to gather the seeds of the earth. He says, "I am a Rastafarian. I believe in God, not myself."*

*Judge Hole sentences Campbell to seven days in prison.*

**Dread, by Joseph Owens:** The sacred character of ganja is accepted by all Rastafarians: they see it spoken of in The Bible; they use it as a sacrament in their worship; they pray devoutly every time they light up the pipe. Much Rastafarian discourse about ganja is studded with biblical allusions and references, and the brethren see biblical foundations from the very first to the very last chapter of the scriptures.

God also said, "See, I give you every seed-bearing plant all over the earth, and every tree that has seed-bearing fruit on it to be your food." (Genesis 1:29)...

...Revelations 22:2: "The leaves of the tree were for the healing of the nations."...

...Even the Lord himself is pictured as drawing mightily of the holy herb: "Smoke rose from his nostrils, and a devouring fire from his mouth that kindled coals into flame." (Psalms 18:9).

**Russell Fairbrother, Napier lawyer and Labour MP:** I met Chris when he was in Wanganui prison. It might have been when he was on remand on the charge. And he didn't want to be represented because he was sure he was right and he thought that if he was right he'd get off. He was persuaded by the social worker Denis O'Reilly, who'd spent a lot of time with the Rastas, that he should be represented. I agreed to on the basis that I would run the defence as I saw appropriate and if at any stage he and I didn't agree then I'd step aside.

So we got right through to the end of the Crown case and I thought his defence was especially well established then, mainly that of self defence and I thought the jury were quite receptive to what we were doing.

The crown had called all their police witnesses and the decision was do we call evidence or not. I was prepared to call Chris. But I wanted him to give evidence in English and to give quite carefully controlled evidence because the story he told me sounded quite plausible.

I don't think Chis Campbell and the others ever saw the full number of the police party. I think they were dealing with people who were yelling at them from the cover of bush. And there was certainly no need for them to be arrested in that manner, in that way.

And that came out in trial. The reason for wanting to speak to them was not clearly established and certainly having the Armed Offenders Squad there was fairly tenuous. And I think during the trial people like Malcolm Thomas kept on giving circuitous answers as to why they were there and why they used those methods.

And that is why I thought we had a good defence. Clearly there was some game-playing going on.

But in the end Chris decided that he wanted to run the case his way as was his right. He felt he needed to speak to the jury in Maori. He needed to explain what his beliefs were. And I knew that would alienate the judge and the jury. And that's when he and I parted ways.

I came back to Napier and then I get a summons from the court requiring me to attend as a witness. And I get into court and I'm about to go in the witness box and the judge asks me to wait by the box. And I did. And he asks Chris Campbell how I can help. And Chris explained that I was the expert, that I'd thoroughly investigated the matter, I knew all about it and the jury should hear from me as an expert as to what had gone on. From his point of view there was a lot of sense in that because I did have a good knowledge at the time. But it wasn't the way to do it in law. So the judge ordered that I couldn't be called. And I went home again.

**Denis Kohn, Gisborne lawyer (retired):** Ultimately, Russell Fairbrother, Doug Rishworth and I, we all got sacked. I think Russell was the first to go and I remember Doug got sacked before I did because there was a Law Society do on in Rotorua and Doug had gone on ahead of me. So he must have been sacked by that stage. And this particular morning, as we had been in the habit of doing, we went down to the cells to talk to the guys. Campbell always wanted to see us. I went down there this particular morning and the screws just quietly told me that there'd been a bit of a rumble in the cell and my guy had been given a going-over. When I saw him, Thompson, he'd obviously had a dealing-to. He didn't have a great deal to say. But Campbell was the one who was delivering all the commands and orders and had been running the trial for the three of them really. And he said that I wasn't required any more because I was obstructing justice. I was obstructing the truth coming out. I think that's what he said.

So I more or less got my marching orders. And I explained to him that I would have to explain that to the judge. Anyway, the jury had been called in and then of course the judge came in. And the court is starting to sit. I had told the registrar what had happened and he had obviously told the judge. I don't know whether the judge was conniving at it or not. I should probably have gone to see the judge in chambers to tell him what had happened. But I was so pissed off with Campbell that I thought, "Well bugger it, the jury can hear this." And I stood up and said that I'd been having consultation with the defendants downstairs and had been told by Mr Campbell that I was obstructing the truth coming out therefore under the circumstances I felt obliged to ask for leave to withdraw. And there was nothing that Chilwell, the judge, could do about it.

**Hata Thompson (July 2001):** If Chris had listened to the lawyers we wouldn't have gone to jail. It's a bit hard for me, that one. At the time I was only nineteen when that happened. I'm thirty-six now. The memory's sort of dim on those days.

**Detective Sergeant Gary Condon:** Campbell would have organised that they all sacked their lawyers. He would have decided that he wanted his day in court and felt that he had the ability to do it. I can always remember when he opened his defence, he did a bloody haka in court. The judge told him to finish it. But he kept going and finally stopped. And then for the next three days or so he ran his defence, called his own witnesses. He wasn't that impressive. He would've been far better off to stick with Russell Fairbrother. I think he was just trying to promote himself.

# CHAPTER 5

## CHRIS CAMPBELL'S KIDNAPPING STORY

*August 26, 1986 (seventh day of kidnapping trial): Chis Campbell tells the court his version of how he, Cody and Hata came to take Laurie Naden hostage. A lot of the action has already been covered in this book from the perspectives of* people like Laurie Naden and Hata Thompson. But I believe the trial notes of Campbell's testimony rank alongside the notes of the Joe Nepe murder trial as one of the strangest documents that has ever been recorded by a New Zealand court stenographer. Apart from that, Campbell is a cracking – and eloquent – storyteller with an incredible memory for detail. For those reasons I am unapologetic about running so much of it verbatim. To be honest, I feel I'm doing New Zealand a favour by saving his version of events from the so-called dustbin of history.

Campbell's defending himself and says he's basing his defence on the fact he and his brethren feel the New Zealand police have persecuted them. He says his concepts of spirituality are in constant conflict with the institutions, which govern society, and that society frowns on his group. He says that in the past the police had also persecuted the prophets Rua Kenana and Te Kooti and the great warrior Te Rauparaha.

Campbell tells the jury that he wishes to be judged by them only if they hold the concept that Jesus Christ rose from the dead. He also speaks about his strong belief in wairua (spirituality), his attachment to the land and his part in a Maori land issue, the return of Mount Hikurangi. He says it's because of his spiritual affiliation with the taonga (treasure) Mt Hikurangi that he finds himself in court. After going on national television on the Hikurangi land issue, he says he became the subject of intense police scrutiny. This affected him and his family, including his brother, Constable Barney Campbell.

Chris Campbell says he felt hunted and was told by a senior detective that his destiny was in the mortuary.

Campbell says that people often describe incidents to him because they consider him to be a leader of the Rastafarians. On one occasion Graeme Mathieson, who had also been accused of burning down Rasta John Heeney's house, had pointed a rifle at a cousin of Campbell's and told him that the horse he was riding belonged to him (Mathieson). His brother Pani (Barney) arrested Mathieson and brought him to Gisborne, "but those fellows down here let him go".

He outlines other incidents: a rock-wielding attack on a house after which a woman gave birth prematurely, and the attack on Paddy and Forli Brown.

On another occasion, says Campbell, Hata Thompson was asleep on a marae when four policemen, including Detective Sergeant Naden, kicked in the door and began to beat him. Thompson was taken outside on to the road. A woman asked what they were doing and Naden said, "This is how we fix these black bastards up."

*Campbell says he's descended from some of the finest fighting men in the world – the Maori Battalion soldiers known as Nga Tama Toa, who had fought Rommel in the desert. He's also related to Moana Ngarimu VC and Colonel Awatere MC. With this sort of bloodline, Campbell says, he's inclined to be a tama toa, or warrior. He says this is an important part of his defence because of the way he reacted when the Armed Offenders Squad came to Whakaahu.*

*About this time, Campbell says, he was involved in a dispute with his elders. They told him Whakaahu was a tapu place and that he shouldn't go there. They felt he was becoming spiritually affected and said he might be suffering from mate Maori, or Maori sickness.*

*Campbell tells the jury that the day before he took Laurie Naden hostage was brimming with spiritual significance. Campbell, Hata Thompson and Cody Haua were riding on horseback towards Whakaahu when Campbell experienced a revelation. He saw half a rainbow under Mt Hikurangi. He interpreted this as a sign of foreboding.*

*They carried on riding. When they arrived at Whakaahu Campbell had a premonition that something bad was going to happen. Their rifles were stolen from one of the vigilantes, and he noticed that the ammunition had been excessively modified.*

*Visions of rainbows are taken very seriously around Ruatoria. Here are two other interview excerpts where the vision of a strange rainbow is given special significance.*

**Interview with Hata Thompson:** *A lot of people talk about Hori Gage predicting a leader to come out of Ngati Porou. When I talk to your mum, she thinks the person's supposed to come out of Mangahanea Marae. When I talk to Sarah Sykes, she thinks the leader's supposed to come out of Te Aowera. Every family thinks it's them that's got the new leader. I talked to John Taituha, a mate of mine from Waihirere (just south of Gisborne). He said, "Don't worry, Gus. My family all think it's me."*

Hata: My thing is in a way I believe that. But you'd just know, ay. In Maoridom, you'd just know if it was the right person. It's a spiritual sort-a thing.

*Well, the impression I get is that Chris thought it was him. John thinks it's him. And quietly Beau thinks it's him.*

They're all barking up the wrong tree, mate. I don't believe that.

*Whadyu reckon? Do you think I'm on the right track there?*

Aw, I wouldn't say you're on the *wrong* track. You'd be pretty spot on...

*So what are the prophecies about that?*

This is something I've never really talked about. I saw one, two, three, four...
I saw a white rainbow with a double rainbow and a single rainbow, on top of
Whakaahu. Yeah. (Hata draws some lines on the table with his finger). The white
rainbow, that's on one side. The double rainbow, it's over there. And there's
another rainbow here like that. And over here we have a little round one.

*Yeah?*

A round rainbow... I'd never seen one in my life and to this day I've never
seen a round rainbow again. And when that happened it was of great spiritual
significance to us. It was like there was a power there or something.

*People talk about white rainbows though don't they? White rainbows mean
something on the coast, ay?*

A white rainbow's death. White rainbows signify death. They signify that
someone's died, someone who's high-ranking for the Ringatu faith. That's the
faith started by Te Kooti and the white rainbow is supposed to be a sign of him.
We're all Ringatu. I'm a Ringatu. And they say, well, why don't you go to
church and pray. Well I don't believe that. Your church is your self. You're the
temple. My belief is your body is the temple of God. If your house inside *you* is
opened towards *Him* then that's the power. That's the power that people can't get
over. I've felt that power. I know that power. That power is what has helped me
with God. I tell you what: ever since that time with those rainbows I've always
felt that power. About twelve of us saw them.

A lot of people look at you like, "They're kookie," sort-a thing, you know. So
I don't talk about it too much. I just keep it quiet. I don't know what a round
rainbow means specifically. All I know is a round rainbow is something very
special. That's all I know. There was a lot of meaning in that round rainbow. I
think it was showing us something. But we just didn't pick it up.

**Notes to myself after a conversation with Sarah Sykes:** Sarah said her
kaitiaki or spirit guide is a white rainbow. She said that her husband and kids
have seen the white rainbow spanning from Te Aowera to Mount Hikurangi. It
blew them away apparently. When she sees it the kaitiaki gives her messages,
and she listens.

On New Years morning at the millennium Sarah said she didn't bother going
up to the mountain through all the mud and rain. But she said that there was a big
ring of lightning around that Te Aowera area, like a big golden ring, like a
wedding band.

She thought that everyone would have seen it. But it was only that Te
Aowera area and members of her family who saw it.

Then she realised what her father had said. "You don't have to go anywhere to find it. It will come to you. The magic and the power will come to you." Sarah says the discs, the swirling circles on the facing board of Te Aowera Marae are Ringatu symbols.

**Chris Campbell in court:** I didn't know where those rifles had come from but it was later revealed to me that they were the property of an active member of the vigilantes. This was relayed to me by a nephew of a chap called Maurice, who was also a vigilante. At this stage several persons had begun to collect various articles of weaponry that were in the possession of these people. The reason being that at one stage we wished to make contact with (journalist) Pat Booth of the Auckland Star in Auckland and show him these various forms of weaponry. With the .3030 rifle were seventeen rounds of ammunition and these seventeen rounds of ammunition were all excessively modified in a way that is detrimental to the Geneva Convention.

I went to the pool that afternoon just on dark. There was still an overwhelming feeling of foreboding hanging over me. I got there. I had a karakia. The karakia lasted approximately twenty-five minutes. I am able to make this observation of the point of time because it takes me approximately twenty-five minutes to perform this ritual every day, three times a day, sometimes four, other times, twelve times a day. After I finished having a karakia – a prayer – I took all my clothes off and waded into the pool. At this stage a very heavy feeling began to come upon me. It was a feeling that it's very hard to describe. And I became frightened. I backed underneath the waterfall and had another prayer. I felt a force come upon me. I got out of the pool and it was a big effort to get out of the pool. I had a feeling that some supernatural force, perhaps, for lack of a better way to describe it, was pulling me back underneath the waterfall.

I got out and had another karakia. It was at this point that I began to realise a profound change come over me. It could be described as a lifting of I think the word is ihihi and ihihi means a fighting spirit, perhaps.

It was at that stage I began to believe that I was invincible. I likened it unto Samson in the Bible, when he quoted when he fought the Philistines and he smote one thousand of them with a donkey's jawbone and he said the spirit of the Lord came mightily upon him. The same occurrence was also mentioned when he slayed the lion. But I knew I was a warrior because I felt it. And it was at that point that I decided I wasn't going to run any more. That I was going to make my stand the way my ancestors made their stand. And at that moment words came into my head and those words were... ... Kohi mati uru – it took me

– e koro o au mate whata koia e mate uru roa. At that time I did not know what that was. Some time later I was able to be given the translation and the meaning. The proverb is the old battlecry of the Ngati Porou people and it means if I should die it will not be as a floundering octopus but like a hammerhead shark, which is the mightiest warrior in the oceans.

I went back to the hut. I did not talk to either of the other two defendants. I do not recall much of the activity of the rest of that evening. I remember having another prayer before we went to bed.

Early that morning I heard a voice in my head. And that voice sounded like it was saying, "Chris Campbell, come out with your hands up. This is the police. I call on you to surrender."

I was wearing a pair of red woollen longjohn underwear and nothing else. I recall a sense of urgency coming over me almost like a feeling of great panic. The next few moments are not quite clear. But I remember thinking that after all these months of running and hiding I had reached the end of my road. The voice appeal was still sounding outside. I jumped out of bed, grabbed the .3030 rifle, which is over there (indicates with head) and bolted out the door.

I saw three policemen standing in the direction, which I hoped to effect my escape. I did not know who these policemen were. One of them had a dog... ... The constable holding the dog yelled out to me to drop the rifle and get down on the grass. He was side-on to me... ... I had the gun like that (indicates pointing the gun). He called out to me to drop it or he would shoot. I stopped and turned around and faced him and it was at that stage that I realised something was wrong with the dog handler. He was pointing his pistol at me and he was yelling out, "Drop it! Drop it! Before I shoot you!" I did not drop it. I began to feel that if I was to be shot so be it. A very, very strong feeling came over me. I knew that I was standing on sacred ground and I began to believe that my tipunas were all around me, great grandpeople. At that point, I believed they could not kill me. I began to believe that they could not kill me because the wairua tapu was covering me. At this stage the dog handler was becoming very erratic in his movements. His dog was barking and he seemed to be having trouble containing it. I also realised that the dog was not pulling in my direction as one would otherwise expect but was wanting to go towards the direction of Sergeant Naden...

... At this stage his gun hand began to falter and wave dangerously around in the air and I thought that at any moment I would be shot. Words were spoken between him and I. I'm not sure of some of the exact words that I said to him, but they were of the nature that if he was going to shoot me he should hurry up and do so. At that point I began to move away from the dog handler and I thought if I got over the bank I would be safe, because then I would disappear into the bush. And they would not be able to catch me because I am good in the bush. I fell over... ... that is where I tripped over. The Winchester discharged into the ground. I lay there, must have been only seconds, and I looked back to where the dog handler was and I saw that he was running away. I remember this incident quite well because of the way he was running. I remember he had his dog in his left arm, his back was to me and he was running up the hill.

Up to that point, I had not thought of the other two policemen that were in the area. I lay on the ground for some seconds and I sort of began to believe that any minute I could possibly be shot while lying on the ground. I recall a feeling of defencelessness coming over me and I recall thinking, "Well, any minute, this is it. I'm going to get it."

I sprung up and made a dash towards cover or where I believed cover was... ... I recall sprinting and diving over the bank and almost colliding with Sergeant Laurie Naden. He had his back to me. He was crouched down behind the bank, his pistol was in his right hand and he was pointing it up in the air like that. When I suddenly jumped over behind him he acknowledged my presence. He did not turn around. He did not take any type of overt movement. He just turned his head side-on to me and said, "You've got me, Chris."

I would have possibly been from here to the Crown prosecutor in distance from him. Sergeant Naden lowered his pistol, put it back in his holster. He still had his back to me. And at that stage I was still not quite sure of who it was that was in front of me.

Because he had a uniform, which was really all black - black jersey, black trousers, black Army boots, he had a black beret on his head and all the skin of his face and neck was blackened with boot polish. The next stage was recognition of Sergeant Naden by myself.

I saw that it was Laurie Naden. I said, "What are you doing here, Laurie? Why have you come here?"

He said, "I didn't want to come here, Chris. I'm only following orders."

He then asked me if he could sit down. We both sat down. He asked me if he could have a cigarette. I definitely recall saying to Sergeant Naden that it would be a good idea if we both had a smoke and try and settle things down a bit. He produced a packet of smokes from his shirt pocket and offered me a cigarette.

I declined and told him that I did not smoke. I asked him if he had any cigarette tissues. He felt his pockets and said no.

I then said, "Why have you come here, Laurie?"

He said, "I don't know, Chris." He then added, "It's a matter of some warrants."

I said, "Why have you come dressed as you have, Laurie?"

He said that it was part of his job.

At this stage probably no more than a couple of minutes had gone past. I was still holding the rifle across my lap. He had his pistol in the holster. I said to him, "You had better pass me your pistol, Laurie, as I believe that you have come here to injure me."

He did this. He passed the pistol to me without hesitation. He passed it butt first, like he was holding the barrel.

He said he was acting under orders from higher-up and personally he did not want any part of these orders that he was carrying out.

I said, "Why didn't you knock on the door, Laurie?"

He said that he had been informed that he wasn't allowed to knock on the door.

I said, "Why didn't you yell out and tell me it was you?"

He said that that's how he personaly would have wanted to hardle the situation but that he had been over-ruled from his superiors. He said to me, "Let me go now, Chris."

I asked him how many police officers were there with him. He said there was the dog handler... ...He said that Dodsy was in the area. I took Dodsy to be a chap named Jeffrey Dods, who I knew from my school days. He also said that Tim Reedy was in the area too. But that's all there were.

Laurie had a battery-powered loudhailer with him and I remember asking him if he was in charge of the scene. He said, yes, that he was in charge of the operation.

I said, "Well, you order your men out of the area, Laurie," because I felt at the time that I would be shot by marksmen holding a rifle. These were the thoughts that were going through my mind. I had heard how the Armed Offenders operated. My oldest brother is a policeman of fourteen years experience. And I often heard him describe operations that he was personally involved in with other policemen. So my feeling at the time was that I could be shot at any stage.

I said to Laurie to call out on the megaphone and order his men to leave the area. At this stage, Laurie had an earplug in his ear with a wire running down to his radio. And there was a type of button instrument on his thumb. I realised that the button activated the radio. He began to speak into his hand, saying, "Dodsy, this is Laurie, clear the area. Chris has captured me." It was at this stage that he began to have difficulty with his radio. It wasn't working. And he couldn't seem to get any response from the Armed Offenders who were present. He disconnected the headphones from off his head and the button part that he had in his hand and put it in his pocket.

I said to him, "How does the radio work, Laurie, to talk to the other fullas."

He said, "Chris, it's no good now because I've got the button and I've pulled it out and it won't work any more."

I said, "Will you use the loud-hailer and instruct the rest of the AOS to evacuate the rest of the area?"

He did so. The first effort was aborted because the volume switch had been turned up on full. He then adjusted it and began a voice appeal.

But they were not responding and he indicated to me during the time that it was part of their procedure, that if anything like this should happen this was the normal course of action taken.

I said, "How don't I know, Laurie, that there is somebody sneaking around."

He said, "No, Chris, while I'm with you they won't endanger me. They'll regroup and try something out."

A few moments passed. I definitely remember Laurie had lit his second cigarette. He was chain-smoking very rapidly. He was nervous. He seemed to be greatly agitated. At this stage he began to take his shirt off. I did not invite him to take his shirt off. He just took it off. The black boot polish on his face was starting to run down through his sweat and it was streaking down his body. It was all over his chest and he was sweating quite profusely.

He said, "Why don't we go back up to the hut, Chris, and talk about things."

I was very distrustful and we talked about this for a few moments.

I said, "We go back up there, Laurie, I will be out in the open and one of your men will put one into me."

He said to me, "No, Chris, I give you my word this will not happen to you."

We went back to the hut. I said, "Sorry, Laurie, I can't offer you a cup of tea. We can't have breakfast because the fire has not been lit."

He said, "That's all right, Chris. I had some breakfast before we left."

He was seated on the bench. He had given me his pistol before he left the bank. I was at that stage in possession of his pistol.

I offered him a drink of cordial out of a bottle. He had a drink... ...I said, "What sort of gun is this Laurie?"

He looked me in the eye and without batting an eyelid he said, "Standard .38 police issue."...

...I said, "No it's not, Laurie, this is a Dirty Harry handgun."

He did not reply.

I then opened the chamber like that (indicates) and saw that it was loaded. I tilted it like that and the bullets fell out into my hand (witness looks at the bullets). Six bullets fell out of the chamber into my hand like that. I looked at them and said, "What sort of bullets are these, Laurie?"

He said again without batting an eyelid, "Standard police issue, Chris."

I said, "Don't lie to me, Laurie. I'm not dumb." I said, "This is a Dirty Harry handgun." By Dirty Harry I mean Clint Eastwood the actor. He acts in a movie called Dirty Harry. He plays the part of a tough detective.

Laurie was sweating profusely by this stage. I said, "Laurie, you're not supposed to have things like this in your possession."

He declined to answer.

I said, "How many of the others are carrying things like this?"

He said, "I'm the only one, Chris. The rest have just got police issue."

He then asked me to let him go. He said to me, and I quote, "Let me go, Chris. Let me go now. This is a very big embarrassment to the police."

I said, "Never mind the police, Laurie. What about now? What about me?"

He said, "Let me go and you, Cody and Hata ride away into the bush."

I said, "I'm in trouble, Laurie. I am in more trouble than I have ever been in my life before."

He declined to answer.

I said, "I know what's going to happen to me. As soon as we let you go, you guys are going to blow us away."

He said, "No Chris, that's not right."

I said, "Why did you lie to me about the gun and about the bullets?"

He declined to answer.

At this stage he was seated smoking, chain-smoking.

I put the shells back in the pistol and began to examine the pistol. I said, "This is the ugliest gun I have ever seen, Laurie, and those bullets are the ugliest bullets that I've ever seen."

He did not comment. At that time I was holding the pistol like this. All of a sudden it was like that (indicates skyward). I don't know how it got like that but it got in that position. Laurie said, "Be fuckin' careful, Chris. It'll go off."

I recall holding it very, very delicately. It was on cock, like that. I said, "Where's the safety catch, Laurie?"

He said, "Hasn't got one, Chris."

I said, "Do you carry a gun around with no safety?"

And he then explained that the safety was this strap here and showed how it worked. I said, "How do you put it back in a safe position?"

He said, "Put your thumb on the hammer, pull the trigger with your other finger, like that, and let it go." He was sitting there looking up at me and I'm standing in front of him holding the gun.

I said, "How do you let it go, Laurie, without it firing off?"

He said, "Put your thumb on the hammer, Chris, take the pressure off, pull the trigger and let it go slowly. But be very careful or it could go off." Those were his exact words. I followed his instructions and I recall putting it back very slowly and it went off (demonstrates) and deafened me and freaked me right out. Yeah. It was a loud, loud bang and it took us a few moments to get ourselves organised again. It was a terrible experience.

At that moment, a voice yelled out to me from out of the scrub. This voice identified itself as being that of Senior Constable Tamati Moturangi Reedy. He said, "Chris, is that you?"

I recognised the voice immediately. I said, "Course it's me. Who do you think it is."

He said, "This is Tim Reedy. This is Tim Reedy, Chris."

I said, "What can I do for you, Tim Reedy?"

He said, "How's Laurie?"

I said, "Laurie's all right."

He said, "Can I speak to him?"

I said, "You can speak to him."

He yelled out to Laurie Naden. He said, "Laurie, are you all right?"

Laurie said, "I'm fine, Tim. Will you clear the area?"

Tim said, "The area has been cleared." He said he had been sent forward after receiving instructions from headquarters to commence a voice contact with us. Tim said, "Chris, remember all those things you and I spoke about before?"

I said, "Come out, Tim Reedy, come out and talk to me face to face."

He said, "I can't do that, Chris, orders from the boss."

I said, "Who's the boss that tells you what to do on your turangawaewae, Tim Reedy?"

He said, "Whiro Ratahi."

I said to Laurie Naden, "Where's he from?"

Laurie Naden said, "Nga Puhi."

I recollected directing an adverse comment about Whiro Ratahi's tribal affiliation. But then I recalled having read in a Tu Tangata Magazine some months earlier that Whiro Ratahi was not from Nga Puhi but was in fact from Taranaki.

I yelled out to Tim Reedy, "Laurie Naden told me that Whiro Ratahi comes from Nga Puhi."

Tim then began to talk about whakapapa with me. He said, "You know, Chris, you and I are one. You and I have a tie. We come from the same subtribe,

266

Te Aitanga a Mate." He said, "You remember, Chris, we spoke about these things together in court last year during your fullas' big jury trial."

I replied: "Great place to talk about such things isn't it, Tim Reedy."

He said that it was unfortunate. We then discussed genealogy for a while. I said, "Do you know who the Nga Kuri Paakaa were, Tim Reedy?"

I then began to tell him about Nga Kuri Paakaa, which means the dogs of war (another source, Rongowhakaata Halbert, uses the term "Nga Kuri Paakaa a Uetuhiao", the ruddy dogs of Uetuhiao, Uetuhiao being their mother). I told him that they were three chiefs from long ago and that it was felt by our Ngati Te Aowera people, which is the hapu Tim Reedy and myself belong to... and I spoke to him about the warlike makeup of these particular people. I told him about the meeting house at Whareponga, that these kuri paakaa were in fact the meeting house at Whareponga known as Ngaronga Toa. He did not know this.

I realised at this point they were keeping me talking, that they were trying to keep me occupied, perhaps. I then renounced Tim Reedy. I said, "Tim Reedy," and I called him a name. I said, "You are a ...... and I refuse to speak to you any longer."

He said, "Don't be like that, Chris. You and I are family."

I said, "Were family. I am renouncing you. I no longer desire to be associated with you in any form or colour or anything."

He replied, "Don't be like that, Chris."

It was quite an emotional discussion we had, him and I. I remember expressing my hurt at Tim Reedy that he should come there as he had, dressed as he was in a uniform of brutality. And I told him I was not prepared to speak with him any longer. I said, "I'm going now, Tim."

He said, "Where are you going to?"

I said, "I don't know where I'm going. I'm just going."

He said, "Don't go, Chris. Stay there."

At this stage another voice was heard and I identified that voice as belonging to Senior Constable Jeffrey Dods of the Gisborne police. He said, "Chris, this is me."

I said, "Who's me?"

He said, "Dodsy."

I said, "What can I do for you, Dodsy?"

He asked how Laurie was. I told him that Laurie was all right. He asked to speak to Laurie. They spoke to each other. He said, "Chris, throw down the gun and give yourself up."

I said, "I can't do that, Jeff, because I might get shot."

He said, "Nobody's going to shoot you, Chris. You have my word on that."

I said, "Have you got a gun like Laurie's?"

He said, "No."

I said, "Are you carrying bullets like Laurie's?"

He said, "No."

I said, "I don't believe you."

It was at this stage that I began to ask for the whereabouts of my brother. I said, "Dodsy, where's Pani?"

He said, "He's not here, Chris."

I said, "Get him up here. I want him."

He said that he would relay the message to base. It was at this time I noticed a movement in the bushes. I recognised it as being an AOS member by the way he was dressed. I saw that he was holding a rifle and that the rifle had telescopic sights on it. I challenged him and he dropped down into the little creek that runs past. Laurie ordered him to vacate his position through the use of the loudhailer. I said, "I can see him there, Laurie. There he is right there."

He said, "Don't do anything silly, Chris."

I said, "Tell him to get out of the area, Laurie."

Laurie ordered him to leave the area. There was a pause and the chap stood up, looked across the clearing towards us, turned his back and walked away into the opposite direction.

I thought, "Well, I should leave this area for the safety of all persons concerned."

I recall asking Hata to go and catch our horses and he did. While they were away, catching the horses, Laurie and I had a general discussion. I said to Laurie, "Did you know, Laurie, that this is an old marae site here you're standing on."

He said, "No, I didn't know that, Chris."

I said to him, "Did you know that you and your friends that have come here today have trampled on the mauri of this place." By mauri I mean sacredness, I suppose, the tapu of it.

He said, "No, I did not know that, Chris." And he expressed a type of apology for having done this.

I said, "Do you know why things have gone wrong for us, Laurie?"

"No."

I said, "All the old people are around here, Laurie," that they were in the hills, that they were in the trees and that I was a mokopuna tamaiti, which means a grandchild. I said, "They are here with me, Laurie, and while they are here with me they will not be able to hurt me in any way."

He said, "Yes, I accept that, Chris."

We then began to speak about my ancestors who were soldiers down through the past generations. I said to him, "Laurie, I am not afraid to die here today."

He said, "Nobody's going to die, Chris. Nobody will die today."

I said, "My culture tells me, Laurie, that there is no greater honour than to face Hine-nui-te-po (the goddess of night, darkness and death, the queen of the underworld, called Great Lady of the Night)." I said that I would die but that I would die with honour and I would die hard whilst standing upon the old marae.

He said, "I know all about that, Chris. Just remember I am from the fellow down the way a bit."

I said, "To who are you referring to?"

He said, "The Nadens of Tokomaru Bay."

I said (in Maori): "Good gracious, you are my relative."

He said, "That is correct, Chris." And from that point on we took a different direction...

...I said, "Laurie, did you know that the Treaty of Waitangi is the most sacred document ever signed between two peoples?"

He did not comment.

I said, "Laurie, did you know that when Her Majesty Queen Elizabeth of England came here on her 1957 coronation visit she said that the Treaty of Waitangi was the most sacred document ever drawn up between two peoples?"

I cannot recall him answering that one.

At this stage, I was just conversing with Laurie to use up the time until Hata Thompson came back with the horses. I categorically and emphatically deny ever making mention or wishing ill intent or physical harm towards the person known as Her Majesty the Queen of England. I might add that I am in fact a royalist.

The horses then arrived. Laurie said, "Where are we going, Chris?"

I said, "Away from here."

He said, "Away where?"

I said, "We are going to a sacred pool where we will humbly beseech the Lord to help me."

He said, "Leave me here, Chris. You guys ride out."

I said, "Laurie, if we ride out they will shoot us from the sky."

He did not reply. He said, "Chris, my daughter turns twenty-one on Saturday. Will I be there?"

I said, "Don't worry, Laurie, you will be there."

He looked distraught. I said, "I know what it's like Laurie for you. I know that you are a family man and that you have a family waiting at home for you."

He did not say anything.

I said, "Laurie, you will be all right. I promise you that you will be all right. As soon as we are clear, you will be released."

We then mounted and rode out down the face of the mountain at a gallop. Laurie was having difficulty hanging on. Ten minutes later we heard a helicopter hovering around in the distance.

We arrived at the pool and dismounted...

... I said to Laurie, "We are going to have church, Laurie. Do you wish to join us?"

He said, "Yes please, Chris."

I said, "I will be praying in Maori, Laurie. But if you're a Naden from Tikurangi way you should understand what I'm saying." He bowed his head and I began to pray to God. I asked God to please guide and protect us on the hill there that day. I asked God to assist because we needed assistance...

...I then had what is commonly known as a wai. I then bent down to wash myself in the pool. Laurie was standing at my right hand. He asked if he could have a wash. I said certainly. Before our very eyes the pool turned muddy brown. I said, "There you are, Laurie, look what's happened."

At this stage a helicopter began to hover overhead. We mounted and rode out at a gallop. It was tough going because of all the bush. The helicopter tracked us. I became worried because I believed there was a marksman in the helicopter.

We rode out up onto the brow of a small hill and I looked up at the helicopter. Laurie Naden began to gesticulate loudly. He seemed to be signalling the occupants of the helicopter to go away. One of his movements was that of bending his head down in a downward fashion, which I assumed he was indicating to the persons in the helicopter the bald part of his head, probably as some form of identification. At the same time he gave that type of motion – a covering of the head – and going like that (raising his arms up to the air). I said, "Laurie is there a marksman in that helicopter?" He did not hear me over the noise of the rotors. We rode away into the bush. And from there I never saw Laurie Naden again until he visited me some months later in the Gisborne police cells.

## UNDER SEIGE

**Chris Campbell in court:** By this stage there were five helicopters in the sky. There was a big black Jetranger I recognised as belonging to Wanganui

Aviation operated by Dennis – a chap that lives in Ruatoria – Hartley. There was a white helicopter. There was a yellow helicopter. There were two Army gunboats, helicopter gunboats. I recognised these as being Army gunships. I had seen them on the movies before. They were in Army camouflage markings. There were two Phantom Skyhawk jets that flew low over Whakaahu. I understood this to be a type of scare tactic used by the police. I let my horse go. He ran home. I began to run through the bush towards the township of Tuparoa, situated directly east of Ruatoria.

Upon dark I made my way to my uncle's house, where a meal and a change of clothing were waiting for me. On dark, he led me through Tuparoa because the Neighbourhood Watch Group were positioned in and around the township of Tuparoa. He said that they were watching for us. He led me over to the wharetipuna, where I met a brother of one of the Neighbourhood Watch persons. He said that he was pissed off with his brother.

I asked him if he could lend me a horse because I wished to travel back into the Whakaahu to locate my brethren (Hata and Cody). He said it was no good to go that way because all the vigilantes were armed with shotguns and various other calibres of rifle and I could get shot. My uncle suggested that I should take the beach route to Reporua, which is north of Ruatoria. From there, cross over to Te Kaha, where I would be helped. He cautioned me that to go around the beach in the dark with the tide in was a very dangerous procedure but advised that it was the best thing for me to do as the police presence the next day would be excessive. We stood on this marae at Tuparoa and we had a karakia. We then saw a falling star and he said, "There you go."

My cousin drove his car up the Tuparoa Creek and there discharged several shots into the night to draw the Neighbourhood Watch persons. I travelled approximately fifteen kilometres in a northerly direction towards Reporua. I passed many lookout points along the way, fires on the beach with persons sitting around watching the beach. I stopped many times when I thought that I could go no further. Always the sign in the elements led me on. I climbed a cliff after going past Reporua and slept concealed underneath a manuka tree.

I was awakened at daybreak by the sound of an Army gunship flying directly above me. It was a very frightening experience. I spotted a fishing boat anchored below, which I believed to be owned by Detective Steve Dimery of Gisborne. I also saw the HMS Monowai sail by. I stayed undercover right throughout the day. At dark I crossed over on to a property known as Tui Mara, directly northeast of Ruatoria. I observed a police patrol on this property. I avoided this police patrol. I walked down the stream that passed through Koka Station. It would have been possibly the early hours of the morning by the time I got on the road. I am able to tell this because all the houses I passed were in a state of sleep. I walked towards Te Kapapa, directly northeast of Ruatoria. I stopped at the meeting house there and asked my tipuna to help me.

I made my way thereafter in a westerly direction towards Orangi Ngata, where it was my intention to go into the bush. I arrived home, I'm not sure when. I was met by my father and by my mother. Constable Pani Campbell was coming. I said that I feared for my safety and that I had in my possession bullets, excessively modified bullets and a .357 calibre Smith & Wesson Magnum, which up to that time I was not aware of being used by the police in thiscountry.

Other members of my family arrived from various parts of New Zealand, and a hui hui of sorts took place. A hui hui is a Maori term for meeting. I told my family that the police had come to Whakaahu to kill me.

My brother said, "Chris, I have spoken to my boss and he has assured me that you will not be killed."

I said, "What about these bullets?"

"What about them?"

"What about this gun?"

"Give it back."

I was not convinced by my brother's assurances that my safety was guaranteed. I said, "No, I know they want to kill me," whereupon he fell upon me and effected an arrest. It was a very emotional time. I called out to my father to order him to release me. I called out to my mother to order him to release me. All my sisters were crying. My younger brother challenged my older brother to release me. Members of the Armed Offenders Squad then arrived. I was in a very emotional state. I was crying. I was pleading with my brother not to deliver me up. He said, "Here they come, stand up, be a man. Don't let them see you like this." I did that. I abused the Armed Offenders when they came to get me. I was then escorted by the Armed Offenders to a waiting police car that was situated at the beginning of our road.

I travelled to Gisborne with my brother, Eric Newman and Detective Flaus. I said to my brother (in Maori), "Everything is all right."

A short time later I was visited by Sergeant John Robinson of the Gisborne Police. He said he abused (was upset by) the vigilante presence in Ruatoria. He said, "The order had gone out, Chris. They wanted you brought in dead." He then left. I went to prison.

I came back from prison and was visited by Senior Detective Jeffrey Dods, stationed here in Gisborne. He said, "Chris, can I talk to you? The way we used to talk to each other before." We began to talk. He said, "Why don't you get back on TV, Chris, and change the story."

I said, "I can't do that. Because what I said on television was only the truth."
I said, "Why have you come to my house now, Jeff, twice in the past twelve
months with black boot polish on your face?"

He said, "It's my job."

I said, "I don't go to your place with black boot polish on my face."

He said, "That's right." He said, "Give it up, Chris."

I said, "Give what up?"

He said, "Whatever it is that you're trying to do."

I said, "What is it that I'm trying to do?"

He said, "What about all these cut fences?"

I said, "What cut fences?"

He said, "You know."

I said, "I haven't been cutting any fences."

He said, "Think about what you're doing to your parents."

I said, "You think about what *you* are doing to my parents."

At that stage, the conversation seemed to take a different direction. He said,
"Chris, I want you to know right now personally I've got nothing against you."

We shook hands.

He said that he had become affected by what had happened up on the hill.

I said, "In what way are you affected?"

He said that he had been having trouble sleeping, that his conscience was
troubling him, and that he wasn't very happy with the way things had happened.

I said, "You'll be having to get up and give your evidence, Jeff."

He didn't reply.

We spoke about several Maori issues and he said, "Don't forget, Chris, I
married one."

I said, "I haven't forgotten."

He said, "All the best, Chris. I wish you well."

And I said, "Same to you." And that is the conclusion of my evidence, sir.


## BROTHER V BROTHER


*Chris Campbell cross-examines Barney during the kidnapping trial. He isn't
happy that his brother had been observing him up at Whakaahu the afternoon
before the Armed Offenders Squad moved in or that his brother hadn't made
contact with him in the early stages of the siege. He taunts Barney, saying he*

*isn't in touch with his Maori culture. It has also emerged that, while Chris was on the run, he had left Laurie Naden's gun with the soft-nosed bullets in a shed at their parents' place with instructions for it to be given to Auckland journalist Pat Booth.*

*Here are some excerpts from the cross-examination.*

Chris: Do you know who Apirana Ngata (the famous Ngati Porou politician) was?

Barney: Yes.

Chris: I want to read you a little quotation here. "A Maori who knows neither his own language or history and despises both should have his face bleached." Do you agree with that?

Barney: No.

Would you agree with me if I would say to you that Sir Apirana Ngata was the greatest Maori that ever lived? Do you agree with that?

He certainly was a great Maori by all accounts. Whether he was the greatest that ever lived remains to be seen. We judge people differently.

I am judging him from the Maori perspective.

Well I would say I am not proficient in things Maori so I am unable to judge him on that point.

Do you despise things Maori?

No. I never said that.

Do you pursue your culture?

It was one of the reasons I transferred back to this area. Lately I haven't had the time.

Is that because your duties as a police officer restrict you? In the pursuit of your culture?

No they don't restrict me in the pursuit of my culture.

You just haven't got the time?

No.

You don't really know anything about being a Maori do you, Constable?

Well I am one…

…Do you agree with Apirana Ngata with what he is reputed to have spoken or written? "A half-pie Maori who pretends a knowledge he does not possess is clearly dishonest. And that class is increasing in numbers and pretentiousness." Do you agree with that?

Who am I to disagree with that?…

…Are you proud of your Maori heritage?

Certainly.

274

You have had occasion to frown upon my pursuit of the culture, haven't you, Brother?

To frown upon?

My application of the culture.

It's not the application I'm frowning on; it seems to be the practice.

And what is the practice you frown upon?

The very reason that you're here in court today.

And what is the reason?

You are charged with criminal offences.

What would have made you reluctant to approach me at the hut on Whakaahu?

The Bench: When?

Chris: On the 17th.

The Bench: Well, first, were you reluctant to approach Mr Campbell on the 17th of February 1986?

Barney: Sir, I was sent up there to observe.

Chris: If you had observed me at the hut, would you have approached?

No.

Why not?

I was sent up there to observe and to report any sightings to the officer in charge...

... Did you arrest me?

When?

Earlier this year?

No, I can't remember arresting you.

Did you take me into custody? During February of this year?

Yes.

What was my reaction to being taken into custody at that time?

Which day?

The day in February when you took me into custody.

What was your reaction? You came, but at times rather reluctantly.

Very reluctantly?

Well, you walked to the vehicle of your own free will.

Did I ask you to release me?

Yes, I do recall one part where you did ask to be released.

Did I tell you that I believed the police were trying to kill me?

Yes I seem to recall you saying something along those lines.

Did I tell you that I had material proof that the police were trying to kill me?

You may have. I can't remember you saying it in those words.

Did you not say to me you had spoken to your superiors? And that they were in fact not going to kill me?

Who said we were going to kill you?

I said to you the police were going to kill me and you said, no, they are not. That's right, yes.

Then did you say if you had spoken to your superiors?

I wouldn't have had to speak to my superiors to know that the police were not going to kill you.

Did you say to me you had spoken to your superiors and they told you they were not going to kill me?

Yes.

Yes you had spoken to your superiors?

Yes.

And they had given you their assurance that they were not going to kill me?

If certain conditions existed perhaps they may have had to revise the situation. But the situation as I had informed them was that nobody was going to shoot anybody.

Were you present on Whakaahu on the morning of the 18$^{th}$?

Yes.

Where were you positioned?

Up on the ridge?

Why didn't you come down? I was sent up there to observe.

On the morning of the 18$^{th}$?

Yes.

Before the Armed Offenders Squad arrived?

Yes.

If you had been asked to make contact, would you have made contact?

On what day?

February 18$^{th}$.

The day Laurie Naden was taken prisoner? Yes. I most probably would have if I had been asked by the OIC.

Who was the officer in charge?

Mr (Whiro) Ratahi.

Are you aware that during the siege I asked to see you?

I have since read that that is what you did. At the time, no, I was not aware.

You were up on the ridge?

Yes.

Nobody told you that I had given instructions that I wished to see you?

I don't recall being told by anybody that was the case, not while I was on the ridge.

Did you see the bullets that Naden was carrying?

On that day?

Yes.

No.

Did you go with Constable (Mal) Meihana to our parents' farm?

Yes.

To collect a .357 Smith & Wesson magnum handgun and seventeen rounds of ammunition?

Yes.

Did you see the bullets?

I saw the pistol and the belt but I just can't recall seeing the bullets. And the Winchester, I think that was there, too.

You didn't examine them?

Constable Meihana had them, as I recall.

Would you accept it if I were to say to you that our father examined the bullets, that our sister examined them and that our brother in law examined them and other members of our immediate family examined them? Would you accept that?

No I can't.

Who did you retrieve the handgun and bullets from?

The shed.

Which shed?

The shed at home.

Did our father ring you to come and get them?

Yes.

Was Constable Meihana with you?

Yes.

Is Constable Meihana a very good friend of the family?

I would say so.

You say you didn't examine the bullets?

I didn't examine them, no.

Would you recognise them if you saw them again?

I'd probably recognise similar bullets but I wouldn't recognise the ones there on the day, no.

Did I tell you that those bullets should be taken and shown to Pat Booth of the Auckland Star?

I don't recall you telling me that, no.

Do you recall me telling our brother in law to do this?

No.

Have you been in the Armed Offenders?

Not recently, no.

During your fourteen years in the force?

Yes.

How long did you serve in the Armed Offenders?

Just over a year.

Wellington?

Yes.

What were the arms you carried when you were in the Armed Offenders?

Just the Smith & Wesson hand pistol.

387?

Yes.

Ever see a .357 magnum before today?

Yes.

The ammunition used?

Yes.

Would you accept it if I were to say those bullets are in direct contravention of the Geneva Convention?

Bench: There is no evidence of that Mr Campbell. What you would say about it is certainly not evidence.

Chris: Our brother in law was an Army man before he married our sister?

As far as I know, yes.

Do you recall a conversation between myself, yourself and him in the shed at home?

On what day?

The day you arrested me.

I never arrested you. I recall my part as listening.

Did you hear him say that as far as he knew it was illegal to chop the nose off any bullets?

Bench: Don't answer that question.

Chris: Very well, sir, I withdraw that question.


... Do you know who Te Kooti Arikirangi was?

Barney: I know of the man. I've read about him.

Would you accept it if I was to say to you that habeus corpus was totally disregarded...

The Bench: Don't answer that question. It is irrelevant...

278

... Are you familiar with the Bible?

Not really.

Have you read Matthew?

No.

Would you accept if I was to say to you that I consider it an honour to have been delivered up by my brother?

Can you repeat that please?

Would you accept it if I was to say to you that I felt honoured that...

The Bench: Excuse me for interrupting but he can't feel your feelings. Did Mr Campbell say he felt honoured to have been handed over by you?

Barney: No, I don't recall him saying that at the time, sir.

Chris: Would you accept it if I said to you that Christ said in the Gospel of Matthew chapter 10, verse 36...

Bench: Well, what does it matter whether he accepts it or not?

Chris: I would know if he did accept it or not.

Bench: I can't see that that has got any relevance to what happened at Whakaahu on the 18th of February.

It has got plenty of relevance actually.

I'm telling you it hasn't.

Could be a convenient time, sir (for an adjournment; the judge declines and the cross-examination continues)...

...Chris: If I say to you that Christ said that a man's enemies would be in his own household...

Bench: Don't answer that. It is irrelevant.

Would you accept if I said that you are still my tuaka, my elder, and I still respect you as such and I still love you as my tuaka and nothing will ever change that? Do you accept that?

Well, that's what you're telling me. Your feelings are going to be erratic at the best of times.

I have never ever shown you any ill-will before today have I? Personally, between you and I?

No.

Never, have I? No?

Bench: How can he answer that?

Chris: Nor will I ever.

Bench: You will not say that.

I will say to my tuaka that I love my tuaka and I forgive him everything that he's done to me. Is this a convenient time?

Bench: No.

Katepi.

Bench: What is that you said? Would you translate that please?

Everything is all right. (Maori). My heart is breaking to you, my tuaka. Katepi. I forgive you for everything you have done to me. (Maori).

Bench: Have you ever done anything to him which requires forgiveness?

No sir.

How has this affected our family?

Bench: The question is irrelevant. Don't answer it.

How has this affected our mother?

Bench: Irrelevant. Don't answer it.

Do you know that our mother left home some weeks before the incident at Whakaahu?

Bench: Do you know that your mother left home before Whakaahu?

Barney: I think she went for a holiday somewhere. I can't remember the exact date.

Chris: Would you accept if I was to say to you the reason she left home is because of the immense pressures that were being put on to our family?

Well, she never told me why she left home. All she said was she was going for a holiday.

Bench: What frame of mind did she appear to be in? Happy? Despondent?

Barney: Tired, sir...

...What did I instruct you, brother?

To seek forgiveness from the Lord.

I have no more questions.


# CHAPTER 5


## HOW THE COURT WAS FOOLED


**Hughie Hughes, Ruatoria electrician:** Chris Campbell was a bitter man. He hated everybody. I never saw him smile. And I felt sorry for Barney, his brother, who was one of the policemen here. The cops should have shut Barney out of it right at the start. In the end the whole thing destroyed him. And he was a bloody good cop, one of the best cops I've ever worked with. I'm the coroner up here. And if you asked me who was the best coroner's constable I'd say Barney was the best I've ever struck.

They should have just said, "Barney, pick up your family. We're gonna find you a house for six months in Taranaki," or something like that and got him out of it. But they left him here and he was caught in the middle of it. Then people were scared to talk to the cops in case Barney somehow let it slip to his brother. Nothing against Barney, but it might have worked against the cops to have him in the middle of that situation.

**Denis Kohn, Gisborne lawyer (retired):** I remember the Laurie Naden kidnapping case quite clearly because it was quite a big item around Gisborne at the time. I think probably the one highlight in the thing that I really remember was Chris deciding he wanted to call Tom Te Maro, who is the old kaumatua from up at Ruatoria. And Tom obviously wasn't happy about being involved in all of this.

And the day that he was called I can remember clearly this little man, apparently very frightened and timorous, carefully picking his way from the back of the court down to the witness box and looking around in bewilderment at everybody.

And I forget how it came about. It must have been when the registrar came to get him to take the oath, Tom was still pretending bewilderment. And the judge perceived that there was a difficulty with language because of this old fellow dressed in what I remember now looked like an old Army greatcoat, looking around the courtroom. And he said to Chris, "Do we have a language problem, Mr Campbell?" which of course was right up Chris's alley. And Chris said, "Yes."

And then it was quite obvious that we weren't going to be able to get a translator. We didn't have translators on standby. So after conferring with the registrar the judge said to Chris, "Will you tell Mr Te Maro please that we can't get a translator at the moment. We'll recall him after lunch and he can give his evidence then."

So Chris then, in plain *English*, told Tom that they couldn't get a translator, he could go away and have some lunch and come back after lunch and they'd hear his evidence.

They did get hold of Charlie Kutia, who was the translator at the Maori Land Court, and it was all done in Maori.

I was able to follow quite a bit of it. I have a nodding acquaintance with the Maori language. And there was one stage there where Chris mentioned something about the girl Pewhairangi from up the coast. She'd written quite a lot of songs and was very highly respected. And Tom went right off his tree about "mentioning that girl's name in these halls". And he gave Chris a real blast and called him for want of a better word a real mongrel for doing that. It came out in such an effusive rush that Charlie was having difficulty keeping up with the translating. And a lot of this calling Chris a bastard for mentioning the girl's name, Charlie didn't get it. But I did. Poor old Terry Stapleton, the prosecutor, of course, didn't know what was going on. But I think from memory we had four Maoris on the jury. And I just quietly looked over to see if they were understanding. And there were a couple of them grinning and nodding. They knew what Tom was saying, but Charlie had missed it. Tom was making it clear he felt that Chris was grandstanding and turning the whole case into a sideshow. Plus Tom didn't want to be there.

I had a talk with Tom outside at the top of the stairs at some stage. And he was real shitty about being called up for all that sort of rubbish. I know Tom and I had known Tom from a long way back. And Tom was normally a completely different person to the Tom who appeared in court that day. Tom's not frightened of being in public at all. Get him on the marae and that and he's quite a showman. And he's got a very sharp sense of humour. I saw him in the supermarket just a couple of months ago and we embraced and remembered each other from way back. Aw, he's a bloody rascal, old Tom. He wasn't going to be put on the spot by what he called a useless waster.

*Thursday, October 16, 1986: Chris Campbell is sentenced to seven years in jail for kidnapping Laurie Naden, using a firearm to avoid arrest, threatening grievous bodily harm, aggravated robbery and theft of a police radio and gas grenade. His response is to declare he'll never eat again.*

*Hata Thompson gets four years for kidnapping, unlawfully taking a car, unlawfully entering premises and theft.*

*Cody Haua gets two years for kidnapping.*

*"This is the law of man, not the law of God," says Campbell, "and the Bible tells me the law of man is the law of Satan."*

**Phil Dreifuss, Gisborne lawyer:** I remember Doug (Rishworth) had been involved in the trial. He'd been sacked as counsel and for some reason Denis (Kohn) stayed behind. Denis was disappointed that he couldn't come to the law conference at Rotorua because of this. So we were in Rotorua and we got a call from Shirley Stephens. She was a secretary with us. Shirley had received a call from Denis: "Just tell Doug, seven, four and two." She thought it was a tip for the horses, not realising it was the respective sentences the Rastas had received, because Denis wouldn't tell her what it was to do with. He just said, "Doug will know what it's about." She was sure it must be a hot tip. So she put however many dollars on the trifecta. And she won twelve hundred dollars. So she actually won the money by picking seven, four and two in the big race meeting that weekend. It wasn't until we came back from Rotorua the next week that she said, "That was a bloody good tip of Denis's wasn't it. I won twelve hundred bucks."

**Russell Fairbrother, lawyer:** And then Campbell was convicted and remanded in custody and he was sentenced in Auckland.

The judge I'm sure was Chilwell, who was a fairly old school judge. And I didn't attend the sentencing. But I understand it took about a day because Campbell was totally confrontational insofar as repeatedly calling the judge a bald-headed fuckwit. And in those days a baldhead was a bit of an insult. I think he got seven years for that. I don't think Campbell was ever scared of going to jail. Going to prison wasn't the problem. He saw what he was doing as almost his God-given right. And it didn't matter where he was. And I think he was quite successful at recruiting people in jail. So that wasn't his problem. His problem was not being understood or being misunderstood.

You always think you'd have got them off when you're not put to the test. But I remember at the time arguing with Chris that I should stay on the case because I thought we were in a strong position. I thought it was worth standing my ground because I thought the trial had gone particularly well.

I still to this day cannot remember a single justification, other than fear by the police, as to why they went up there to the bush-line with a loudspeaker with the Armed Offenders Squad telling Campbell to come out with his hands up because they were armed. It was a very aggressive approach. There aren't that many ways up that mountain. They could have waited for them to come down. It was just a show of force and an attempt to try and bring matters to an end through intimidation.

**Phil Dreifuss, lawyer:** I didn't work on the Laurie Naden kidnapping trial but I sat through it all. And the really interesting evidence was the defence evidence. Really, if they hadn't sacked their counsel they might have had a chance because they had some pretty good justification for what they were doing. The police had no right to be there. Campbell had been told that he was going to be killed. Brown bread was the term that Hemi Hikawai used. "You'll be brown bread." And suddenly it's unfolding right in front of his eyes. There they are. He's not wanted by the police. He's in the middle of nowhere, up on Whakaahu. And he's surrounded by the Armed Offenders Squad. I mean... I think he was totally justified in what he did. And Laurie Naden was pretty well treated. He was the one that got to ride the horse. They walked through the bush. He sat on the horse. Okay, he had his hands tied behind his back and they had his gun. But they never hurt him and when they felt they were no longer at risk, they let him go. So they took a hostage purely for reasons of self-defence. So they should never have gone to jail for that, I don't think. But when Chris took over the trial the courtroom became a political platform and jurors just tire of that.

# CHAPTER 6

## THE LOST CHAPTER

*In 2018, ten years after I launched the first of the Ngati Dread books, the phrase The Blue Line popped into my head for some reason. Suddenly I had a moment of panic. I grabbed copies of the three volumes off my bookshelf and began thumbing through them with mounting dread. Nowhere could I find the phrase The Blue Line in the books, let alone an explanation of what it was and how it had affected life in Ruatoria. I remembered doing the research and writing up the subject many years earlier but for some reason it was no longer included. I'm a slow reader but I spent a few weeks reading through the three volumes and sure enough, no mention of The Blue Line. It was a mystery what had happened to this part of the story – I figured I had written it but later accidentally opened an earlier version of the manuscript on my computer and carried on working in that instead - but I felt the series was incomplete without that information. Unfortunately, I didn't have a copy of what I'd originally written so I gathered together all the notes I'd made on the subject that I could still find and set about recreating it from scratch. So here it is, belatedly.*

*In the midst of a reluctant interview, farmer Colin Williams told me that the Ruatoria Troubles all started because of The Blue Line.*

*"What's The Blue Line?" I asked innocently.*

*"What's The Blue Line?!" he repeated, horrified. He'd just finished trying to convince me that I shouldn't write this series of books, that no one should write about what had happened. "You want to write about the Ruatoria Troubles and what's happened with the Rastas and you don't even know what The Blue Line is?!"*

*I had to make a split-second decision: bluff that I actually did know what The Blue Line was or come clean. "No, I've never heard of it," I admitted.*

*Colin was obviously not impressed but he gave me a brief rundown and I went away and did my own research. I spoke with his relative Jeremy Williams about local farming history. I spoke with a researcher at the Poverty Bay Catchment Board and obtained a copy of the "Taylor Report" and as I write, I also have open on my computer excerpts from the book Landslide Hazard and Risk edited by Thomas Glade, Malcolm G Anderson and Michael J Crozier, Te Ara.govt.nz and Parliamentary Debates, Volume 395 from 11 October to 8 November 1974 (God, I love the internet!) and the following segment is a mix of stuff I've either nicked, rewritten or spliced together from those sources.*

*So what I can tell you is The Blue Line was basically a line that was drawn on maps of the East Coast in a report officially published in 1970. The "Taylor Report" (named after the committee chair Norman Taylor, a geologist and expert on different types of soil) persuaded the Government to take decisive action to try to stop the devastating erosion in the Poverty Bay-East Cape district. The idea was to stabilise land beyond a "blue line". On one side of the line: 346 thousand acres of land where farming was deemed impractical and where forestry was preferable. This was the Critical Headwaters Area, in the highest and steepest country where the rivers started and there was the most rainfall and the most severe erosion. On the other side of The Blue Line was The Pastoral Foreland. This was lower land and most of it could be farmed although of the 1.2 million acres in this area, 120 thousand were deemed non-agricultural and sub-marginal, 720 thousand needed work such as tree planting, and only 370 thousand acres had no outstanding erosion problems. Some farmers who had land in the vast area put aside for forestry, on the higher side of The Blue Line, were frustrated and angry because they hadn't been consulted and they still considered those parts of their property to be financially viable.*

*But before we get into more of that, we'll jump back in time a bit to get some context and try to edge closer to why Colin Williams believed you couldn't tell the story of the Rastas properly without mention of The Blue Line. I suppose it's similar to the belief many have that you can't tell the story of the Ruatoria Rastas without mentioning the devastating losses taken by local Maori in wars fought for New Zealand over the years and particularly by the Maori Battalion's C Company in World War II. The common denominator is: decisions were made by society's leaders and lawmakers and many believe the results of those decisions had a detrimental effect on the East Coast and the people who lived there for generations to come.*

**Jeremy Williams:** When the early European settlers felled the bush, they had a million years of humus underneath that bush. (Humus is the dark organic matter that forms in soil when dead plant and animal matter decays. It has many nutrients that improve the health of soil, with nitrogen being the most important). So it was like incredibly well fertilised pasture every year for 70 years until it ran out. Labour was cheap. Fencing material was cheap. You just paid a few men to chop a few trees down and you could make all the batons and posts. They used to go in and they'd pick out a prominent hill and they'd chop down a few totara trees. They'd split them and they'd dig a big pit and bury all these posts and batons. Then they'd go through and cut down all the undergrowth. Everything under six inches was actually chopped down. And then they would go through and they'd scarf every tree. So they'd take a wedge out of every tree all the way up. And when they got to the top of the hill they'd chop the top one down and you'd get the domino effect and it would take the whole lot down. That's what they call a run. And it would go boom, boom, boom, and then halfway down the hill it would stop. So some poor bugger would have to go and cut the next tree down and hope like hell he didn't get squashed. And that's how they did it. Then you leave it for a few months. All the mingi mingi and other low shrubs are already dry. Then they'd have a gang of 50 to 80 men going around lighting fires. And they'd have these huge burn-offs. So that's how they got the humus.

There was an old fulla called Ernie Reedy who shepherded for our families most of his life. He was a very able stockman. And he ended up in hospital as an old man. I talked to him when I was in hospital having my arm operated on. And he was telling me about a block in the back of Wairongomai Station, near Ruatoria, which now is cold, wintry gutless sort of stuff. In fact it's been planted in Douglas fir. Anyway, he says they fattened ten thousand lambs just after they burnt the bush there. Well, until recently, you wouldn't have fattened any lambs up there. There's no guts left in the soil. The natural fertility's worn out. So those old-timers when they felled the bush, they were left with perfect soil. They also had no tax to pay. Product prices were high. And they made fortunes.

And this idea of landed gentry in New Zealand; that's where it came from. Some of them could go from nothing to being millionaires within 10 years, which it's extremely hard to do now by farming.


*The region has always been susceptible to severe storms and, with global warming, the storms seem to be getting worse and more frequent. In the year I'm writing this, 2018, Tolaga Bay's rivers, beach and many farms were clogged by forestry offcuts that flowed down from the hills during a storm. Some evidence suggests the East Coast's erosion problems began during the early settlement by Maori. But the rate of erosion multiplied many times with the arrival of the European settlers and their farming practices. They began clearing the native forest in the 1880s and by the 1920s all but the highest and most rugged hill country had been cleared. Though some forested areas were logged, most were burnt, then oversown with introduced grass species. Such a drastic change in vegetation cover from forest to grazed pasture accelerated erosion. Slope stability declined as the root systems of the native forest began to decay. With the removal of the forest, the interception of rain by the forest canopy ceased. Soil moisture levels increased and soils remained wetter for longer and were thus more prone to mass wasting. By 1980, the East Coast had the distinction of being one of the most erosion-prone regions of New Zealand and in the world.*


*In July, 1963, the Soil Conservation and Rivers Control Council set up a committee to investigate and come up with solutions to the erosion problems in the Poverty Bay-East Cape district. It concluded that the "unstable terrain much in evidence throughout" and "particularly notable in the back-country hill areas", had an "adverse effect upon the whole district, sociologically, productively, and economically".*

*Dr R. E. Dils, a Professor of Watershed Management from Colorado State University, had a dire warning for the committee. "Unless remedial action is initiated soon, the ultimate cost to New Zealand may far exceed the cost of treatment now."*

*The committee noted that rural areas in the district showed an abnormal and long-continued rate of decline in population, and land values in back-country areas were extremely depressed. The effects of the erosion were "widespread, entering into nearly every phase of activity in the district and hindering its growth and well-being". They undoubtedly contributed to "stagnation and regression" in some areas.*

*The committee said large sections of the eroding back country were unsuited to farming but could be effectively afforested. "Benefits from such diversification will accrue to all sections of the community and to the nation."*

*The Taylor Report said that although the "potential of the district was relatively high", its condition at that time was "indeed poor". It noted the drift of population, adding, "Away from Gisborne, the district offers little to attract the new settler." It went on: "Various reasons, such as isolation, land tenure, racial incompatibility, lack of educational and other social amenities, are given to account for the current state of affairs. Undoubtedly all of these have operated in the past and are in varying degree contributing to the problem today. However, similar difficulties have been encountered during the development of other districts but have been or are in the process of being gradually and successfully resolved. The difference between this and other North Island districts is that here the position has been complicated by the rapid acceleration of erosion and sedimentation before New Zealand was geared up to deal with the problems involved. Land use practices unsuited to the needs of an unstable terrain led to gullying and slipping, which in the north and west reached a scale beyond the possibility of farmer/catchment board control, while the accompanying sedimentation destroyed stream and river flats. Accelerated erosion and sedimentation have accentuated the numerous other difficulties commonly encountered in district development. Farming gradually became more perplexing and uncertain... ...Overall production became static, with the consequence that townships that would ordinarily have developed to meet the needs of a progressive countryside failed to do so. Hence social amenities necessary for progress became gradually more and more inadequate. A lack of confidence in the future of the district was inevitable."*

*As Jeremy Williams mentioned, the boom times for farmers on the East Coast were when the forest had just been cleared and the soil was still healthy and full of nutrients. But as times got tougher, many European families left, literally in search of greener pastures.*

**Jeremy Williams:** If you look back over history, European families have been leaving the East Coast since the 1930s, maybe even earlier. A lot of those leases went from the early 1900s to about '35. And the leases fell in and a lot of the families lost money in the big depression. So they started leaving. At Whakaangiang Valley, there were a dozen Pakeha families. And all but a few of them left in the 1930s. A lot of them left Mangaoparo Valley in the '60s, when I was a kid. Tapuaeroa Valley, a lot of them left. And there's been a gradual progression away from the coast. But it's partly to do with the downturn in the rural sector.

*And Colin Williams believed the drawing up of The Blue Line drove out many of the remaining European farming families.*

**Colin Williams:** We purchased this place here in Gisborne in about 1972 with the eventual idea of coming to live here. We started looking to move away from Ruatoria and the East Coast as early as 1968 when the forestry started to move in. All our country out the back there like Pakihiroa, up under the mountains, was affected when they drew that Blue Line in '68. That Blue Line is what really started the exodus from the coast. The Government decided that all the country up there was rubbish and they were gonna plant it in pine trees. And it came out on TV, this Blue Line. It started at East Cape and virtually ran right down to Gisborne. And all that good East Coast hill country was all behind The Blue Line. And they said, "This country has to be planted because it's physically unstable because of the erosion," which was a load of bullshit. Most of the best country on the coast was behind The Blue Line. And that started the general exodus.

*Maori families making a living from land above The Blue Line had to make tough decisions as their livelihoods were also threatened. Those who left the district were following well-worn paths. In 1966, Maori made up 56 percent of the rural population in the Gisborne and East Coast district and owned more than 30 percent of the land. But people were moving away in droves. In the decade leading up to 1966, the population of the rural areas in the district underwent a decrease of 15.4 percent, while rural areas in the rest of New Zealand had a 9.2 percent rise. The downturn in the rural sector forced many Maori in their teens and early 20s out of the district to look for work. Most of the female teens moving away from the East Coast counties went to Gisborne, but statistics suggest the young men tended to go further afield, looking for work.*

*In May, 1978, the East Coast Project developed from the Taylor Report. It said that while The Blue Line was essential initially and had served its purpose, it was now recognised as being too general. New studies of the land resource data were available and a better regional land use pattern was discernible.*

*The East Coast Project recommended best long-term use of different areas in three categories – large scale afforestation, farm scale afforestation and farming. In other words instead of splitting the East Coast with a blue line, it broke it up into lots of little pockets, each of them fitting into one of those three categories.*


**Colin Williams:** After we moved back to Gisborne, we sold our main station up the valley to the Maori Affairs Department. Now the actual boundary of Pakihiroa Station encompassed most of Mount Hikurangi. And I made it a condition of sale in the agreement when I sold it to the Government that the mountain and the bush around it were to be kept in trust for the Ngati Porou forever.

Now look at this. It's clause 10 of the purchase agreement from when I sold Pakihiroa to the Maori Affairs Department. It says: The purchaser undertakes to ensure that Mount Hikurangi and its immediate surrounds, which are at present undeveloped for pastoral farming, are preserved for the Ngati Porou people for all time.

That meant not only the bit that I sold them, but also the back of the mountain, which was crown land. That bit there should also be in that reserve for the Ngati Porou.

And there it is. It's signed by the two Maori politicians, Koro Wetere and Terakatene Sullivan, among others.

I felt that would have gone a long way towards alleviating some of the problems up there because they've always considered it as their special mountain. It always has been. They've got songs they sing about Hikurangi. They've got the Hikurangi football team. A lot of their action songs are based around the mountain. I thought it might've helped to settle down all the problems. But it didn't really. The problems still went on after that.

But Ngati Porou own the whole farm now. It was made over by the Maori Affairs Department to Ngati Porou. I don't know whether my agreement had anything to do with that. It was out of my control by then anyway. But I'm glad that it has happened. It's a beautiful block of country and it has been well farmed by Bill Poi, who used to work for us when we purchased the property in 1963 from my aunt...

...In 1968 and '69 they planted the first trees on the Rip Station (Raparapararariki Station), which was next door to our property up there. And I said to Jacquie, "One of these days we're gonna have to go. They'll probably plant our farm too." So we bought this little place here, which was pretty cheap at that stage, and leveled this house site. And by the end of '84 nearly all our mates had left from up there, all our generation. Most of them had gone because of the forestry. They'd sold their farms and gone because the Government had said, "We're gonna plant this country." And they felt insecure because of that threat so they sold their country and came away. By then we were about the last of our generation to leave.
And it really hurt. I was about third generation up there. My grandfather had made his home there. Anyway, we decided we'd do it. And we got the carpenter to start on this place at the beginning of '84, expecting to be in it at the end of '84. It was finished in October '85 and we moved out. That's why we came. It had nothing to do with all the troubles with the Rastas in Ruatoria.

I hated it as we drove away from our home up the coast. My grandparents and my aunt and my uncle and our first little boy are all buried there and that's all very much a part of both of us. We felt terrible leaving.

# LIST OF MAIN CHARACTERS & INTERVIEWEES IN VOLUME 1

Danny Batchelor: Police photographer
Sonny Brown: Hamana Brown's dad
Chris Bunyan: Policeman and former schoolmate of Chris Campbell
Barney (Pani) Campbell: Former Ruatoria policeman and Chris's
brother Chris Campbell: Rasta leader
Ike Campbell: Chris's brother
Joe "Boots" Campbell: Chris's brother
Gary Condon: Former police officer
David Conway: Gisborne Herald
reporter
Luke Donnelly: Shot Chris Campbell dead (explored fully in volume
3) Phil Dreifuss: Gisborne lawyer
Russell Fairbrother: Napier lawyer
Pop Gage (Hori Keeti): Late tohunga, who prophesied the coming of a
great spiritual leader on the East Coast
Norm Gray: Former head cop in Ruatoria
Rex Harrison: Former Gisborne CIB detective with family ties to the
Rastas Cody Haua: Rasta, kidnapped Laurie Naden
John (Hone) Heeney: Campbell's right hand man in the
Rastas Tom Heeney: Ruatoria deputy fire chief and John's
dad
Hemi Hikawai: Former CIB detective who investigated most of the
Ruatoria crimes
Lyn Hillock: Former Gisborne deputy fire
chief Tiger (Tika) Hongara: Rasta
Gallace Hongara: Rasta
Alex Hope: Former head cop in Ruatoria
Hughie Hughes: Pakeha electrician in
Ruatoria
Bob Kaa: Neighbourhood Support Group ("The Vigilantes")
Hone Kaa: Priest and expert witness on Maori culture in Joe Nepe's murder
trial Sammy Keelan: Rasta
Hori Keeti (Pop Gage): Late tohunga, who prophesied the coming of a
great spiritual leader on the East Coast
Denis Kohn: Gisborne lawyer

Lance Kupenga: Was beheaded by Joe Nepe

Paetene Kupenga: Lance's dad

Bruce Laing: Former Ruatoria traffic officer

Ken McKinnon: Ruatoria Fire Chief

Bob Marley: Late Rastafarian singer/songwriter

Eruera Ranfurly "Tuck" Morice: Rasta who was accused of arson

Laurie Naden: Former CIB detective kidnapped by Rastas

Joe Nepe: Rasta who beheaded fellow Rasta Lance Kupenga

Sue Nikora: Early influence on the Rastas

Junior Paul: Friend of the Rastas, who became their victim

Raewyn Rickard: Beau Tuhura's sister

John Robinson: Former policeman respected by Rastas and colleagues

Haile Selassie: Late Emperor of Ethiopia, considered the Second Coming by Rastafarians

Gordon Sutton: Childhood friend of Chris Campbell

Sarah Sykes: Secretary of Te Poho-Te-Aowera Marae, south of Ruatoria

Victor Takarangi: One of the main "vigilantes"

Te Kooti Arikirangi Te Turuki: 19th century rebel prophet, founder of Ringatu church

Ed Te Rauna: Former Rasta

Malcolm Thomas: Detective

Chris Thompson: Hata's brother

Hata Thompson: Rasta, kidnapped Laurie Naden

Laura Thompson: Hata's mum (Aunty Ga-ga)

Steve Tresidder: Former Ruatoria policeman

Beau Tuhura: One of the early Rasta leaders

Kate Walker: Aunty of Rasta John Heeney (victim of arson)

Glynn Walker Findlay: Policeman who helped interview Joe Nepe before his arrest

Genevieve Westcott: TV current affairs reporter

Colin Williams: Pakeha farmer, member of pioneer family

Jeremy Williams: Pakeha farmer, member of pioneer family

Peter Williams: Auckland defence lawyer for Joe Nepe

Stuart Williams: Pakeha farmer, member of pioneer family